PRAISE FOR *CONFLICT IS NOT ABUSE*

"Schulman's book could not have come at a better time ... *Conflict* is a balm against comforting explanations for violence and abuse, ones we know aren't true, just easy." —*Village Voice*

"*Conflict Is Not Abuse* presents a gestalt shift in thinking about conflict, power relations, harm and social responsibility." —*The Globe and Mail*

"*Conflict*'s publication could not be timelier ... A sharply observant and relevant text that is already getting its wish for action granted." —*Lambda Literary*

"*Conflict Is Not Abuse* should prove to be essential reading for people interested in psychology, group dynamics, and social justice activism." —*Global Comment*

"A compelling call out of call-out culture and everything that it messily dredges up, brings forward, and shunts away." —*Canadian Art*

"Schulman's new work is a provocative rethinking of intimate and civil discourse for a rapidly shrinking world ... a rallying cry for civil engagement and engaged civility." —*Gay City News*

Conflict Is Not Abuse

Overstating Harm, Community Responsibility, and the Duty of Repair

Sarah Schulman

Is Not Abuse

Arsenal Pulp Press | Vancouver

ELEVENTH PRINTING: 2023

ARSENAL PULP PRESS
Suite 202 – 211 East Georgia St.
Vancouver, BC V6A 1Z6
Canada

arsenalpulp.com

Arsenal Pulp Press acknowledges the xʷməθkʷəyəm (Musqueam), Sḵwxwú7mesh (Squamish), and səlilwətaɬ (Tsleil-Waututh) Nations, custodians of the traditional, ancestral, and unceded territories where our office is located. We pay respect to their histories, traditions, and continuous living cultures and commit to accountability, respectful relations, and friendship.

Cover and text design by
Zab Design & Typography

Edited by Brian Lam
Editorial assistance by Linda Field

Printed and bound in Canada

LIBRARY AND ARCHIVES CANADA
CATALOGUING IN PUBLICATION

Schulman, Sarah, 1958-, author Conflict is not abuse : overstating harm, community responsibility, and the duty of repair / Sarah Schulman.

Issued in print and electronic formats.
ISBN 978-1-55152-643-0 (paperback).
ISBN 978-1-55152-644-7 (html)

1. Conflict management. 2. Social conflict. 3. Social psychology. 4. Difference(Psychology).
I. Title.

HM1126.S34 2016 303.6'9
C2016-904334-7 C2016-904335-5

This book is dedicated with love to Hindeleh Pivko, who was only a little girl.

"I am grateful to the men and women who create books,
and I forgive the men and women who make books necessary."
— VOICE AT QUAKER MEETING, Peterborough New Hampshire

"It is not only that we may not choose with whom to cohabitate, but that we must actively preserve the unchosen character of inclusive and plural cohabitation; we not only live with those we never chose and to whom we may feel no social sense of belonging, but we are also obligated to preserve their lives and the plurality of which they form a part. In this sense, concrete political norms and ethical prescriptions emerge from the unchosen character of these modes of cohabitation."
— JUDITH BUTLER, *Parting Ways: Jewishness and the Critique of Zionism*, 2013

"Shunning is so often the go-to tool of people dealing with problems or conflict in queer communities, which only contributes to cycles of dehumanization and abuse. It's the easy, simplistic response too often deployed for all manner of interpersonal and inter-community conflict."
— COOPER LEE BOMBARDIER, Facebook post, January 2015

"I want people to be open to the little power that they do have."
— LISA HENDERSON, personal conversation, 2015

CONTENTS

Introduction | A Reparative Manifesto

Not everything that is faced can be changed; but nothing can be changed until it is faced.
— JAMES BALDWIN

AS I BEGAN THIS BOOK during the summer of 2014, the human community witnessed systemic repetition of unjustified cruelty with exhaustion and frustration. We watched white police officers in Ferguson, Missouri and Staten Island, New York murder two unarmed Black men: Michael Brown and Eric Garner. We watched a rich and powerful professional football player, Ray Rice, beat his wife, Janay, unconscious in an elevator. We watched the Israeli government mass murder over 2,000 Palestinian civilians in Gaza. It quickly became apparent that the methods we have developed collectively, to date, to understand these kinds of actions in order to avoid them, are not adequate.

As a novelist, in order to create characters that have integrity, I apply the principle that people do things for reasons, even if they are not aware of those reasons or even if they can't accept that their actions are motivated instead of neutral and objective. Using this principle to examine those events, I have to ask myself what the white police officers, the wealthy football player, and the militarized nation state *think* is happening that produces and justifies their brutal actions. As video and witness accounts attest, neither Michael Brown nor Eric Garner did *anything* that justified the way they were treated by the police. Eric Garner sold loose cigarettes and Michael Brown walked down the street. Both men tried to offer the police alternatives to cruelty. Eric Garner informed the police of the consequences of their actions on him, when he told them eleven times, while in an illegal chokehold, "I can't breathe." Michael Brown raised his hands in a sign of surrender and said, "Don't shoot." But something occurred within the minds, impulses, and group identities of the white police officers, in that they construed the original non-event compounded with these factual and peacemaking communications as some kind of threat or attack. In other words, these policemen looked at *nothing*, the complete absence of threat, and there they saw threat gross enough to justify murder. Nothing happened, but these people with power saw *abuse*.

We know from security camera footage taken in a casino lobby and elevator that Baltimore Ravens running back Ray Rice and his wife were having a quarrel. As much as we don't like quarrels with our partners, and wish they wouldn't happen, disagreement with one's lover is a normative part of human experience. It is impossible to live without it ever taking place. Intimate disagreement is, as they say, *life*. Yet, Ray Rice experienced normative, regular conflict that exists in every relationship, family, and household in the world as so overwhelmingly unbearable and threatening that he hit his wife, knocking her unconscious, and dragged her limp body by the ankles out of the elevator, leaving her lying inert in a hallway. He looked at normative, everyday conflict, and responded with extreme cruelty. He looked at the regular, even banal, expression of difference and saw *threat*.

The Israeli government has kept the Palestinian Gaza Strip under siege since 2005. This has made daily life unbearable for its inhabitants. In the late spring of 2014, the government of Benjamin Netanyahu escalated pressure on the already suffering Palestinians, and some factions within Gaza responded with rockets that were of such poor quality they had only symbolic impact. The Israeli government re-reacted in turn to this response with over fifty days of aerial bombing and ground invasion, causing mass death and massive destruction of literal, cultural, and psychological infrastructure. The Gazans were reacting to a state of injustice that the Israelis had created. The Gazans were *resisting*. They were refusing to go along with unbearable and unjustifiable treatment. The Israelis experienced this resistance to ongoing unfair treatment as *attack*.

Brown and Garner did absolutely nothing but be Black. Janay Rice expressed normative conflict. Gazans resisted unbearable treatment. In all of these cases the police, the husband, and the nation overstated harm. They took Nothing, Normative Conflict, and Resistance and misrepresented these reasonable stances of difference as Abuse. From the most intimate relationship between two people, to the power of the police, to the crushing reality of occupation, these actors displayed distorted thinking in which justifiable behavior was understood as aggression. In this way they overreacted at a level that produced tragedy, pain, and division. It is this moment of overreaction that I wish to examine in this book. My thesis is that at many levels of human interaction there is the opportunity to conflate discomfort with threat, to mistake internal anxiety for exterior danger, and in turn to escalate rather than resolve. I will show how this dynamic, whether between two individuals, between groups of people, between governments and civilians, or between nations is a fundamental opportunity for either tragedy or peace. Conscious awareness of these political and emotional mechanisms gives us all a chance to face ourselves, to achieve recognition and understanding in order to avoid escalation towards unnecessary pain.

Methodology

I ground my perspective in the queer: I use queer examples, I cite queer authors, I am rooted in queer points of view, I address and investigate concerns and trends in queer discourse. I come directly from a specifically lesbian historical analysis of power, rooted generationally in Audre Lorde and Adrienne Rich, in which sexual, racial, material, emotional, colonial, and gender dynamics were seen as continuous and interrelated. Audre, in particular, in her classic *Zami: A New Spelling of My Name*, which she called a "Biomythography," addressed the question of genre directly by simply inventing her own. So I continue the tradition of creative writers using non-fiction to address their observations, feelings, contexts, histories, visions, memories, and dreams. It is a category of the literature of ideas that stands apart from academia, and yet is useful to it and frequently incorporated into classroom reading, serving as a subject of academic analysis and inquiry while not being a product of it.

I also grew up in feminism, in which the meaning of the private sphere is organic to the meaning of the larger frame of power, and one is understood as consequential to the other. So to see and then examine the relationship of individual anxiety to its geopolitical expression is an historically consistent impulse. In the contemporary moment, this lens enables me to recognize the transition of "gay" from a severely oppressed, once broad category of people, to the more recent phenomenon of select sexual minority sectors getting access to the state's punishment apparatus, often based in whiteness, citizenship, normalizing family roles, and HIV negativity. The implications of these shifts are informative to all who are able to learn from queer experience. This trajectory from oppressed to oppressor is central to the content of this book. Just as unresolved, formerly subordinated or traumatized individuals can collude with or identify with bullies, so can unresolved, formerly subordinated or traumatized groups of people identify with the supremacy of the state. In both cases, the lack of recognition that the past is not the present leads to the newly acquired power to punish rather than to the self-transformation necessary to resolve conflict and produce justice.

My range of consideration is broad. Queer intellectuals and artists are no longer required to stay within our subject ghetto. We no longer have to choose between queer subjectivity and the world. The world, at least the world of ideas, now understands that the two are integrated. In some arenas I can claim "expertise," but in others I have something deeper to offer. As an artist I offer the reader an eclectic way in. I do not practice the "one, long, slow idea" school of thought. Instead, through three decades of books, plays, and movies, I have evolved a style of offering the reader many, many new ideas at once. Some of them will stick, some will be rejected, and some will be grappled with in a manner that creates even newer insights on the part of the reader. Historian Nan Alamilla Boyd helped me to understand that my lack of academic training makes me literally "undisciplined." This news was very freeing, and a gift I wish I had been handed decades before. I now am able to ask you to read this book the way you would watch a play: not to emerge saying, "The play is right!" but rather to observe that the play reveals human nuance, contradiction, limitation, joy, connection, and the tragedy of separation. That the playwright's own humanity is also an example of these unavoidable flaws. These chapters are not homogenous. As a creative writer I have long understood that form should be an organic expression of the feelings at the core of the piece. Each chapter here serves a different function and that is represented in its tone, genre, style, and form. Some are journalistic, some analytical, some are speculative, others abstract, some are only feelings. As a novelist, I know that it is the cumulative juxtaposition that reveals the story.

This is not a book to be agreed with, an exhibition of evidence or display of proof. It is instead designed for engaged and dynamic interactive collective thinking where some ideas will resonate, others will be rejected, and still others will provoke the readers to produce new knowledge themselves. Like authentic, conscious relationships, truly progressive communities, responsible citizenship, and real friendship, and like the peace-making that all these require, it asks you to be interactive.

Facing and Dealing with Conflict

The examples of racist police violence when nothing is happening, men beating their female partners unconscious in response to normative conflict, and the mass murder of civilians when acts of resistance against intolerable conditions are taking place, are all extreme but daily acts of injustice. By the time these cruelties occur, the situation is already completely out of control. For that reason, I am interested, in *this* book, in examining the phenomenon of overstating harm where it begins in its earlier stage as *Conflict*, before it escalates and explodes into tragedy. Disaster originates in an initial overreaction to *Conflict* and then escalates to the level of gross *Abuse*. It is at the Conflict stage that the hideous future is still not inevitable and can be resolved. Once the cruelty and perhaps violence erupts, it is too late. Or at least requires a level of repair outside of the range of what many of us will do without encouragement and support.

Conflict, after all, is rooted in difference and people are and always will be different. With the exception of those natural disasters that are not caused by human misdeed, most of the pain, destruction, waste, and neglect towards human life that we create on this planet and beyond, are consequences of our overreaction to difference. This is expressed through our resistance to facing and resolving problems, which is overwhelmingly a refusal to change how we see ourselves in order to be accountable. Therefore how we understand Conflict, how we respond to Conflict, and how we behave as bystanders in the face of other people's Conflict determines whether or not we have collective justice and peace.

At the center of my vision is the recognition that above all, it is the community surrounding a Conflict that is the source of its resolution. The community holds the crucial responsibility to resist overreaction to difference, and to offer alternatives of understanding and complexity. We have to help each other illuminate and counter the role of overstating harm instead of using it to justify cruelty. I suggest that we have a better chance at interrupting unnecessary pain if we articulate our *shared* responsibility in creating alternatives. Looking for methods of *collective* problem-solving make these destructive, tragic leaps more difficult to accomplish. People who are being punished for doing nothing, for having normative conflict, or for resisting unjustified situations, need the help of other people. While there are many excuses for not intervening in unjust punishment, that intervention is, nonetheless, essential. Without the intervention that most people are afraid to commit to, this escalation cannot be interrupted.

In other words, because we won't change our stories to integrate other people's known *reasons* and illuminate their unknown ones, we cannot resolve Conflict in a way that is productive, equitable, and fair. This is why we (individuals, couples, cliques, families, communities, nations, peoples) often pretend, believe, or claim that Conflict is, instead, Abuse and therefore deserves punishment. That the mere fact of the other person's difference is misrepresented as an assault that then justifies our cruelty and relinquishes our responsibility to change. Consequently, resistance to that false charge of Abuse is then positioned as further justification of even more cruelty masquerading as "punishment," through the illogic at base of refusing accountability and repair.

While people are punished at every level of human relationship for doing nothing, for normative Conflict and for resistance, simultaneously we have the overwhelming reality of actual violence and real Abuse. There is an enormous existing literature that analyzes and quantifies actual violence and real Abuse. There are political movements like Black Lives Matter and Palestine Solidarity that respond to this real violence and actual Abuse. And on the individual and family level there is a financially and culturally significant Recovery Industry with books, podcasts, videos, workshops, and a wide variety of practitioners and healing practices. Because discourse on actual violence and abuse and the recovery process is already embedded in the commercial and cultural realm, I am not going to repeat that information here. Instead, in *this* book I am looking at something quite different. Without in any way minimizing the role of violence in our lives, I am looking, *simultaneously*, at how a heightened rhetoric of threat that confuses doing nothing, normative conflict, and resistance with actual abuse, has produced a wide practice of *overstating harm*. And that this overstatement of harm is often expressed in "shunning," a literal refusal to speak in person with another human being, or group of people, an exclusion of their information, the active obstruction to a person being heard and the pretense that they do not exist. I am examining the inaccurate claiming of "abuse" as a substitute for problem-solving. I make plain how this deflection of responsibility produces unnecessary separation and perpetuates anxiety while producing cruelty, shunning, undeserved punishment, incarceration, and occupation. The title of this book, *Conflict Is Not Abuse*, recommends mutual accountability in a culture of underreaction to abuse and overreaction to conflict. I am motivated to separate out the cultural phenomena of overstatement of harm from harm itself, because this separation is necessary in order to retain the legitimate protections and recognitions afforded the experience of actual violence and real oppression. This book offers many, many examples that I hope will help clarify the negative consequences of conflating Conflict with Abuse.

Positive Change Can Happen

Because I have participated in, contributed to, and witnessed progressive paradigm shifts, I know from the fact of my own lived experience that, while perfection is never achievable, positive change is always possible. Resolution doesn't mean that everyone is happy, but it does mean that perhaps fewer people are being blamed for pain they have not caused, or being cast as the receptacle of other people's anxieties, so that fewer people are dehumanized by false accusation. Or as Matt Brim suggests, that when we are in the realm of Conflict, we can move from the Abuse-based construction of *perpetrator and victim* to the more accurate recognition of the parties as *the conflicted*, each with legitimate concerns and legitimate rights that must be considered in order to produce just resolution.

At the beginning of the AIDS epidemic, people with HIV were among the most oppressed people on earth. In addition to oppression by race, geography, class, gender, and sexuality, they faced a terminal illness for which there were no known treatments. They had no laws of protection, no services, no representation, and received no compassion. Their lives did not matter and their prognosis was unabated suffering and inevitable mass death. Millions suffered and died without care, comfort, or interest, vilified by cruel projections, neglect, and unjustified exclusion and blame. They were systematically shunned, their experiences and points of view viciously excluded from policy, representation, dominant cultural mores, and law. I witnessed this firsthand.

Only when people with AIDS and their friends intervened against the status quo and forced an end to the shunning by forcing interactivity through zaps, sit-ins, initiated agendas, actions, interruptions, shut-downs, exposes, research, and demonstrations, did systemic progress begin to be made. The state theorized this unwanted insistence on appropriate treatment as an act of violation, calling it "disorderly conduct" instead of resistance, an illegality to be punished and stigmatized. They shunned people with AIDS and therefore did not hear what they had to say to about how they were being treated. As a result, thousands of arrests took place of people trying to save lives, many of whom fought passionately until the day they died. In other words, it was the mistreatment and shunning of people with HIV that produced their illegality. If the powers that be had invited people with HIV into their halls and said, "We have a conflict here. Therefore we need to sit down together and solve it," people with HIV would not have had to do civil disobedience, for which they and their supporters were arrested by the police. It was the shunning that made them have to do this. It was the immoral shunning that criminalized people with HIV.

Today, we understand that those people's acts of resistance were necessary, heroic, and socially transformative; that just because they were forbidden to speak doesn't mean that they were obligated to obey those unjust orders. As a consequence, the experience of being HIV-positive has changed dramatically for many, though absolutely not for all. Attitude, treatment, laws, public opinion, social responsibility, and representation have been transformed in significant ways. The two primary obstacles in place now are stigma and economics: the greed of pharmaceutical companies and health care industries in a context of global capital. What remains to be addressed is a question of political will so that existing effective treatments can be extended to all regardless of nationality, location, or class. Today, the renewed stigma of HIV criminalization looms. It relies on the fundamental dynamics addressed in this book: *The conflation of Conflict with Abuse, and the overstatement of harm as a justification for cruelty*, even while revolutions in attitude, and the experience of HIV, evolve simultaneously.

It is clear from history that progressive cultural and political advancement is not natural or neutral and does not occur on its own momentum. As Jim Hubbard and I showed in the film he directed and we co-produced, *United In Anger: A History of ACT UP* (2012), these changes for people with HIV/AIDS, within one generation, were accomplished by radical, effective, creative, and diverse political activism on multiple fronts. Change requires awareness to propel a transformation of attitude. Once there is even a glimmer of awareness, it implies the ownership of an injustice, and a consequential responsibility for its solution, which must be expressed through behavior, not just feeling. Yet, as was learned by the AIDS crisis, significant attitudinal change, while inhabited by many, is propelled by a *critical mass*, a small diverse collection of individuals with focused intent and effective action who rise to the occasion to literally change our minds.

In the summer of 2014, the Palestinian people of Gaza were slaughtered by Israelis in the face of worldwide abandonment. Palestinians are, today, among the most victimized, scapegoated, and attacked people in the world. I watch as their suffering and mass murder is propagandized through pervasive dehumanized representations that falsely position them as "dangerous" when, in fact, they are the ones endangered and in desperate need of outside intervention. Although I quote extensively from Palestinians in Historic Palestine and the diaspora in this book, I do want to start with a piece Jewish journalist Amira Haas wrote in July 2014 in the newspaper *Haaretz* addressed to her fellow Israelis:

> If victory is measured by the success of causing lifelong trauma to 1.8 million people (and not for the first time) waiting to be executed at any moment then the victory is yours and adds up to our moral implosion, the ethical defeat of a society engaged in no self-inspection, wallowing in self-pity over postponed airline flights and burnishing itself with the pride of the enlightened.

Haas identifies the key elements found in many group supremacy formations, whether families, cliques, or nations. It's what Canadian Jude Johnson names "meritocracy, entitlement, enemy mind." One group deserves the right to be unquestioned and they are entitled to dehumanize the other whom they misrepresent as "a threat" while using this distortion as the grounds for self-congratulation, indifferent to the pain they cause and the long-term negative consequences of their actions.

While every context has its specificities, I remember when people with AIDS were universally treated as dangerous pariahs, inherently guilty, accused of being predators, excluded, silenced, and threatened while being refused research, protection, or kindness and therefore condemned to suffer and die in the millions. Many of my friends numbered among them. Many more are haunted for life by the specter of that suffering. There can never be a direct comparison, only the resonance of historic memory, but I know that the persecution, mass death experience, and abandonment of Palestinians, justified by similarly aligned false representations, unjustified claims of Abuse, the projection of Trauma caused by others, Supremacy ideology, and distorted thinking, can all be transformed. But first these constructions have to be recognized. Any pain that human beings can create, human beings can transcend. But we have to understand what we are doing. This transformation also requires a critical mass, a small, effective, focused, and inspired group of people who can combine clear moral thinking with the taking of responsibility, as expressed through direct challenge to brutality and organized action. It can be a small group of conscious friends helping a person conflating Conflict with Abuse find alternatives. It can be two family members who don't jump on an unethical bandwagon falsely construed as "loyalty." It can be a vanguard of activists in a city, or a minority stratum in the world who object to victimization and intervene to create change. In a society, this can be a few thousand or even hundred people. In one person's life, or the life of a family or community, it can be two friends.

Tom Bartlett, writing in the *Chronicle of Higher Education* in July 2015, memorialized the massacre at the Bosnian town of Srebrenica by reviewing some recent research by social psychologists studying conflict resolution. The findings seem obvious, and yet are rejected by many people. "More contact between groups reduces prejudice," Bartlett concludes. "The status of the groups must be respected as equal. Those in authority must be supportive. The contact must be more than superficial." A meta-analysis of 515 studies involving a quarter of a million people concluded that

> intergroup contact fosters "greater trust and forgiveness for past transgressions." The effects are evident regardless of gender, age, religion, or ethnicity. They seem to hold even when the contact is indirect—that is, you are less likely to be prejudiced against a certain group if a member of your group is friends with a member of that group. A 2009 study

> published in *American Psychologist* found, somewhat incredibly, that simply thinking about positive interactions with a member of another group reduces prejudice. Imaginary contact may be better than none at all.

Yet over and over again, self-righteousness and the refusal to be self-critical is expressed as dominance reliant on the ability to shun or exclude the other party. Those seeking justice often have to organize allies in order to force contact and conversation, negotiation. Trying to create communication is almost always the uphill struggle of the falsely blamed. And entire movements are structured around the goal of forcing one party to face the reality of the other, and thereby face themselves. And of course this power struggle over whether or not opposing parties will speak is an enormous smokescreen covering up the real issue, the substance of what they need to speak about: namely, the nature of and resolution to the conflict.

In the realm of geopolitics, that human impulse to end cruelty and create repair is represented, in one example, by the Palestinian-led Boycott, Divestment and Sanctions movement founded in 2005. This is a non-violent global movement rooted in the action of withholding economic, academic, and cultural support from the Israeli war machine to force basic human rights: the rights of refugees, the right to free movement, the rights of basic autonomy. This is an achievable goal reliant on community conscience and action, and towards which consumers, students, churches, employees with pension plans, artists and performers, and companies with investments must contribute. For Americans who oppose these cruelties and dishonorable actions, one goal is ending US military funding for Israel's occupation of Palestine.

This book starts in the most intimate realm of personal difference that confuses anxiety with threat: sexual fear, domestic disagreement, individual projection of past experiences onto the present, or lack of support from friends and family to dismantle distorted thinking. It then moves on to the second tier: the relationship between overreaction and the state and the responsibility of community to help individuals progress towards repair without capitulating to the power of the state. It is here that we find the roots of the problem: Overstatement of Harm, False Accusations of Blame, Punishment for Resistance, Projection, Shunning and Exclusion, Group Bullying, Bad Groups, False Concepts of Loyalty, Cruelty over Accountability, Distorted Thinking/Mental Illness, and the stigma around acknowledging it in people we love or could love. It is in the personal realm of people we know, institutions we interact with, and authorities we empower that these transformations can be made. Right now, the state and shallow group relationships collude to escalate Conflict and obstruct repair. As I try to show over and over again, refusing to be self-critical in order to solve conflicts enhances the power of the state. We can resist this process. As individuals, we have enormous power in the ways we abandon the scapegoated, or instead stand up for them. We have power to change the ways we encourage shunning and instead do the work to facilitate communication. Simple shifts in personal behavior and their expressions in political structures of power, produce changing public norms which can make huge differences in individual and collective experiences.

For example, when I was sixteen in 1975 and faced the brutality of my parents' homophobia, I went to my high school guidance counselor. He told me not to tell my classmates that I was a lesbian because they could shun me. In other words, instead of intervening, he upheld the distorted thinking, unjustified punishment, and exclusion. Today, when I hear about familial homophobia from my students, I connect them to relevant aspects of the LGBT community, provide alternatives in my classroom, and offer to speak to their parents, i.e., to intervene and stand up to brutality in order to protect its recipient and transform their context. I do this in the midst of a critical mass of other teachers taking the same action, and in this way there is a paradigm shift, where the school that, in my case, was part of the oppression system can become part of the resistance and solution. This is the kind of step that I am asking for, and which I believe is possible both inside and outside of institutions and with friends. The move from complicit bystander to active participant for change is the same kind of attitudinal shift that many of us went through in relationship to people with AIDS, and must go through in relationship to Palestine. But I am not asking for this on a disaster by disaster basis, but rather as a shift in our collective mindset. By differentiating between Conflict and Abuse, we can become advocates with our friends, families, communities, workplaces, localities, religions, and nations against scapegoating and shunning on the small and large scales, and contributors to a group dynamic of accountability and repair.

In this book, I bring fifty-seven years of living and thirty-five years of writing to a critical conclusion: that from the most potent potential for intimacy between strangers, to intimate domestic moments between lovers, to the claims of the state on its citizens, to the geopolitical phenomena of mass murder, we witness a continuum. Namely, false accusations of harm are used to avoid acknowledgment of complicity in creating conflict and instead escalate normative conflict to the level of crisis. This choice to punish rather than resolve is a product of distorted thinking, and relies on reinforcement of negative group relationships, when instead these ideologies should be actively challenged. Through this overstatement of harm, false accusations are used to justify cruelty, while shunning keeps information from entering into the process. Resistance to shunning, exclusion, and unilateral control, while necessary, are mischaracterized as harm and used to re-justify more escalation towards bullying, state intervention, and violence. Emphasizing communication and repair, instead of shunning and separation, is the key to transforming these paradigms.

PART ONE | *The Conflicted Self and the Abusive State*

Chapter One lays out the fundamental differences between Conflict and Abuse in the realm of the heart, the intimate: the flirt, relationships, households, and surrounding friendship circles. Here we begin the conversation about what happens when Conflict is wrongly represented as Abuse in the personal realm, and how the new technologies corrupt potential affections, understandings, negotiations, and love.

In Chapter Two, I enter the arena of the state, learning from the work of anti-violence advocate Catherine Hodes to understand the difference between Conflict and Abuse in relationship to social service providers.

Chapter Three begins the application of these ideas by examining an expression of *overstating harm* in which the police are called or the state is invoked in matters where Conflict is misrepresented as Abuse. In trying to understand how the police became the arbiters of our relationships, I look at the historic evolution from the creation of the Feminist Anti-Violence movement in the 1960s to contemporary state control of the domestic realm. How resistance politics became part of the state apparatus of control, often using the same words. I examine how differences in race and class impact contemporary legal and social approaches to intimate partner abuse, and how the individual's inability to problem-solve serves the interests of the state.

Chapter Four expands these foundations through the surprising example of Canadian HIV criminalization, showing how the "moderate" presentation of a neoliberal society can cover up extreme scapegoating of Conflict, and exploitation of sexual anxiety initiated and aggravated by the state itself. Here I examine some ways that governments collude with citizens to misdirect anxiety (from Latin *angustus* meaning "narrow") into claims of criminal wrong.

PART TWO | *The Impulse to Escalate*

Once this relationship between overstating harm and the Abuse by the state is established, I start to unravel some of the reasons why people are compelled to escalate. The centerpiece of this dynamic is the role of "bad" groups in encouraging bullying and shunning instead of peacemaking. Escalation is the key consequence of refusing to problem-solve or negotiate, and it demands our attention as a central obstacle to peace and justice.

In Chapter Five, I examine how Traumatized behavior and Supremacy ideology resemble each other, how both produce distorted thinking that seeks unreasonable levels of control over other people and does not tolerate self-criticism or difference. I propose a release of the stigma around recognizing mental illness, distorted thinking, and anxiety, and suggest that they be publicly and commonly recognized as contributing sources of this intolerance and control. And I try to look at the cultural denial of these manifestations of distorted thinking as a strategy for the enforcement of dominance.

Chapter Six further deepens this discussion by taking up the contemporary concern with "triggers," i.e., the moment of escalation, especially in sequence with shunning. Here I look at four diverse systems of thought that all recognize the trigger + shunning sequence as the centerpiece of injustice and pain: Traditional Psychoanalysis, Contemporary Psychiatry and its commercial counterpart Pop Psychology, Mindfulness, and Al-Anon, the counterpart to Alcoholics Anonymous focused on partners and families of Alcoholics. I examine how each of these perspectives understand the role of the "bad" group (couple, family, community, friends, religion, nation, peoples) as enforcers of escalation driven by overstated harm. I look at how these divergent systems of thought unite by offering what Stephen Andrews calls "realignment" from "bad" groups, and centering delay as a method for avoiding unjust escalation.

In Chapter Seven, I examine the role of the family as a dangerous place of production of this group-based negative loyalty, male control, and violence. I suggest that the rising legitimacy of some LGBT people in relationship to the state through the traditional family structure reinforces some of the problematic aspects of that structure. And how, in particular, the assumptions of the mother role remains antithetical to power sharing, even in the queer family, and its relationship to the state. This alignment between family and state makes us increasingly complicit with a governmental apparatus of punishment that does not address the actual sources of conflict, and instead relies on overreaction instead of repair.

PART THREE | *Supremacy/Trauma and the Justification of Injustice: The Israeli War on Gaza*

Finally, in Chapter Eight, I represent the first three weeks of the Israeli war on Gaza as witnessed from afar through social media in the summer of 2014. I analyze it as a production of all the elements discussed and accrued throughout the book. I will show how refusal to take responsibility for participation in creating both Conflict and Abuse and unilateral false stories about one party's righteousness in combination with the negative bonds of the "bad" group, reinforced by shunning and propelled by both

Supremacy ideology and Traumatized behavior, produce what Israeli historian Ilan Pappe calls "incremental genocide."

In the Conclusion, I explore how people with social commitments have a special responsibility to intervene to end shunning, facilitate communication, and do the work to reveal complex views of human behavior as we practice self-criticism and stand up to negative groups. I detail the tasks and gifts of real solidarity towards peacemaking and its necessity for those of us with visions for a better future. "The Duty of Repair" belongs to us all, but especially to those who claim access to a social conscience.

SARAH SCHULMAN
March 2, 2016
New York City

PART ONE | The Conflicted Self and the Abusive State

Chapter One | **In Love:** Conflict Is Not Abuse

A possible life is one that wills the impossible.
— MAHMOUD DARWISH

OF COURSE IT IS NOT ONLY the police, wealthy football players, or colonial occupiers who can feel abused in the absence of actual threat. It is not only the dominant who feel endangered when faced with normative conflict or when their own unjust actions are responded to with resistance. In fact these distorted reactions occur in both the powerful and the weak, the supremacist and the traumatized, in society and in intimacy. In arenas in which real abuse could conceivably take place, there are those who feel persecuted and threatened even though they are not in danger, and they often lack help from those around them to differentiate between the possible and the actual. Bullies often conceptualize themselves as being under attack when they are the ones originating the pain. Everywhere we look, there is confusion between Conflict and Abuse.

If a person cannot solve a conflict with a friend, how can they possibly contribute to larger efforts for peace? If we refuse to speak to a friend because we project our anxieties onto an email they wrote, how are we going to welcome refugees, immigrants, and the homeless into our communities? The values required for social repair are the same values required for personal repair. And so this discussion must begin in the most micro experience. Confusing being mortal with being threatened can occur in any realm. The fact that something *could* go wrong does not mean that we are in danger. It means that we are alive. Mortality is the sign of life. In the most intimate and personal of arenas, many of us have loved and trusted someone who violated that trust. So when someone else comes along who intrigues us, whose interests we share, who we enjoy being with, with whom there could be some mutual enrichment and understanding, that does not mean that we are going to be violated again. And experiencing confusion, disagreement, frustration, and difference does not mean that we are being violated again. Experiencing anxiety does not mean that anyone is doing anything to us that is unjust.

Now, recognition and consciousness about these differences brings us the opportunity to truly face and deal with the problems of intimacy that we couldn't resolve before. Awareness of these distinctions gives us the chance to appreciate and enjoy the gifts of intimacy and difference, that perhaps we took for granted before, or of which we were once over-critical. Of course, some people just give up. They internalize a story about themselves that they are unlovable or incapable of loving an equal, or that they are perpetual victims, or that they "can't do" long-term relationships, but thinking these things doesn't make them true. In order to "protect" ourselves by keeping our lives small and shutting out intimacies, we could actually be hurting ourselves, missing out on a transformative experience of the heart, and sabotaging our small but crucial contribution to making peace. And the withholding also mis-trains those around us to not see us and others like us as sexual, loving adults who have the right to be in intimacy with equals. Relationships of all kinds, after all, are the centerpiece of healing.

Some of the fear is based in earlier experience. If we were in a car accident, we can become afraid of cars. If someone close to us died, we could become terrified of normative loss. If we experience sexually alienating encounters, we could construct ourselves as not sexual. If we are physically violated, we could imagine that every person who reminds us of the assailant is going to assault and violate us. If we are socially oppressed or marginalized or punished, we could mistrust everyone from the category of the oppressor. But this fear of potential threat is not always based in actual experience. It can also be a political construction, one that is fabricated and then advertised through popular culture and entertainment, or enforced through systems of power, like Islamaphobia, or generalized rhetorics of "terror." We are often made to believe through repetitive official and sub-cultural messaging that certain kinds of people are dangerous, that certain kinds of social interactions are threatening, even though the only thing they might actually threaten is an established power structure. Or when it is we who wield the unjust upper-hand, we are reinforced in falsely conceptualizing the other party's resistance as the originating threat.

Why do some of us need to feel and act as though we are being assaulted when we're not? It's a big question, and one at the core of so much hostility, fear, projection, and punishment. The more I look at this inflationary process, the more I see how central it is to unnecessary separation and pain. Confusions between projection, discomfort, and threat appear in every realm from the most intimate to the global: from the first ping of desire, to the bombardment of civilians. Seeing danger that isn't there leads to escalation and overreaction, which can destroy people's lives spiritually and literally, individually and collectively. So because the question is so big, I start in the smallest place. With the flirt.

The Dangerous Flirt

I'm at a table with relative strangers. I notice the woman in the opposite chair; she is attractive and smart. Her imagination is surprising. She has insights that are attention-grabbing. And she displays herself in a way that may be aimed at the larger group but is having an effect on me. We are all talking business, but she is a bit naughty. This is a professional gathering inside an institutional building. Yet the woman across the way uses the word "G-spot." Now, queer people have a sexualized vocabulary in professional spaces that many straight people might find inappropriate, so this stands out as a bit showy, but it's not that unusual. Later, though, she insists on it. She wants attention for this word and we all give it to her. She smiles, she is bold, she commands but she is also soft in her command. Now I am thinking about her sexually. I am thinking about the word *G-spot*, its mythologies and implications. The more she insists that we think about this, the more I begin to think about penetrating her and I am also thinking about her penetrating me. Is she flirting with me? I am the stranger here; the others are her workmates. I don't know if she is always like this, if she is flirting with someone else at the table, or if this is for my benefit. Is this "inadvertent" or is it "intentional." Is she *innocent* of being sexually suggestive or is she *guilty*?

A different person, perhaps one with a history of a specific kind of sexual abuse, processed in a specific way, especially if it pertained to suggestible language, could find her speech inappropriate and upsetting. They could find it harassing. It could be a "trigger." However, I find it inviting. I am enjoying her and I am appreciating her. If I attempt to follow up in order to discover if this was actually aimed at me, I too could be seen as a harasser; after all, this is a professional relationship. Human Resources could be called in to hurt me. Or, just as easily, my interest could be reciprocated. I have to be very, very careful. One false move and I could be the sad object of an outraged story on the dreaded grapevine: "Sarah Schulman came on to me. It was so inappropriate." The story would never be "I liked her, I flirted with her, she understood me, and then I was scared I would be hurt like I have been before." Depending on her character, self-concept, history, and logic, depending on how she chooses to act, or if she is conscious enough to have choice, I could be accused of desire. And so could she. Given the institutional setting, I could even have charges brought against me. Or, things could go very well.

Being accused of desire is as old as history itself, and is central to the queer experience. It has been very, very dangerous. Both seeing and imagining queer desire in another has and can cost us our lives, our homes, our families, and employment. We have been excluded, shunned, imprisoned, and murdered for knowing or believing that desire is reciprocated. Sex workers, especially trans women, often lose their lives expressly because they were desired. And certainly "homosexual panic defense" has been used successfully in courts to justify the murders of gay men, perhaps gay men who had absolutely zero sexual interest in their assailant; or cis women, trans women, or gay men who responded to another man's wanting. And of course many of us have been violated by the person we most loved and desired, and who loved and desired us. We are accused of desire when it never manifested, and we are accused of desire when it is full and free. Being desired is not the same as being harassed, and we do not have to punish or shun the person who sees what is special about us. Just because you want me, doesn't mean I have to hurt you. Especially if I also feel attractions that I don't pursue for reasons of projections from my past. I don't have to avoid you, ignore your call, refuse to return your email, or block you. We can actually talk to each other, and find the other ways and realms in which to connect. We can be people. We can deal with it. We can build friendships, collaborate, and just be nice to one another. Uneven desire is not a crime, it is not rude, it is not an assault or grounds for shunning or being hurtful. It's just life and we can still be friends. For real. Even forever. But we have to talk.

Being falsely accused of desire also has its own more extended history, one more deeply rooted in race. There is already a long, known tradition of white people repeatedly concocting accusations of desire to justify specifically racial violence. Black men, as we all know, have been lynched, tortured, castrated, incarcerated, and murdered by the white state since they were brought to the continent as slaves, and one of the chief channels has been through the false accusation that they desired white women. Of course intrinsic to white Supremacy is the internal fantasy and external projection that Black people want what white people have. So while Black people are the ones who are endangered, they have been falsely positioned as dangerous and threatening to whites in order to justify white cruelty. White people can't face our need to subjugate and diminish others, so we create a claim that they have done something wrong which justifies this punishment. We take our anxieties about our own negative impulses and unjust deeds and mask them with untrue stories about Black people's characters, actions, and intent, including in the realm of desire.

I think of the complexity expressed by actress Sarah Paulson's deep and multi-dimensional performance in the movie *12 Years a Slave*. As the white wife of a pathologically cruel slave owner, Paulson's character cannot understand that her real problem is the frame of white and male Supremacy in which she lives. So she projects her uncomprehending pain into the substitute arena of jealousy over her husband's sexual abuse of a Black slave, played by Lupita Nyong'o (who won an Oscar). The white woman is not a slave owner herself as she cannot own property, human or otherwise, but her husband owns this Black woman whom he openly sexually abuses. This white woman excuses her husband, overlooks white Supremacy and slavery, and instead aims all her pain and rage at the Black woman, causing her to be brutally whipped. In this way Paulson's character finds the wrong solution for the wrong problem. Nyong'o's character is, of course, shunned. She is not allowed to communicate, to speak or to express her experience, point of view, and/or understanding. Her position as a specter is a unilateral creation of the jealous white woman who does not imagine or consider that the Black woman does not want to be understood or treated this way. Political problems become diverted and expressed as intimate problems and anxieties get aimed at the wrong person.

As stark as the racial example is, we certainly don't need the historic cataclysm of slavery to find projections of social evils catapulted onto intimate personal relationships. They are everywhere. There is a pervasive inability to see the big picture, to look at psychological make-up, to imagine economic consequences, or to ask about other people's real motives and objectives. This lack of information, communication, and understanding produces unnecessary fear and then cruelty, while refusing contexts and explanatory histories and avoiding scapegoating. The refusal to actually ask someone *what they think is happening* and to instead insist on unilateral interpretations compounds misunderstanding and then injustice.

The use of accusations of desire as an overstatement of harm is a prototype with powerful trickle-down application. After all, many of us are never supposed to express erotic feeling or its discrete and different counterpart: erotic interest. Women, of course, risk all kinds of slander and are tagged as predators for revealing erotic feeling. Mothers are not supposed to have desires that could disrupt their sacrifice to their children. Queers have been taught all our lives that erotic feeling is wrong and that it will subject us to ridicule, exclusion, and punishment. People who feel erotically towards forbidden objects—like those other than partners to whom they have pledged monogamy, or those who are the wrong age, who work in the same sexually prohibitive workplace, who are transgender, or sex workers, who are generally desexualized by the dominant culture, or who are "off-type" (as in not as butch as one's femme identity demands in a partner)—can motivate them to hide feelings, even to themselves. Telling the truth of interest means taking the risk of being accused.

There have been times in my life when I was attracted to someone and didn't want to admit it, or that I was attracted to or even in love with her, or at least loved her, and had no awareness of this. It is not that I was lying, but that I was *defended*. I blocked access to my own real feelings. I did this to *defend* a story about myself that I felt safe maintaining, even if it wasn't true. But sometimes the other person saw the truth that I was unable to access or be accountable for. Part of peace-making is acknowledging that we can't know everything about ourselves, and sometimes we reveal things to others that we are not ready to accept.

Sexism has exploited this truth into the lie that men always know more about women than we know about ourselves. But refuting male Supremacy does not mean pretending that we all understand ourselves completely. What if she reciprocated or expressed what I was not developed enough to express? What if I became angry, or denied the reality? Blamed her as a substitute for examining myself? What if she tried to help me recognize or be accountable to that reality? Certainly this dynamic of defended refusal is a normative part of many people's coming to terms with their sexual imaginations and can in fact continue after sexual identity is well in place. Is the act of honest pushback a kind of "harassment," or is it a gift?

Of course, people come to themselves in their own time, but what if the denial manifests in something harmful to the other person? What if I was flirting but didn't realize what I was feeling and doing? What if she responded? What if I became angry or withdrawn at her recognition of a truth I could not recognize? What if I blamed her and asked her to carry the burden of my own dishonesty? What do we call that? Of course, I should not feel expected to kiss someone I don't want to kiss. But what if I don't want to want to kiss her but still want to? Then is the other's forward response an invasion? I don't think so.

Email, Texts, and Negative Escalation

This central role of anxiety in escalating Conflict is one of the reasons why, in our contemporary time, email and texts are so often the source for tragic separations of potentially enriching relationships. First of all, email and text are both unidirectional and don't allow for return information to enhance or transform comprehension. We must speak to each other, especially when events or feelings are fraught. I wish that all the people of the industrial world would sign a pledge that any negative exchange that is created on email or text must be followed by a live, in-person conversation. And clearly we have a responsibility to encourage our friends and colleagues to not make negative judgments based on email or texts. So many relationships are ruined by the artificial nature of these obstructive walls, especially when one party makes a negative power-play by refusing to speak to the other in person. They then create the false problem of whether or not the two conflicted parties will speak at all, which makes addressing and progressing to the real source of anxiety impossible. Refusing to communicate has always been one of the main causes of false accusation as it guarantees negative fantasy about the other, especially in arenas that are particularly loaded like sexuality, love, community, family, materiality, group identification, gender, power, access, and violence. Email and texts don't allow us to go through the human phases of feeling that occur when we actually communicate face to face.

Refusing to speak to someone without terms for repair is a strange, childish act of destruction in which nothing can be won. Like all withholding, it comes from a state of rage, and states of rage are products of the past. As some say, "If it's hysterical, it's historical." By refusing to talk without terms, a person is refusing to learn about themselves and thereby refusing to have a better life. It hurts everyone around them by dividing communities and inhibiting learning. When we have terms (e.g., "You stole my money to buy drugs so I will talk to you about this when you have three years sober"), they may not ever be met. But at least there is always a possibility of repair. Withholding this possibility makes normative conflict or resistance the primary source of injustice between us. It is designed to hurt, and it does hurt, with nothing gained but pain.

Without conversation, it is the person with the most limitations who is in control. The desirable goal for all of us is not to restrict those who can, but to bring more communication skills to those who can't. Refusal through email, texting, and other technologies keeps the person who doesn't know how to problem-solve from learning how. It keeps them imprisoned in their own imagined negative fears about the other, and their fantasies of their own potential humiliation or demise if they were to talk to the other person and thereby understand what the other person is thinking and feeling. Often these blocks are instigated over Nothing, Normative Conflict, or Simple Difference. It gets elevated in importance in the blocker's mind because they are too anxious to negotiate, or are paralyzed by negative fantasy about actually speaking to the dehumanized other. But because they also deny these internal conditions, negotiation becomes impossible. They cannot advance, and anyone who is controlled by their refusal cannot advance. If we can recognize that relationships are necessary to human peace and society, then friends or family would say, "What is the worst thing that could happen if you talk?" or "How can I help the two of you communicate?" Unfortunately, it is the distorted social norm to see the wish to repair as an assault, and the projection of negative fantasy to be a right.

A banal illustration from my own daily life: You live in another city and we have a long-standing date for lunch when I come to town. But we made the date by email, so there was no discussion and I had no idea that you were squeezing me in between really high-pressure events. If we had spoken on the phone, even for ten minutes, we could have talked this through and I would have realized where you were at, and rearranged things so you could be better accommodated. But I don't know anything about it. And your secret makes you feel as though you are being pressured ... by me. Even though that is not what is happening, the actual source of the pressure is that we didn't speak. So, the mere fact that we planned our get-together by email has set us up for failure.

I am excited to see you. I have invited you for lunch and have been thinking about what I will make for you. I know you are a busy single parent and assume that few people make meals for you so I want it to be a nice change. But the day before you cancel by email. This is approximately what you write:

> So sorry but the evening after our lunch is the party for my son's graduation and my family is in for the festivities from out of town and they are staying with me. Then in two days I am taking him out of town, and I have a lot of projects to finish I am sorry Sarah.

Now if we had spoken, even for a few minutes, we could have cycled through the normal reactions. 1. I am disappointed. 2. I only realize now how kind it was of you to try when you had so much going on and I want you to know that I now recognize this so you can feel appreciated. 3. I brought you a little gift. What is your address? I will mail it to you before I leave. 4. Now that the business is taken care of, we can cycle into connecting. How are you? Are you excited to be taking him on a trip? And finally, Appreciation. 5. I am so glad I had the chance to hear your voice. Grand total of time expended to connect, communicate, and respect: five to ten minutes.

But with email, none of this is possible. Only one feeling can be conveyed, in place of the natural progression of feeling that conversation allows. So if I respond to your email with one of my own: "I am sad, but let's talk on the phone before you leave"—that could cause the cataclysmic catastrophic end of all ends. Instead of just calling me, you can decide that I am abusing you. That I am pressuring you, guilt-tripping you, you are too busy to phone, you can't text, you're too mad, hectic. You have too many things to think about. We simply will not be allowed to evolve. All your anger about your family and who will and won't be at your party for your son, your conflicts about your life, all of that converges on me and the horrible transgressing demand I have made on you by asking for us to talk. I am actually your friend, but you turn me into your foe. You therefore don't answer me, and now we're fucked up.

Email creates repression and anxiety. No one is seen and no one is affirmed. The only way to recreate the normal human cycle of response is to send even more short emails or texts in a row, each with an evolved position. The next one assures you that I understand, as I am afraid that you are misconstruing me. And the final one wishes you a good trip. And, sadly, I have only made it all worse by now being in the arena of what I know is going to be simplistically called "too much" when in reality it is frankly and literally not enough. Five texts are culturally stigmatized as excessive, but they only cover a minute or two of conversation. And people need interactive conversations, even short ones, in order to understand each other.

Most Americans have cell phones now. They can return phone calls on the walk from the subway station to their apartment buildings, from the car to the mall. There is no reason why people do not return phone calls except for the power-play of not answering. It certainly does not save time. It is tragic that we have evolved a social custom that people need to email in order to ask for permission to make a phone call. Just call! Emailing to ask for permission to speak privileges the rage, Supremacy, and Trauma of withholding over the human responsibility to communicate and understand. I say, let's get back to the first one hundred years of telephone culture, where people looked up each other's numbers and called. The now "forbidden" ten-to-twenty-minute phone conversation could save the subsequent months or years of misplaced bad feeling. All this terrible loss, for nothing.

In another example from other people's lives, sometimes angry, supremacist, or traumatized people send emails commanding, "Do not contact me." I want to state here, for the record, that no one is obligated to obey a unidirectional order that has not been discussed. Negotiation is a human responsibility. Little children order their parents around: "Mommy, sit there!" When adults give orders while hiding behind technology, they are behaving illegitimately. These unilateral orders do not have to be obeyed. They need to be discussed. Two people in a situation means two experiences, two points of view, two sources of information, two voices. And talking through conflict saves time, because having email/text-produced enmity with someone with whom one's life could be enriched, wastes years if not lifetimes. So sending a person an email that says, "I don't want to talk to you" and then refusing to discuss the problem at hand, or even to interact at all, resolves nothing. In fact, it creates anxieties, fears, antagonisms, and pain that can be long-lasting.

The performative conceit at the root of this kind of assaultive action is the melodrama that email orders are a "last resort" in response to some horrible transgression. But the opposite is more likely true. Often a real conversation would illuminate nuances and correct misunderstandings. The real question is: Why would a person rather have an enemy than a conversation? Why would they rather see themselves as harassed and transgressed instead of have a conversation that could reveal them as an equal participant in creating conflict? There should be a relief in discovering that one is not being persecuted, but actually, in the way we have misconstrued these responsibilities, sadly the relief is in confirming that one has been "victimized." It comes with the relieving abdication of responsibility. There is something in the person who hides behind email that *wants* these offenses to be true. They want to feel victimized. Then they don't have to look at themselves critically or think about the other person with complexity. There is no guilt or responsibility if one is an email victim.

Similarly, email "apologies" can also be uni-directional, and create even more complication because of lack of affect. An apology that doesn't allow the other person to talk is not an apology. People need to speak, look, smell, touch, experience vocal tone, facial expression, make jokes, sit back, shift gears, and evolve their ideas and feelings in front of each other in order to produce meaning. They need to eat together. As the old Jewish joke goes, "Comrade Stalin, you are the true leader of Russia" could also be, "Comrade Stalin. *You* are the true leader of Russia???"

Reductive Modes of Illogic

We have developed these reductive modes like email and texts to accompany reductive ideas that are supposed to serve large social functions but are not based in human complexity. They seem to be time savers, but avoiding real communication produces long-lasting problems that can endure forever. Shortcuts and speed-ups define our moment, and yet they simply do not address human reality. For example, there are common slogans in general use which are essentially shortcuts with high aims, something like the advertising slogans of old. *Blondes Have More Fun* is a message about white Supremacy. *Things Go Better With Coke* is a false claim on loneliness that contributes to malnutrition and obesity. Only now, the reductive quality of advertising slogans is applied to extremely serious social messages about human rights and safety. They are not there to sell us dishwashing liquid, but are rather designed, for example, to help women protect themselves from male violence. But because of the resonant lack of subtlety, they also can become reinforcers of denial. The contradiction is a difficult terrain of nuance that we must embrace if we are to be functional, decent, and sincere.

One of these is "Believe women!" We have this slogan in circulation because so many women are not believed when they tell the truth. But what about when they are not telling the truth? Are we still supposed to believe them? The histories of racism and colonialism remind us regularly that white women lying have been used to justify all kinds of cruelty against people of color, especially Black and Brown men in the United States. When we insist that we must "believe women" no matter what, we do help people who are telling the truth about violations they have experienced. But there are all kinds of truth. Sometimes "telling the truth" means representing one's self as flawed or mistaken, and there is often punishment for this productive and generous act. So insisting that women are telling "the truth" that we are in fact not allowed to tell can deny them the possibility of more nuanced, complex stories about themselves, which may be the only thing that can help them get closer to leading integrated lives. What about when women say things that aren't true because they don't understand themselves, ourselves? Being defended, of course, is rarely deliberate when we are not self-aware, self-critical, accountable, or psychologically sophisticated. Are others still required to obey?

There is a contemporary, quite visible, collectively agreed-upon, almost traditional social model of "abuse" where a man invites a woman to respond to his desires when she does not return those desires, nor has she suggested or advertised that she does. He is supposed to recognize that she never felt nor suggested those feelings. If at this point in the narrative he physically or, more interpretively, psychologically forces her in some way, we all agree that this is Abuse. It is "power over." Usually the alternative ending offered is that instead of force we expect him to have recognition, to apologize for the misunderstanding. Then she can leave and tell everyone that he "hit" on her, but she turned him down. That is the "happy ending" version of this scenario. Given constraints on women's behavior, she retains her purity, her appropriate female lack of erotic feeling. She gets to announce that she is attractive, as women are supposed to be, but she is not attracted, as women are not supposed to be. But what if she was attracted to him and did show it, and won't acknowledge that? And he doesn't want to live with the "he hit on me" narrative. As a writer, I know that there is, after all, the right to be described accurately. What he wants is the "I was attracted to him but I wouldn't acknowledge it, so I got confused" version. We don't have language or methodology for that option, because it immediately becomes her "fault." In a world based on blame, women have to be clear to be clean, unfortunately, so avoiding blame means avoiding complexity, contradictions, and ambivalences.

There are some women, often in the bourgeois class, who now perform that public event commonly recognized as "abused," with ease: that the other person, male or female, wanted something from me that I did not want and so "I was abused." It is a shortcut. They may select some details and omit others; they may rearrange the order of events so that consequences are reconstructed as causes; they may refuse to engage sequence, objective. I recite those few words: "I was abused" or "she was abusive" or "it was an abusive relationship" and it is immediately understood that I am right, and I am violated, and I am in danger and therefore deserving of group acclaim. While the other s/he is wrong, a harasser, s/he had desire and I didn't, so I am clean and s/he is abusive. And if they wanted to straighten this out, or discuss it until more complexities are revealed, then s/he is a stalker, while I am clean. I am not sullied by desire or sexual curiosity, I have done nothing wrong, and therefore I am a victim. I am an ethical virgin.

I acknowledge this from my own experience on both sides of the coin. I have been attracted to someone and then pretended I wasn't, or denied that I was. I remember one person saying to me, "You shouldn't say you aren't attracted when you are." She was right and it has stayed with me. Now when I hear "When a woman says *no*, she means *no*," I know that that is too simple, because I have said *no* when I didn't mean it. And I am a woman. When I have said "no" there were times when I did not know that I actually felt "yes" and there are times that I *did* know that I actually "felt" yes. People do not always know what they feel, nor do they acknowledge what they really know. Sometimes we say what we think we are supposed to say, or what we are used to saying; we don't give the actual moment a chance. Sometimes we just try out saying certain things. Consequently, making an accusation does not make us right, being angry does not make us right, refusing to communicate does not make us right. In fact, all those things could make us very, very wrong.

There is a range of persuasion narratives to the experience of "romance." Sometimes there is a seduction involved, which is a winning over. Sometimes there is a reassurance process. Sometimes a person starts out resistant but then opens up, or realizes that they are confusing their past with their present, or that they are simply afraid of change. Sometimes one party can see clearly into the future while the other's vision is obscured by unresolved but ancient experiences. Sometimes someone needs to be courted. Sometimes one party has the wrong impression of the other person, cannot see their gifts.

In the movies we watch the story of the single mother, fiftyish, who was grotesquely hurt by her spouse. She never wants to be hurt again. She conceptualizes herself as a romantic failure. She devotes herself to her children, her aging parents, her work. She develops a protective notion about herself. She comes to believe that she will never again have a relationship with an equal party, a lover, someone with whom to think, share, enjoy the last conversation (in person or by phone) of the day. She cannot even imagine constructing an equal relationship with an adult that could actually make sense in her life. So when she finally meets someone she enjoys talking to, and who enjoys her, she cuts it dead. Or once there is real potential, she sabotages it. Or she begins the relationship and when she finally acknowledges that she loves, she concocts a false reason to destroy it. In the movie version, of course, the other person can see more clearly than she can. They understand what is happening; they are not insulted. They see the potential for relationship and persevere, gently but with commitment. Life is not forever, after all, and how often do we actually meet people we want to talk to? And at some point, the woman too comes to understand that she can let go of her self-punishment. She can be taken care of too. She can have intimacy. She can care. She can reciprocate. She can have a real life. Cut to credits.

Yet our contemporary bourgeois discourse of "threat" now prohibits this trajectory. In the movie, the potential lover goes, knocks on the door, says "Wait," and the reluctant party waits.

"Listen," she tells her. "I know that someone, your ex or your father or someone, told you a story about yourself. That you don't know how to love. But I am here to tell you that it's not true."

Unfortunately, in our contemporary confusion, at the point where the other knocks on our protagonist's door, they are a "stalker." We are no longer allowed to drop by unannounced when things are fraught. She can't call on the phone to deliver the monologue of persuasion with an open heart, because our heroine hides behind voice mail. She can't send it by email, because it will either be deleted, or forwarded to thousands. If she has knocked, called, and emailed, she is now officially, in the era of overstating harm, a "harasser." The person who fights for honest conversation that can heal, such a well-known and beloved character of yore, is, alas, no more. And so Ms. Reluctant never gets the affective reality, the skin, the voice, the tone, the eyes, the smile, the jokes, and especially the back and forth, the interactivity that reminds her of what it feels like to let someone in, the interactivity that produces a revelation that her future is not impossible. Instead, past pain dominates over possibility. To suggest otherwise is forbidden.

If the movies replicated these restrictive values, movies would be even worse than they are already. No surprises. First impulse, only impulse. But in reality, romance doesn't always start off on the right foot, two people don't always see the potential in one another at the same time, and thankfully, other people can change us with their hope, forgiveness, and optimism. We can make each other's lives better, despite all our fears. Sometimes one of us knows that before the other. There are positive surprises in life too. And just because our heroine decided that she would never be able to construct a relationship with someone that would make sense, she doesn't have to stick to that belief. While unrecovered trauma is so often a prison of inflexibility, some people do have choices about how to respond. And someone else might make that shift possible by daring to imagine what to us may feel unimaginable. Which can be love. As a novelist, I simply cannot abandon the possibility of reversal.

When I think about it deeply, I can see multiple moments in each day when I have the option to act hurt, to act put-upon, to be offended, to make accusations. Anyone can point to any little thing and turn it into a moment of outrage simply by calling it so. There is an arbitrary element to rejection. I remember I once said to a friend, "You know, I was thinking about going to San Francisco for a week." "What do you mean, *You know?*" she said, incredulous, offended. "How am I supposed to know?" Of course I meant *you know* like *uh, um*. But she needed to construct me as someone doing something bad to her. Assuming. And of course this made any fun conversation about San Francisco impossible, because now I was wrong. At any conflicted moment that is available to interpret one's self as somehow transgressed, there is often the option of not seeing it that way. Or of asking the other person what they mean. There are all different kinds of choices. Many, many times a day we could say *yes* instead of saying *no*, or find something interesting or revelatory or enlightening instead of offensive. To talk instead of shun. Of course, to *always* respond this way is problematic because then we never stand for anything on our own. But while recognizing that for socially marginalized or demeaned people, exclusion and silencing are everywhere and must be addressed, we still have choices about how to understand each other.

And, of course, there are all different kinds of desires. I spend my life talking to a lot of people, and yet I am always looking for those very few with whom I really want to be in conversation. Such occasions are rare, but when it happens, it is a special kind of love. Once, after a stunningly comfortable and enriching lunch with someone where there was no potential for a romantic relationship, I asked the woman, in a follow-up message, if she would like to continue to talk on the phone. "Please feel comfortable to say no," I wrote. She answered that yes, she would like to, that she'd "enjoyed our conversation too." So then I texted her to see if she wanted to talk on Saturday. "I have plans," she answered. "But let's talk soon, okay?" In my mind, I now had two yesses evidenced by the phrases "I enjoyed" and the words "talk soon, okay?" So I wrote back, "How about when I get home tomorrow?" She never answered. Now what? She'd said yes twice. I waited and then offered her a way out. "If your life is too full, just let me know. Otherwise what about the 25th?" She didn't answer. If I make contact again, am I a harasser? From my point of view, I believed what she said. I'd asked her and she said yes. We both acknowledged to each other that there was an understanding, a pleasure. Then she disappeared. Yet, I still gave her a graceful way out.

Don't people have some responsibility to be accountable? Or does the new victimology require me to interpret yes as no, and silence as "I changed my mind"? No answer is not an answer. It is unreasonable to expect other people to interpret our silences. That, I think, is an unfair burden. I think she should have told me, "I said yes, but I realize now I am afraid, not as interested as I thought I was, shy, intimidated, afraid of being hurt again, don't want the responsibility, *whatever*." And I could have said, "Thank you for letting me know." Or, even better, we could have talked through the anxiety. You know, helped each other. But there was no answer. So what is the dynamic we have here? Is asking for some kind of response being "stalker-ish"? Not responding puts all the responsibility on the other party.

I have long felt that withholding produces anxiety, and accountability creates relief. But some anxiety is a consequence and other anxiety is a cause. Why not have a common value of resolution? Let's imagine that this person did become accountable and in the end chose mutual kindness/accountability over accusation. She realized that she was mad at me for no reason caused by me, that this was old stuff acting itself out in new places, and so she did the right thing and picked up the phone. We talked. We saw each other, and the friendship was allowed to become important. So, happy ending. Out of a single phone call.

The problem is that silence is not accountable. Feeling confused, feeling the anxiety of attraction to a body or a mind, feeling that someone has come along who I was not prepared for, these are not signs that someone is doing something bad to me. The woman who told me, "Don't say you aren't attracted when you are," was not harassing me. She was not taking agency away from me, overpowering me, or being controlling. Instead, she gave me a gift. She offered me a code of decency.

Chapter Two | **Abandoning the Personal:** The State and the Production of Abuse

Criticism must think of itself as life enhancing.
— EDWARD SAID

SOMETIMES INVOKING the language of abuse is an avoidance of responsibility, just like speaking in metaphors. Like when people say, "I feel like I've been raped," to mean they are upset. In reality, what they feel is nothing like what they would feel if they'd been raped. It's a turn of phrase that means they don't like what is happening and don't know how to make it better. It's an overstatement of harm using Abuse tropes. And sometimes we are so insistent on our right to overstate that we do things that are not merited by the actual dimensions of the conflict. Sometimes, when we are upset, we pretend or convince ourselves that Conflict is actually not only Abuse, but a crime. Sometimes, we really do not want to face ourselves, our own participation, our own painful pasts, the facts of our own projections, distorted thinking, mental illness. When we have nowhere to go but inside ourselves, and when that self that we inhabit is convinced that it cannot bear to be seen, we call the police. And then we are in the arms of The State. And there we are.

On a freezing, snowy day in 2014, I was invited to a workshop run by social worker Catherine Hodes. A native New Yorker in her fifties, Hodes is an experienced professional with over twenty years of development and leadership in what was once known as "The Battered Women's Movement" back when she was called an "activist." The field has since transformed, first into "Domestic Violence" and then "Intimate Relationship Abuse Advocacy" where she is now known as "a service provider." Intimate abuse is a real crisis for many New Yorkers. *The New York Times* reported in November, 2014 that the police receive 284,660 intimate abuse calls a year, which is about 800 a day, and make 46,000 intimate abuse arrests every year. Citywide, almost half of all felony assaults and one-third of all rapes in New York City are related to intimate abuse, the overwhelming majority conducted by men against women and children. According to Jane Stoever, writing in the *Vanderbilt Law Review*:

> While an overreliance on gender as the explanation for domestic violence undermines efforts to address same-sex domestic violence, most abuse is committed by men against women, with approximately eighty-five percent of victims being female and ninety percent of perpetrators being male.

Stoever concludes that, in the United States, every year 1.3 million women are physically assaulted by a male partner at a rate that is higher than "automobile accidents, muggings and stranger rape" combined. Given these complex quantitative and emotional realities, in order to be able to serve clients maximally, social workers need a sophisticated understanding of what constitutes intimate abuse, what causes it, how to respond to it, and how to prevent it.

This training was held in a pristine classroom with stained glass windows at a classic Gilded Age Protestant church on Fifth Avenue in Greenwich Village, far away from the normal daily routines of both Hodes and her young students. Becoming a social worker is often a first step by new immigrants into the professional class, and these young men and women in their twenties came from Sri Lankan, West Indian, West African, Cambodian, Russian, Chinese, Albanian, and Dominican backgrounds. They were sincere, committed, and working in community-based services, often within their own neighborhoods and ethnicities.

It was a fantastic class, offering wisdom and provoking a lot of re-thinking. In an environment like New York City that is filled with violence, Hodes had boldly started to notice that clients were increasingly confused about what the word "Abuse" actually means. That it was overused. The paradox is, of course, that many women are unable to recognize that they are being abused, or cannot get acknowledgment of this reality from others. But at the very same time, Hodes found that some women were applying the term Abuse to situations that were really something else. Increasingly, she noticed that women who did not know how to resolve a problem sometimes described that feeling with the word Abuse. So this session had been convened to address that trend directly with service providers.

Hodes' focus was to help social workers differentiate between Abuse and Conflict so that they could be effective, and directed in helping clients in ways that would speak to their real experiences. While identifying Abuse is essential to saving lives and providing services, differentiating Conflict from Abuse is also essential to meeting clients' real need to learn how to face and deal with obstacles, and to develop truthful assessments of themselves and others. Hodes offered many insights rooted in decades of work on the issues of violence and nonviolence in New York, many of which shook the foundational assumptions that the young social workers and I shared despite a thirty year age difference. The centerpiece of her presentation emerged early and with simple clarity. She started by making us look at common misuses of the word "Abuse." For example, Hodes told us:

"There is no such thing as mutually abusive relationships."

Of course this was startling, because the concept of "mutual abuse" is so commonplace in our culture that its construction is never questioned. Don't we all often get into fraught situations with other people where we both have a role to play? In fact, in our contemporary world, it is a sign of maturity and decency to acknowledge that often all parties participate in making mistakes that can produce discord. In our time, recognizing this fact is part of being an honest person of depth. It helps us understand that trouble between people gets transformed when everyone takes responsibility for their part. Negotiation is a process, first of acknowledgment, and then adjustment to the new information produced by that acknowledgment. Recognizing mutuality of cause is a principle that allows progressive change without scapegoating. Scapegoating, after all, is often rooted in the false accusation that one person or group is unilaterally responsible for mistakes that are actually contributed to by multiple parties. So what did she mean by undoing an insight that so many of us have spent years learning how to apply?

What's wrong with this concept, Hodes quickly clarified, is not the recognition of mutual *responsibility*, but rather the use of the word Abuse, because once the dynamic is mutual, it is not Abuse, which inherently implies one person's domination.

"Differentiating between *Power Struggle* and *Power Over*," Hodes explained, "is the difference between Conflict and Abuse." Abuse is Power Over and Conflict is Power Struggle.

As we students discussed and grappled with this insight over the course of the day, my understanding consistently deepened. While obviously significant abuse does take place in life, where one person is being controlled by another or by a group in a manner that the recipient has not contributed to and can't change, the word "Abuse" has become overused:

- People may feel angry, frustrated, upset. But this does not mean they are being abused. They could, instead, be in Conflict. Instead of identifying as a victim, they might be, as Matt Brim suggested, Conflicted. Therefore the fact that one person is suffering does not inherently mean that the other party is to blame. The expectation that we will never feel badly or anxious or confused is an unreasonable expectation and doesn't automatically mean that someone else is abusing us. These emotions are part of the human experience.
- People may not know how to make things better, how to look at their own participation, how to deal with feeling badly about themselves. They may not know how to understand their own actions, and are afraid of the implications of their actions on the meaning of their lives. And this may be devastating, tormenting, and painful. But this is not being Abused. It doesn't get resolved by organizing punishment of another person. And someone who feels conflicted in this way does not

have the right to take punitive actions against another person because they feel bad.

- People may be part of negative friendships, families, or communities who attack outsiders instead of being self-critical. They may be receiving encouragement to blame and scapegoat others. They may live within groups, relationships or families that do not tolerate the admission of mistakes, and that reinforce Supremacy ideologies about each other in order to maintain illusions of righteousness. This pressure, resulting in the action of collectively deflecting blame, does not mean that the person being blamed is abusive. In fact, it says nothing at all about that person, except that they are in turn being caused great pain for no reason. And in my mind, they have the right to resist that unilateral blame. In this way, group bullying is multiplicative of injustice, even though it is done in the name of nation, family, friendship, or distorted renditions of "loyalty."
- Being in a negative moment with another person can be destabilizing, hurtful, and stressful, especially if a person's self-concept requires them to think of themselves as perfect. But it is not, by definition, Abuse. It could be Abuse, if one has power over another, but if not, it's a Conflict. And being in a Conflict is a position that is filled with responsibility and opportunity.

"All human relationships have power dynamics and that is neither good nor bad. Power is not the problem," Hodes said. "It's how it is wielded." There is a "difference between volatility and abuse," she added. "But not enough understanding of that difference." The discussion went on to carefully examine the consequences of over-simplifying and obscuring these definitions. Hodes made clear that "as a victim advocate, my *first* concern is always for those being abused." But that part of this responsibility is to find out *if* anyone is actually being abused, or if instead the person is mired in Conflict that they have some role in escalating and consequently some power to resolve. And Hodes' job is to assist these young service providers "in being able to do better and deeper differential assessments."

Her insights produced new knowledge in me, and I saw clearly that this confusion between Abuse and Conflict exists in our historic moment in all structured relationships: from the most intimate partnerships to the government's relationship to its own people, and to the geopolitical dynamics between nations. Her primary concern that afternoon, of course, was specifically between the State of New York and its individual residents. After all, social workers are licensed by the government, often employed by the government, and certainly have influence on the government's findings and conclusive actions regarding very crucial issues in people's lives. Social workers can influence immigration, incarceration, custody, benefits, health care, housing, food, education, and other services. Their misapplications of the word "Abuse" can have profound consequences on how individuals are treated by the state and are viewed by their communities, and thus also on their lives and the lives of the people around them.

In order for people who work with the state and for providers, friends, and community members to actually *help* others, they must have crucial information about specific events and a deeper understanding of power dynamics. In this way they can identify "Power Over" situations and intervene before calamity strikes. Or they can identify "Power Struggle" situations of Conflict and not only avoid the unjustified punishment and stigma of those falsely accused of Abuse, but they can also help people who simply can't problem-solve because they lock themselves into a victimized self-perception. Lacking the support and encouragement to successfully negotiate does not mean that someone is being victimized. True, we have to recognize that the frustration of not knowing how to solve problems and only knowing how to escalate can feel like a response to an outside force, but it is, in fact, internal. Differentiating requires awareness, and we may be dependent on our surrounding communities, including social workers, to achieve this.

Understanding Is More Important than Producing a Victim

"When a provider is trained, they are told what domestic violence is," Hodes said in her presentation. "But I was never told what it is not. And based on what I was taught, I could have looked at every relationship I know and called it *abusive*."

She suggested that social workers change their methodology, and instead of simply asking, "Are you abused?" ask clients questions that would elicit more information. She encouraged the workshop's new professionals to create interactive conversation with clients, rather than narrow experience down into easy categories. This strategic evolution reveals a newly articulated goal to stop organizing the conversation in a way designed to automatically produce the pre-determined revelation that the person is being abused. Instead, the conversation should be redirected to elicit a deeper and more multifaceted factual understanding of what is *actually happening*, in order to reveal more nuance and dimension that could lead to real solutions. Knowing what really happened is more important than deciding who to punish. One suggestion was to ask the client: "Are you unsafe, or are you instead uncomfortable, angry, or hurt?"

People who describe themselves as "Abused" when they are actually in Conflict are not lying; they usually don't know the difference. We're not talking here about the tired false cliché of the vindictive woman who "cries rape" or diabolically constructs the other as an abuser while knowing full well that the charge is false. What we have instead is a devolved definition of personal responsibility, which constructs avoidance as a right regardless of the harm it does to others. This negative standard persuades some people to feel that being uncomfortable signals that they are being Abused, because they don't have the option of describing themselves as Conflicted. So asking a distressed person if they are unsafe, or rather, uncomfortable, angry, or hurt provides them with an alternative idea that might fit better with their actual experience. It not only elicits helpful information, but encourages the individual to start to think about themselves in a more adult, complex, and responsible manner. What I learned at this point was that if we stop asking people, "Are you being Abused?" and start asking key questions about *what actually occurred*, we can move forward from a fixed expression of victimology, and determine the true nature of events, which could be Abuse, or it could be Conflict. If the person is part of a negative clique, community, family, or group, this maturation is an implicating and therefore forbidden endeavor and will require overt support from the social worker.

The question "Are you unsafe or uncomfortable?" was very inspiring. Does the person feel unsafe when they are not actually unsafe, but rather because the other party, with whom they are in Conflict, is bringing up issues about their life that are troublesome and therefore initially feel overwhelming and difficult to face. Accusations of Abuse, when it is in fact Conflict, can be a smokescreen, obscuring the real problems at hand and making effective response difficult. Are they being asked to confront the consequences of childhood sexual abuse on how they handle conflict as an adult? That is not an instance of Power Over. Are they being asked to recognize that they or a family member have addiction or mental health issues? That too is not Power Over. Or, on the other hand, is the person physically unsafe because the other party beats them, possesses a gun, or makes real and credible threats, as many have actually experienced? Does the other have so much psychological power and control over them that they are unable to exercise separation or independent action? Is the person being confronted with emotionally terrifying threats such as kidnapping their children, exposing their undocumented status, withholding medication, calling the police for no reason, interfering with their banking, credit, or benefits, or organizing others to shun them? Which kind of *safety* are we endorsing here? Is it the safety from psychological "power over" and actual harm? Or is it the safety from being made uncomfortable by accurate information that challenges one's self-perception?

If it is the latter, it is an assertion of this book that we owe it to each other to help one another tolerate the temporary discomfort that is necessary for the personal and social change produced by positive, interactive problem-solving. In fact, helping each other negotiate is the bedrock of a healthy and active community, clique, family, country. Instead of shunning, shutting down information and scapegoating from a place of non-responsibility, the Conflicted must express, focus, listen, and transform. It is my claim that in situations of Conflict, accusations that attribute sole responsibility to one party and then construct them as deserving of punishment or shunning are unjust.

In my book *The Gentrification of the Mind: Witness to a Lost Imagination* (2012), I discussed the phenomena of mixed, interactive, dynamic neighborhoods being characterized as "dangerous." I address how homogenizing those neighborhoods through displacement and cultural flattening was falsely characterized as "getting better." The gentrification mentality, which I showed to be a product of suburbanization (gated communities, privatized living, gendered and racially segregated social strata) involves understanding difference as discomfort, and being uncomfortable is equated with being abused or in "danger." Those who avoid change view this discomfort as a threat. Certainly no good can come from us continuing to treat the discomfort of social and personal insight as Abuse.

Asking, "What exactly are you afraid of?" can produce answers that reveal either Conflict or Abuse. Avoiding a complete shutdown and instead encouraging a client or friend's thorough exploration of anxiety is beneficial to the accuser and essential to their object of punishment. A woman stating that she is "afraid" of her partner may produce a knee-jerk superficial reaction confirming her as a *victim* and her partner as a perpetrator because she used *fear* terminology. This resonates with the government's use of the vocabulary of "terror" to keep citizens from looking at the consequences of our national policy on other people's lives, or causing us to racially profile people of color, Muslims, and others. But if instead, enough of a conversation of depth ensues to produce concrete articulation of what exactly she fears, or that citizens fear discovering about ourselves, more layers may emerge.

For example, "I am afraid that she wants me to confront my son's depression, exploitative behavior, or supremacy" might actually be at the core of the Conflict. "And I live inside a community which would make me feel responsible for his anxiety, if I acknowledge it, which is more guilt than I can face." If deep and nuanced support produced this insight, the situation would be revealed as Conflicted. On the other hand, if the same person says, "I am afraid that she will run me over with her car," it could be Abuse. What makes the difference is if the latter is a substitute for the former, that is, if she suggests a scenario of victimization *because* she doesn't have the support to face the actual issue. Real conversation will reveal quickly if the partner has threatened this action, implied or suggested it, or has any history of running people over with cars. But real conversation can also reveal that the partner has never owned a car and the fear is overwhelmingly a deflective projection, which requires yet another path of response. Shallow engagement by a social worker, service provider, or bad friend with the accuser produces outcomes that are detrimental to her, to the person she is blaming, and also to her son, whose stasis remains ignored by the smokescreen of misdirected blame.

Authentic Relationships of Depth vs. Bonding by Bullying

Hodes' illuminations brought many complexities to light about how we, as a community, respond to accusation. Sometimes a person in our lives—a friend, a student, a neighbor or relative—makes negative insinuations about a third party ("He's a stalker" or "She's abusive") and they want us to shun, be cold to, exclude, or in other ways punish this person. Our first responsibility is to determine if they are in physical danger from real violence. If not, then we ask to think with them about the *order of events* so that the complexities of the situation and how it unfolded can be revealed. It is unethical to hurt someone because we have been told to do so. We are required by decency to ask both the complainant and the accused how they understand the situation. And this, I truly believe, requires an in-person discussion. Asking hard questions and creating an environment in which complexities can be faced is, after all, what a real friend does. The possibility that the person is not in physical danger but is experiencing their reasonable needs being over-powered and controlled by others will be revealed by this process. Similarly, discussion will also reveal if they are blaming, scapegoating, or punishing the other and imposing unjustified conditions of harm. What if we cared enough and took the time to have the full conversation, focusing on details? Not only could we get away from the buzz words and their implied helplessness or innocence, but we could finally do what friends, teachers, caseworkers, family, and community members are supposed to do: help the person to understand what is actually happening in their life, their role in it, and the impact of their past experiences on their present perceptions so that they can produce real choices about how to create peace and resolution. In other words, we could have honest relationships of depth. We could be truly "supportive."

"The question *Are you being abused?*, at this point, can be a meaningless question," Hodes said. Instead, she advised her students to take an entirely different path and suggested alternative questions:

- "What was happening when the behavior occurred? What happened before? What was the outcome? What is the context?"
- "How would you describe your partner?"
- "Who makes the decisions? What usually leads up to a fight and how do they usually end?"

This real engagement will reveal whether the person is being Abused or is Conflicted. It will not obscure Abuse, but it also will not assume it. These questions not only elicit information for the advocate, but more importantly, they help the person in distress look at their own participation and acquire a different level of understanding and inquiry.

Again, I was inspired. Instead of encouraging people to label themselves either as *victim* or as *abuser* when that may or may not be the case, the role of the friend, caseworker, family member, or witness here was not to reinforce distorted thinking or justifications of punishment and victimology, but rather to elicit a truthful and complex telling, at the base of which is something that novelists, like myself, know very well: Truths can be multiple and are revealed by *the order of events*. As I teach in my creative writing classes, each moment is a consequence of the previous moment. So truths can be complex, and complexity is articulated by its details. Anyone who refuses to hear the details is making a deliberate decision not to understand.

"She yelled at me; she's abusive."

Is that an originating action? Or is that a response? Were you sitting innocently eating your breakfast and she yelled at you because there was no milk, and you are responsible for serving her at every turn, which would be Abuse? Or did she yell at you because you stole her milk money in order to buy drugs? Which would mean that *you* created the originating action and the yelling was a consequence of that action. So there is Conflict about *your* addiction, and the Abuse accusation is a smokescreen to avoid facing it. Or were you so traumatized from being demeaned constantly as a child that as an adult you can't tolerate difference, and any normative challenge is perceived of as an assault or threat? Is it that, in fact, nothing really happened, and yet you feel terrible? And maybe, rather than face the betrayal of your parents, it's a lot easier to put the whole thing on your partner?

Only by examining the details, asking interactive questions in person (and not by email), and understanding the order of events can we differentiate between these three possible interpretations of the same complaint. The most destructive answer, of course, is "She yelled at you? I will hurt her," which is a shallow relationship manifested as bullying. The best answer is, "If you two can't communicate right now, let me talk to her in person and see how she understands what is happening." Or, "How can I help you sit down and talk this through with her?"

Of course, conflicted people can mutually agree that limiting contact between them is best. Or someone in Conflict (not Abuse) may not have the skills or sense of self to be able to communicate productively for some period of time, and can responsibly and kindly request a limit with terms. For example, "I'm not able to act responsibly; let's have a separation and meet in three weeks and ask our friend Joe to help us communicate." Even in an Abuse situation, terms should be responsible and reasonable. For example, "You stole my money to buy drugs, therefore when you have three years sober, we can get together and talk." But if shunning in the context of Conflict is detrimental to the other person and has no terms, it is purely employed as an act of cruelty/punishment or avoidance/denial of responsibility, and is not justified. At all times, Hodes says, there needs to be articulation of "context, objective, impact."

Just because one conflicted person wants to hurt the other through shunning does not make it a right. For example, if Al wanted to organize a group shunning of Bob overtly because Bob was Black, very few people would theorize that as a right. Nor if it was because Al owed Bob a thousand dollars that he didn't want to pay and so created a diversionary smokescreen. If Al wants to shun Bob because "Bob has three legs," that is not a right. After all, Bob does not have three legs, but even if he did, it would not be legitimate grounds for punishment. If Bob finds the shunning profoundly detrimental and unjustified, he has the right to resist and oppose this form of bullying. Refusing to be shunned for unjust, nonexistent, or absurd reasons is not "stalking." Resisting unjustified punishment is not Abuse. And people who are being asked to stand by and passively allow shunning to take place certainly should know exactly what the accuser is claiming and exactly what the shunned party is experiencing. Without that information, the decision to be a complicit bystander is an unjustified one.

Simply *wanting* to exclude, silence, or dehumanize someone through forced absence is not an inherent right. In the case of Conflict, saying "I refuse to speak to her" can be a behavior that performs the role of "righteous victim of abuse" without the actor actually being in that situation. As always, the people who determine whether or not unjust shunning take place are the surrounding community—they can refuse to participate, or they can blindly endorse it. In my book *Ties That Bind: Familial Homophobia and Its Consequences* (2009), I go into this in detail, using the example of the shunning or exclusion of the queer family member by the homophobic family. There, the family members falsely claim that homosexuality is the Abuse, when in fact the homophobia of the family is the real pathology. This is the perfect example of a process that can only be disrupted by third-party intervention.

At the root of these questions is the responsibility of the caring listener. A shallow relationship with a friend, relative, co-worker, or advocate means that they will not take the time to ask the meaningful questions and to help the person involved overcome shame, anger, and disappointment so they can get to a complex truth about their own participation and how to achieve repair. Who the person talks to is an essential factor in whether they understand or claim their Conflict as Abuse, and establishing the moral standard within the group. *Are we a family who scapegoats outsiders to avoid facing our own long-standing problems? Do we join in on cruel practices of shunning and punishment as a bond of false loyalty? Or, Are we a family whose standard is to support each other in taking responsibility for dysfunctions and developmental problems and not project them onto other people who see them clearly?* It is up to each family member to decide what kind of group their family will be. The same is true for a group of friends, a workplace, a legal apparatus, a government, or a national or ethnic or religious identity, as well as for those constituted by their HIV status or citizenship. Members have to actively take responsibility for the ethics and moral values that their small or large group claims to represent and actually enact this responsibility. And nothing reveals this more clearly than how difference is treated. Is difference a welcomed perspective to keep the relationships honest, or is it a threat to shared myths of Supremacy or vulnerability? How questions are asked fundamentally reveals the value systems at play, particularly whether or not there is a real desire to know what's true.

In my 1999 interview with Kate Kendell, founding director of the National Center for Lesbian Rights (reproduced in my book *Ties That Bind: Familial Homophobia and Its Consequences*), she made an observation that has haunted me to this day. We were discussing a subject that was quite prominent at the time, the trend for lesbian biological mothers to use the absence of legal relationship recognition to deny custody to former female partners who had fully participated in raising a child. We were discussing the cruelty to the former partner and to the child, the vindictiveness, the destruction of the community, the endless longing and irresolution that it produces, and I asked Kendell how these women justified these actions.

"It's the cadre of friends," she said.

This insight has stayed with me ever since. There is often a "cadre" of bad friends around a person encouraging them to do things that are morally wrong, unjustified, and unethical, because endorsing each other's negative actions is built into the group relationship. Kendell recognized how crucial the surrounding community is in determining if a person will insist on false claims of harm or, the opposite, face their own participation.

Therefore, to Hodes' list of questions, I would add a trope of my own, something that I think a good friend, family member, or citizen would ask: "What would the other person say happened? What would she say is going on here, and how does she understand it?"

Again, this is my perspective as a novelist, where my job is to convey how each character experiences their own life. If the complainant can't reproduce the other person's understanding, then they don't have enough information to complete their story.

Just last night as I was writing this book, my friend Dirk told me about a friend of his whose female partner, the mother of a young child, was "stalking" him. He described how the woman came to his friend's workplace with her seven-year-old, and "made a scene," jeopardizing the man's job.

"Why did she do that?" I asked.

"I don't know. She was harassing him."

Now, I can think of a lot of reasons that could produce the moment where a woman feels she must bring her child with her to talk to her boyfriend at work, in front of others, about a wide range of concerns: she didn't have childcare, she was locked out of the apartment, she had been evicted, there had been a fire, her child was too distressed or unwell to be separated, she was on her way to the doctor and needed cash. Perhaps she wanted to remind her boyfriend of who their child really was, how vulnerable, how beautiful, how loving, how hurt, the child missed his father, and so on. He had an obligation to fulfill and was avoiding it by refusing to answer the phone or talk. There are many imaginable scenarios where this *Conflicted* couple could have substantive difference, the resolution of which would make the man uncomfortable, so he could imagine or employ the language of Abuse in order to avoid taking responsibilities. No one in the community surrounding this couple can start to understand if this is Abuse or Conflict if they never talk to the woman in question.

According to my logic, Dirk has an ethical responsibility to understand what the woman's motive and objective were when she came to his friend's workplace in order to be able to evaluate the events *before* he reinforces his male friend in the accusation that she was "stalking" him. Once Dirk and I started actually discussing the situation, he revealed that this responsibility was something that simply never occurred to him. He somehow had gotten the wrong message that "being a good friend" meant *not* asking questions that reveal truths. Instead he was expected to join in, uninformed, on the condemnation of the woman. Instead, Dirk could have tried to understand the motives and objectives of his friend's girlfriend, who was obviously already in a place of distress and pain, something that his male friend may have helped to create.

In other words, despite the fact that Dirk's friend *said* that he was being "abused" and "stalked," and that he may even believe that his girlfriend talking to him about conflicts at work means that he is her victim, many other things could be taking place. They could simply be Conflicted; involved in a disagreement that needs to be faced and dealt with, perhaps with helpful outside parties who can produce meaningful communication. Or, even more importantly, her actions could be *resistance* to his unfair and unjustified behavior. He might be blaming her for something she did not do or blaming her for something that never happened, which is not anyone's *right*. He could be projecting onto her from traumas caused by other people earlier in his life, which, if harmful to her, is not his right. Or he could be overreacting to normative conflict and, by overstating harm, finding justification for his own excessively punitive or cruel behaviors.

"Lack of understanding," Hodes underlined for the class, "about the difference between Conflict and Abuse has negative outcomes."

When the Community Encourages Overreaction

I once had a young male graduate student from a marginalized and oppressed community whose work I very much liked, and whom I liked personally. One day I learned that he had a blog where he wrote that he was in love with me. These were in the early days of the internet, and I didn't even know what a "blog" was, revealing our generational differences. There he made comments about my appearance, discussed his feelings about me, and shared information about my life. Coincidentally, one of his criticisms of an aspect of my appearance hit exactly a place where I felt insecure, something he could not know. And I was so embarrassed, I actually made changes in myself in response to his statements. Although I felt bad, I was still clear that if I hadn't already had a pre-conditioned history of sensitivity to this area, his comments would not have affected me in the same way. They could, in fact, have been benign.

All of my colleagues, with one exception, described his actions as "stalking." None of these people suggested that I talk to him in order to understand what he thought he was doing. None of them offered to have that conversation with him themselves. All but one (a woman from the same oppressed group as the student) assumed as a matter of course that I should expose him to the administration, humiliate him, perhaps endanger his career, and most importantly make accusations against him through authoritative channels. At first, I assumed they were correct. His actions, on the surface, fit behaviors that were undesirable and in response I felt uncomfortable. I, too, lived inside the paradigm where being uncomfortable was grounds for accusing someone of abuse. I contemplated following what seemed to be the obvious, convenient, and socially condoned path of accusing him of "stalking" followed by condemnation, cut-off, and punishment. I accepted the group's offer of approval based on the idea that I was an innocent victim of someone who should, therefore, be hurt.

But at the same time, I discovered that I was disturbed by the rapidity with which my colleagues drew conclusions, the viciousness of their suggestions, the unquestioned reliance on punitive authorities, and their own sense of themselves as superior to him at the root of these impulses. I was most disturbed by them drawing these conclusions *without ever speaking to* him. I realized that, in fact, I had two clearly different options of how to respond. I could solidify my relationship to the group by being outraged, violated, damaged, angry, and fearful and elevate them into rescuers, loyal protectors of my womanhood. Or I could find out what he thought he was doing, and perhaps discover that he had made an error in judgment that we had to address. I realized that I actually had a choice about how to respond, even though my professional community was pushing me toward victimology. In this particular case, I was uncomfortable, in part because of him, but also in part because of earlier experiences in which he had played no part. I thought over my colleagues' advice, and then refused it. I knew that "stalking" was and is a real thing. That ex-husbands and other aggrieved types like fans of movie stars sit outside their homes with guns, and actually do murder people. To use this word, which represents a literal experience of real violence, metaphorically, to describe discomfort or a situation that merits conversation in order to be understood, was absurd.

In fact, I did the opposite. I avoided all third parties, all institutions of power, and took the time to speak to him directly so that we could negotiate a resolution. I told him that I could no longer be his thesis advisor because his comments made me uncomfortable. I made myself available to him for in-person conversation (not through email or third parties) and conveyed that I was transferring him to someone who was appropriate to his project, and that I still supported his work. I told him that I was available to discuss this matter with him until he felt it was resolved. And I kept my word; we had a few conversations. I refused to shun him, or to limit our conversations because my goal was mutual resolution, not punishment, dominance, or assertion of either my victimhood or Supremacy.

A few things surfaced that I could not have known without talking it over, and this new information was enriching. First of all, I became more aware that younger people had a different relationship to the internet than I did. Talking about difficult feelings and sharing information on this level was generationally culturally appropriate for him. That based on our different age positions, we experienced those actions differently. I also learned that I was the first authority figure to take him seriously, from his marginalized position, as an artist and intellectual. And that this had overwhelmed him with feeling, perhaps at a level that maybe should have been contained, but wasn't.

Once he saw that I was establishing a new parameter for the relationship by resigning as his advisor, but that at the same time I was neither punishing him, invoking authority, shunning him, nor withholding, we transitioned positively into the next phase. I was invited into victimology, but I am very glad that I found the strength to resist the image of myself as being more aggressed than I actually was. While my discomfort had multiple sources, he was only one of them. So falsely projecting that my partner in Conflict had sinister intentions, which my colleagues felt sure they could automatically intuit, would have been an error. Instinctually, I applied what Catherine Hodes would years later articulate as "context, objective, impact." Now, more than a decade after these events, this man and I are active friends in the same arts community. But for years I have been grappling with my colleagues' almost prescribed instinct to punish, using the language originated initially by a radical movement but now co-opted to deny complexity, due process, and the kind of in-person, interactive conversation that produces resolution.

I discussed this with my therapist, now deceased, who had treated victims of McCarthyism later on in their lives. He told me that some of his patients had found themselves caught up in the whirlwind smoke of shunning and innuendo, whisper campaigns and exclusions. No one ever sat down and told them what they were being accused of, and they never had a chance to discuss or inform or respond. Instead, group pressures, intimidations, and false loyalties produced a climate of mysterious chill, in which they were denied jobs, kept out of social events, shunned by acquaintances. People were mean to them without ever saying why, and no opportunity for clarification or repair was ever presented. These people found both the material and emotional consequences overwhelming, but even more so they were hurt by the amorphous nature of the problem. Not being able to know exactly what they were charged with, not being able to talk through the accusations, never knowing where they would face these hostile expressions drove many people to extreme suffering. Even later when classic McCarthyism was dismantled and delegitimized, these unnecessarily broken relationships could not be healed. My therapist explained to me that taking extreme bullying actions, like signing a petition against a friend, or denouncing a colleague to others or to the state, as often happened under McCarthyism, was so extreme in its pathology that the participants could never repair. They were so defended against the reality of the injustice of their own action that they couldn't reconcile it to their false image of themselves as righteous. In listening to him, I came to believe that the same personality type who would ice out or attack someone without talking to them first out of false "loyalty" would be the same person who would later be unable to apologize. It's a character issue that becomes the building blocks of fascism or any supremacist construction. And for those people, a commonly held expectation or standard of asking targeted people what they feel or how they understand their experience could be a life-enhancing or even life-saving corrective.

False Accusations and the State

The lack of engaged, compassionate conversation of depth by the community surrounding an accusing party and by the authority to which the accuser would turn has terrible consequences. These include, interestingly, as Hodes informed us, "Perpetrators, themselves, [who] often initiate the complaint of abuse." The legal apparatus that has been put in place ostensibly to assist a victim can and often is used to extend the cruelty as well as to keep the perpetrator from facing their own issues. The system by which we help people step out of conflict is so flawed, and the general understanding in the population so over-simplified that, for example, when the police answer a distress call to a private home, "Survivors may be arrested at the scene," Hodes said. "Or cross complaints may be issued."

Perpetrators increasingly are the ones to call the police, threaten legal action, send lawyer letters, or threaten or seek restraining orders as part and parcel of their agenda of blame and unilateral control. It is an agenda designed to avoid by any means necessary having to examine their own behavior, history, or participation in the Conflict. Actively violent and truly abusive people are hard to convict, and innocent people are convicted of crimes every day. At the same time a targeted victim may rarely be convicted and incarcerated based on exclusively harassing uses of the law, but the stigma, the anxiety, the expense and fear caused by cynical manipulation of police, lawyers, and courts can be the punitive, avoidant goal. The state's protective machine becomes an additional tool of harassment.

"Anyone can use the apparatus," Hodes said. "Including abusers, to mete out punishment."

The National Coalition of Anti-Violence Programs' 2014 report on LGBTQI Intimate Partner Abuse noted that "in 2013 the police mis-arrested the survivor as the perpetrator of violence" in over half of all queer domestic abuse arrests. There are particular dangers in misidentifying the perpetrator in same-sex relationships. The one who is butch, of color, not a mother, not a citizen, is from another culture, or HIV-positive can be falsely construed as the assailant. In all cases, the perpetrator may get control of the Abuse discourse as a denial, defense, or deflection of their own behavior. And just because someone doesn't call the police certainly does not mean they are guilty. There is often the false assumption that the one calling the police is innocent and the one who doesn't call the police is guilty. The real violated party may refuse to engage with the legal system for ethical reasons, or fear of the police, or they may refuse to grandstand on that level of language, punishment, or intimidation. They may simply recognize that the trouble is a Conflict and therefore inappropriate for punishment. And in cases of Conflict, where Abuse is not present, service providers from the New York LGBT Anti-Violence Project told me that false accusations and illegitimate claims to orders of protection were present among the client base, and that they understood these actions of overstating harm as consequences of "trauma."

"Threats," Hodes points out, "are an effective means of control." So just because someone makes the charge of Abuse, organizes group shunning or even generates lawyer letters or calls the police, it is not in any way proof or evidence that they are being "abused." They could be mischaracterizing the other's attempt to straighten things out, to communicate, to de-escalate because they fear the information that real negotiation would reveal. Or they may be so expectant of obedience and successful control of the other that that person's *resistance* to being scapegoated, shunned, or bullied gets called Abuse. Despite the assertions of Supremacy ideology, projecting onto another person or blaming them for things they have not caused, punishing them for things that never happened, organizing group shunning against them, or any other manifestation of mislabeling Conflict as Abuse are not "rights." "In court," Hodes said, "survivors do poorly in forensics and perpetrators do well." Reactions to scapegoating, assault, shunning, the denial of due process, i.e., assertion of what Hannah Arendt called "The right to appear," can all be spun through the language of victimology.

Since perpetrators may refuse to participate in negotiation, group shunning is often one of their strategies. "A perpetrator can isolate their partner from the community," Hodes offered. They can organize or instrumentalize that community to punish or shun the partner, thereby restricting further the partner's ability to provide information, details, ask for help, or engage in negotiation. Hodes advocates for clients to be asked, "What did *you* do? What was the purpose behind your behavior?" Over and over again she recommends an analytical focus on the self: one's own actions, their chronological order, their intent and outcome.

"Abusers externalize," she says. "It's always somebody else's fault." So if the parties are able to spell out and honestly discuss their own roles, then they are more able to create solutions, which is what the abuser fears.

In the workshop we discussed a then-recent case in Connecticut where two men married to each other were issued cross-restraining orders. They both had serious crystal meth problems; there was a lot of acting out, and they each, in a grandstanding way, went to the police asking for protective orders, thereby avoiding the actual problem, which was the drug addiction. Of course, being the one to receive a restraining order in no way means that he is the one being "abused." It may simply mean nothing more than that he wanted to and was able to get a restraining order. Another personality, in the same position, may feel that getting a restraining order would be an escalation and an overstatement. But in this case, both parties decided to overstate harm, with the exaggeration augmented, or perhaps even caused, by addiction. Because the courts were confused by the question of determining who was "the" aggressor when there were two men involved, they were both given restraining orders by the state.

"There should never be cross-restraining orders," Hodes said. That's like saying *we agree to not see each other*. Restraining orders should only be issued if one person is deemed to be a perpetrator and the restraining order is necessary to save the other from Power Over. It's not a tactical strategy designed to prove a point. If both people are contributing to the problem, then it is *mutual* and therefore Conflict, and the intervention of the court is unreasonable. And asking for that intervention is similarly unreasonable. In this case, both men manipulated the Abuse apparatus as smokescreens to avoid dealing with the real issue, addiction. And the state happily enabled them, by reaffirming Abuse claims without providing an investigative process that would have revealed and focused on their drug use. Of course, in this mangled set of missteps, disaster ensued. When they came together again and had another conflict, the police arrived and ridiculously enforced both restraining orders; absurdly, both men were arrested. Unfortunately one had a heart attack while in jail and died. As we learn over and over again from police violence in the United States, calling the police over Conflict can result in violence and death.

"Mainstream Domestic Violence advocacy," Hodes said in a correspondence later that year, "is committed to assuming that *the victim is telling the truth*, and any exploration around that trope is met with heavy resistance. Historically, that makes sense for a host of reasons. But *this* analysis is not about disbelieving, it's about pinpointing where the problem lies."

One of Hodes' many valuable suggestions is to lower the bar for what must happen in a person's life for their suffering to be acknowledged.

"The current paradigm is encouraging all of us to think we are in abusive relationships," Hodes explained. "And if you are not in an abusive relationship, you don't deserve help. Being 'abused' is what makes you 'eligible.' But everyone deserves help when they reach out for it."

This is a strikingly humane idea: that the collapse of Conflict and Abuse is partly the result of a punitive standard in which people are made desperate, yet ineligible, for compassion. This is a non-cynical reading of a human condition in which people who have suffered in the past, or find themselves implicated in situations in which they are afraid to be accountable, fear that within their group acknowledging some responsibility will mean being denied their need to be heard and cared for. So they fall back on the accusation of Abuse to guarantee that they will not be questioned in a way that confirms these fears. Especially vulnerable to this are those who experienced profound disapproval and criticism early on as children, who are later locked into self-righteous families or Supremacy communities with negative bonds. Ultimately, the blurring of Conflict and Abuse, Hodes says, "is epidemic, and leads to everyone identifying as a victim, which is paralyzing the search for solutions."

I was moved and enlightened by her insight that conflicted people have to prove they are "eligible" for compassion. No one can negotiate without being heard. Shunning, therefore, is designed to maintain a unilateral position of unmovable superiority by asserting one's status as Abused and the implied consequential right to punish without terms. This concept, of having to earn the right to have pain acknowledged, is predicated on a need to enforce that one party is entirely righteous and without mistake, while the other is the Specter, the residual holder of all evil. If conflicted people were expected and encouraged to produce complex understandings of their relationships, then people could be expected to negotiate, instead of having to justify their pain through inflated charges of victimization. And it is in the best interest of us all to try to consciously move to that place.

Chapter Three | **The Police and the Politics of Overstating Harm**

AFTER LISTENING to Catherine Hodes, I realized that I had no idea of how and when so many of us have come to accept the state as the ultimate authority in our personal conflicts. I was also curious to explore how this benefits the state's own power. So I started looking at the interwoven history of consciousness about relationship Conflict and relationship Abuse, and how these both became entwined under the exclusive terrain of the state. I started with the recognition that when I was born in 1958, a woman who was raped required corroboration in order to press charges. New York Penal Law provided that, "No conviction can be had for rape or defilement upon the testimony of the female defiled, unsupported by other evidence." In other words, the woman's statement alone was not enough.

The cultural status quo of behavior for apartment building living at that time was that if a neighbor was heard "beating his wife," it was "their" business. Sometimes the police would take the guy for a walk around the block to cool him down, but there was no broad social convention that violence in the home was wrong, or that other people had a responsibility to stop it. Terms like "domestic violence," "sexual abuse," "harassment," and "stalking" had not been articulated, and were not conceptualized by most people as common subjects of public discourse. There was no agreed upon social responsibility for third-party intervention. The separation of the home from the society, the isolation of the family, and male prerogative were the dominant factors in determining right from wrong. Men's behavior towards women and children was practically untouchable by community, society, or the law.

Today, at the same time that violence against women and children is still an everyday experience, the legal and state apparatus to address partner abuse and family violence is extensive. The existence of assault and abuse is well known and commonly represented in mass entertainment, as these terms are part of common parlance. Statistics are widely available and easy to obtain. While much, if not most, crime against women remains obscured, women reporting violence to authorities is widespread and a well-known option. New York City's official statistics for 2003-2005 show that 44 percent of reported and confirmed cases of violence experienced by women were classified as Intimate Partner Abuse. This is astounding information. Statistics show us that *half* of violence against women in New York takes place within the family. Families are dangerous for women and children in more ways than one. We now understand that being on the receiving end of violence is an organic part of women's, children's, and some men's daily realities and that it can be reported. These facts are the subjects of many, many books, movies, studies, conversations, and ideologies. And while an extensive legal infrastructure has developed to address these events, the analysis that produced it historically has differed enormously from the ideology that underlines it today. The implementation of this ideology has resulted in social confusions and messaging contradictions that can easily contribute to misplacing blame and overstating harm in some corners, while erasing responsibility and avoiding accountability as violence continues unabated in others.

The Police as Arbiters of Relationships

Decades of organized politics by anti-violence, feminist, and victims' rights activists transformed the social understanding of partner/family violence and introduced new terms and ideas into the public imagination. These initial grassroots movements against violence emerged in the 1960s and were often related to other radical organizing toward transformations of power. As University of Florida professor Kim Emery reminds me, because of then contemporary social currents gesturing towards big picture structural critique, the movements were more focused on empowering women than on punishing men. Anti-poverty, anti-racist, and women's liberation movements analyzed violence against women and children within the overlapping of those categories of oppression; patriarchy, poverty, and racism were often cited as roots of violence against women. Feminism brought critiques of the role of women in families to the surface. Women were trapped financially, but also emotionally within concepts of family to which they were expected to sacrifice their own wishes for themselves to the wishes of male partners, male relatives, and adult male children. Analysis of the social constraints that accompany motherhood, its mandatory nature in order for a woman to have self-worth and the approval of her family and of society, were paramount. For the first time heterosexuality was understood as an institution that was propagandized and imposed by force. Inadequate access to reproductive control and an understanding that capitalism produces and is reliant on poverty fueled these political analyses and efforts.

But many initially radical movements in the 1960s and '70s soon became single-issue and reform-oriented, and moved into bureaucratic relationships to the government. As Nancy A. Matthews documents in her 1994 book *Confronting Rape: The Feminist Anti-Rape Movement and the State*, increased consciousness of the right to live without violence, the subsequent enormous demand for feminist services like activist-run hotlines and rape crisis centers, and the expansion of service provision created a need for funding in the late 1970s that went beyond grassroots resources. This led to government funding, professionalization, and a bureaucratization of anti-rape collectives and community-based services. I know from my own experience as a

CETA (Comprehensive Employment and Training Act) worker in a feminist health center that the election of Ronald Reagan in 1980 quickly dismantled this twenty-year-old job-training program that had assisted many grassroots organizations. The search for new funding transformed politically motivated services into containment by municipal, state, and federal agencies. Anti-violence politics, along with other revolutionary impulses, changed from a focus on working to transform patriarchy, racism, and poverty to cooperation and integration with the police. This has proven to be a significant turn because the police are, ironically, the embodiment of patriarchy, racism, and the enforcement of the US class system.

John R. Barner and Michelle Mohr Carney's 2011 review of "Interventions for Intimate Partner Violence" encapsulates the period immediately after Reagan's cuts. The study shows that New York City "Battered Women's" shelters alone reported an 80 percent denial rate due to lack of funding in 1982. State legislatures began to fund shelters in 1994 as a result of the Violence Against Women Act, but these programs have faced opposition over the years such as when California's then governor Arnold Schwarzenegger implemented a 100 percent cut to domestic violence shelters in 2009, requiring federal intervention. Barner and Mohr write:

> Shelters have moved from a more central position as primary victim interventions to being motivated to seek out collaborations with law enforcement, health care and other social service agencies to provide funding. As a result the institutional response has evolved from victim centered to perpetrator centered treatment focus.

This placement of the authority to "stop violence" into the hands of the police produces a crisis of meaning. The police are often the *source* of violence, especially in the lives of women, people of color, trans women, sex workers, and the poor. And the police enforce the laws of the United States of America, which is one of the greatest sources of violence in the world. US foreign policy is enforced by the military who are a global police, and domestic order is enforced by the federal, state, and city structures of policing. The law is designed to protect the state, not the people who are victimized by the state. So while police intervention can importantly separate violent adults from their victims or each other after violence has begun, this job of "stopping violence" has shifted from stopping the causes of violence to reacting punitively to the expressions of those unaddressed causes.

What was even more distracting and confusing was that the job of punishing the expressions of patriarchy, racism, and poverty was assigned to the police, who also cause violence. This responsibility, in some cases, produced additional acts of violence on the part of the government, like "stop and frisk," and racial profiling that committed violence in the name of claiming to fight violence. These laws also produced more access for the state into the homes and families of the poor, and more incarceration of Black and other poor men. Instead of empowering women and the poor, the fate of the traumatized was increasingly in the hands of the power of the police acting as a group to represent oppressive systems.

Now, we all know that a very short time ago, women and children had no recourse with the state if they were subjected to physical violence or severe domination. And we all know that many women and children are still subjected to unrestrained violence and severe domination without recourse. We also know that the state over-polices vulnerable communities based on race, poverty, legal status, sex work, or being transgender and other contested existences, and therefore the state itself is often the source of violence. So here we find ourselves in a multi-part conundrum:

- Some of us are able to use the police to help resist violence and domination.
- Some of us continue to experience violence and domination despite the police.
- Some of us experience the police themselves as the source of violence and domination.
- Some of us call on the police because we don't know how to solve problems.
- Some of us use the rhetoric of violence and domination to avoid the discomfort of facing our own aggressions.

- Some of us use the police to reinforce our own unjust social power.

These are not "equal" experiences. For some, the pain caused by these imbalances defines the meaning of advantages that the same inequalities create for others. More importantly, the simultaneity of these realities, experiences, and relationships to the state can serve as a model of how to understand that structures can have different meaning for different people at the same time. This is the fundamental reason why everyone needs to be heard in order for conflict to be resolved.

While radical anti-violence movements declined, the police got primary control of the official discourse of "ending violence," at the same time that they were causing violence. Expressions of this confusion appeared on network television. There is the zeitgeist and then there is the corporate zeitgeist. Television shows like *Law and Order: Special Victims Unit* surfaced with a focus on sex crimes and family violence. In a typical episode, a purely innocent victim, who does not participate in creating conflict and is inherently good, is stalked/abused/attacked by a purely and inherently evil predator. The answer to the conundrum is the police. Popular mass entertainment, a corporate entity that is not self-critical, makes the message clear: people are either victims or predators, and therefore the answer is always the police, who are also not self-critical. If some of these people were understood as Conflicted instead of only as victim/perpetrator, then the solution to conflict would be mutual accountability and negotiation, rather than escalation, which would locate authority and responsibility far from the hands of the police.

Unfortunately, the necessary social conversation that could help us to understand how people participate in the escalation of conflict became conflated with the real crisis of blaming victims, even though they are two entirely separate things. As I will discuss later, the issue of how people operating with Supremacy ideology escalate conflict was ignored. And how traumatized, anxious, or addicted people can escalate conflict became a repressed subject in the name of not inflating blame-the-victim rhetoric, since understanding is conflated with blame. The solution? Again, the police. This reductive, dichotomous, bad/good message has been reinforced daily for decades, through corporate entertainment, media, and the arts in a way that justifies the power of the police and falsely presents it as neutral, objective, and value-free.

In the 1980s context of Reaganism, the integration of the Religious Right into the Republican Party (see my book *My American History: Lesbian and Gay Life During The Reagan/Bush Years*) and renewed rhetoric of patriotism and authority, along with questions of how to address the origins of violence were dominated by an expanded apparatus of punishment. Accurate understanding of the role of the police in enforcing inequality and unjust social order became rhetorically marginalized along with the radical movements that produced them. Questions about the efficacy, ethics, and complexities of state punishment got pushed aside. This crisis in meaning produced a condition of absurdity around these issues. The terms of the debate become corrupted—so vague, elastic, and dishonest—that they ceased to have clear-cut meaning. Citizens too could manipulate the vocabulary of violence to cover up their own destructive and cruel injustices, just like their government did. The focus on the causes of both Conflict and Abuse—male Supremacy, poverty, racism, and an inability to problem-solve—require radical structural change in self-understanding and power. Instead, a simplistic and often destructive emphasis on who is right and who is wrong was replicated so that we, who surround the conflict, could know on whom to inflict punishment, thereby proving our own righteousness.

Is there less violence? Yes. At least the government thinks so. According to November 27, 2012 Bureau of Justice statistics, from 1994 to 2010, the overall rate of intimate partner violence in the US declined by 64 percent. Clearly the paradigm shifts in popular expectations and in access to resources, as well as increased education rates for women, no-fault divorce, and other social shifts including increased awareness by the courts and communities, has reduced incidents of real violence. But is this reduction across the board or is it located in only some demographics? Barner and Carney note that with the shift from community-based feminist movement services to law enforcement-centered and criminally-oriented responses, "arrest and prosecution procedures would seem to fall in line with disproportionate racial demographics in the criminal justice system."

As University of Illinois professor Beth Richie crucially

articulates in her book *Arrested Justice: Black Women, Violence, and America's Prison Nation*:

> There is no solid, longitudinal research on the relationship between specialized new laws, legal procedures, or mandatory protocols and changes in rates of violence against women in more disadvantaged communities.

For some women, there may be more punishment, but there may not be more prevention. Calling the police may interrupt real violence, but it is not designed to address the *causes* of actual violence or actual Abuse, nor does it address the confusion between Conflict and Abuse. Instead, putting the police in charge of both domestic Abuse and domestic Conflict creates a punitive response as the primary, and sometimes only, response. How the social structure of gender, race, and class contribute to violence is obscured. How conditions that may be created in part by sexism, racism, homophobia, transphobia, immigration status, disability, and class oppression contribute to both Abuse and Conflict is under-explored. And how early trauma, addiction, and mental illness contribute to Conflict escalation instead of resolution is also obscured.

It is very difficult to measure rates of partner or family violence. It is hard to know if rates of assault are actually rising or falling, or if it is reporting that is rising and falling. We don't know how to understand fluctuations in the numbers of people who actually make complaints, how the police understand complaints, how complaints lead to arrests, and the relationship between arrests and actual convictions. We don't have a clear sense of how the police or the courts differentiate between Abuse and Conflict. The highest rate of reported rape that led to conviction in New York history was in 1992, when there were approximately 5,000 rape convictions. In 2010, there were a little over 2,000. We don't know if this is connected to gentrification, which removes poor people from the city and replaces them with both perpetrators and victims who have more resources to evade both sexual violence itself and the reach of the law. Money, whiteness, and education help perpetrators and victims both to evade state intervention.

We do know that most sexual assaults are not reported, especially those that take place within families. Many people do not understand exactly what sexual assault is. And sometimes legal definitions do not correspond to how people understand their own lives. While some sex crimes are crystal clear, others are entirely about perception. For some women I know, having sex with their partner at times when they feel ambivalent or not fully engaged is defined in their minds as *coercion* or even Abuse. They find it objectionable or even damaging. For others, that is part of the literal *making* of *love*: the idea that we give to our partners in moments when we are not 100 percent engaged, just as we negotiate in other ways within relationships. Or in terms of casual encounters, quasi-unpleasant to negative sexual experiences are devastating to some, and *just the way things go* to others. How previous experiences of trauma contribute to an individual's understanding of whether or not an experience is Abuse is a factor that we do not have a process of integrating into our understanding of objective crime or objective justice. How some experiences permanently mark some people while not affecting others makes objective standards of right and wrong difficult to establish.

Clearly, inaccurate or projected claims of Abuse when in fact Conflict is at the heart of the problem hurt the person being accused, keep the accuser from a progressive confrontation with the self, and divide and destroy communities. But these actions create much more harm than for the participating parties alone. Professor Richie's book gave me some new insights into the larger, more long-range consequences of conflating Conflict with Abuse. Among other revelations, Richie documents how significant "Power Over" is in the lives of many poor women because of poverty. Or what Hunter College Professor Jacqueline Nassy Brown calls "the gendered politic of staying, going and returning." Richie focuses specifically on Black women. Homicide by an intimate partner is one of the most common causes of death for young Black women in America. According to Richie, 25 percent of Black women experience abuse from their intimate partners, which places them at the average national rate of 22 percent, regardless of race. Richie reports that Black women are killed by a spouse at a rate that is twice that for white women, in part because Black women cannot afford to leave. Poverty, of course, creates vulnerability both to other people and to the state. Oppression, which is itself by definition a state of vulnerability, in turn produces even more vulnerability. Lack of mobility, financial autonomy, access to housing, accurate representation in media, entertainment, and the arts, health care, and representation in government: all of these produce more violence and problems, and fewer conditions conducive to the kind of structural problem-solving that poverty both requires and obstructs.

So, sustained, unilateral violent assault—the kind of experience that these laws, definitions, and social paradigms of Abuse were developed to address—affects Black women in America in similar numbers but at a significantly higher level of lethal impact than white women. Therefore, the exploitation, watering down, and casual overuse of these arenas of experience are detrimental to Black women, along with women, men, and children of all races who are truly victimized. One could argue that the misuse of harm rhetoric by men and women of all races is particularly damaging to all women who experience the crimes these laws were created to illuminate. They already have trouble being heard and helped. The rhetoric of overstated harm is especially damaging to poor and/or Black women who statistically need these paradigms while being denied access to them.

People from privileged groups, or who overlap with the groups society is designed to serve, have expectations that their complaints will be heard. Obviously white and bourgeois people are more likely to have their accusations taken seriously than the undocumented, poor, trans, and people of color, whether the accusations are Abuse or Conflict. So I think it is fair to extrapolate that identification with the power hierarchy and state apparatus would make bourgeois and white people feel more entitled to make overstated accusations and have fewer concerns that their access might not be justified ethically. The word "entitled" itself implies an expectation that one can demand something of others and have it be delivered. This includes accusations of Abuse when Conflict is actually what is occurring. So even with complicating those categories, accusations taken at face value without nuance are those most likely to reinforce existing power dynamics. This is especially true when the person being blamed is a non-citizen, a person of color, poor, trans, queer, HIV-positive, not a family member, etc. In this way, uniting around the accusation allows a group bonded in negative ways to enhance its own status. As Ilana Eloit wrote in the London School of Economics blog Engenderings in July, 2015:

> The ability to claim abuse is intricately related to possessing the symbolic and material capital that allows the claim to be heard, and thus does not reflect the proper power of balance that the claim is supposed to unveil.

One of the most emblematic infamous false accusations in American history was that made by two homeless white sex workers, Ruby Bates and Victoria Price, in 1931 when they falsely accused nine Black men of rape in Scottsboro, Alabama. The men were Roy Wright, Andy Wright, Eugene Williams, Haywood Patterson, Ozie Powell, Clarence Norris, Olen Montgomery, Charlie Weems, and Willie Robertson. What Bates and Price had at stake was that rather than merely being people committing crimes, they were criminalized people. Because they had prior convictions for adultery and vagrancy, it was illegal for them to cross state lines into Alabama; so, they themselves were subjected to overstatement of harm. When confronted with the possibility of arrest, they made their false accusations, which became the justification for decades of tragic incarceration and trauma in the lives of the innocent men and their families. What is especially revealing is that Bates recanted her accusation and toured the United States with some of the mothers of the men her lies had landed in prison. She gave numerous public lectures side by side with the Scottsboro mothers, under the rubric of the Communist Party, explaining that she had lied. Yet, because she had no inherent value as a poor woman, her recantation was ignored by the prosecution. Like the experience of most traumatized people who make alliances with bullies, she was only listened to when it served the white male agenda: the ideology of white male Supremacy.

We have learned over and over again, through the almost mechanistic co-optation of a wide range of radical movements and disenfranchised communities, that as long as the system of domination and power remains intact, winning "rights" or realignment in the hierarchy simply means that the most normative elements of any community gain access to the state apparatus. When this happens, the least powerful elements remain the objects of their force. New insiders will create new outsiders if the way we think about our society doesn't change. Conflicting interpretations of the vocabulary of Abuse appeared to address a problem while simultaneously reinforcing the abusive status quo. Some people may get their problems addressed, but others will have their problems aggravated. In this way, the state and the interests it serves, Kim Emery points out, will have their authority both legitimated and instrumentally extended.

"Violence," Violence, and the Harm of Misnaming Harm

The definition of "violence" has now expanded to include a new continuum of behaviors and feelings that are also generically used to ascribe a negative value to a person's actions. The word "violence" has expanded far beyond the field of physical assault to also mean emotional abuse and, unfortunately, emotional conflict where there is no abuse. In recent years, we see "violence" and "abuse" being ascribed to social criticism, efforts to understand phenomena, and social and psychological analysis. "Abuse" is also regularly used to describe disagreement and misunderstanding. Accusations of "policing," "shaming," and other expressions of "call-out culture" demanding "safety" from uncomfortable ideas represent people and actions as laden with blame, refusing interactivity around the content of ideas and perceptions. This is in line with the similar practice of calling racial analysis "playing the race card." Trying to understand and explain structures of pathology is repressed by accusations of wrong-doing. Thinking is wrong. Saying is wrong. Not only are revelations unwanted, they get mischaracterized as harm.

For this reason I propose that as part of an evolved consciousness about not exploiting the rhetoric of victimization, the word "violence" should be used to describe physical violence. Emotional cruelty, shunning, group bullying—these things can be worse than some violence, but they are not the same. If this wide range of precise experiences is all collapsed into the generic word "violence," then nothing has any differentiation, therefore all the variations lose meaning. And as I have been arguing, rhetorical devices that hide details keep truth from being known and faced. Using the word "violence" without metaphor will help with the current discourse of overreaction and help us discern, with more awareness, the differences between Abuse and Conflict.

Recently we have been seeing academic administrations mimicking the role of the state in these matters. At the same time that universities have come under scrutiny for minimizing sexual assault charges, and accusations that the "corporate university" is increasingly involved in gentrification, labor exploitation, and globalization, we see universities playing an oppressive/protective role in repressing emotional content. It isn't beneficial to go into this particular swamp in too much detail here since many others are engaging the question, but in early 2014, at the dawning of the debate around institutional "trigger warnings," I participated in a public roundtable discussion that was itself an expression of the contradictions at the core of the Conflict versus Abuse dichotomy. At issue were the then-recent announcements by Oberlin College and the University of California at Santa Barbara, two schools with well-to-do constituencies, that professors were mandated to issue "trigger warnings," i.e., advisories to students that assigned texts may contain material that would "trigger" or remind them of past traumas, which they then would have the right to decline to read or view.

In a healthy educational forum, students engage materials regardless of agreement or comfort level and then analyze, debate, critique, and learn from them, addressing the discomfort as well as the text. This is why, in my fiction writing classes at the public City University of New York, College of Staten Island, I have a "no censorship" rule. Since this is an art class, students can engage any subject, event, or character and use any language that they feel is appropriate. However, at the same time, any student who has criticism, insight, or objection to these elements has the equal right to express their views in detail. This has been my policy for sixteen years without a single complaint. The problem with shunning is that it keeps information that can be productive out of the realm of consideration. Healthy discourse means dealing with what exists and coming into some kind of relationship of understanding with reality. Defended discourse forbids or shuns certain perspectives or contexts to information. The focus of these trigger warnings was usually on sexual violence, but the constraints, by implication, could lead to students being exempted from materials describing colonialism, racial Supremacy, Occupation, or anything that they might find upsetting, even from a Supremacy position. Certainly, we have seen the rhetoric of Abuse used by Zionists on college campuses to restrain open discussion of the Palestinian Boycott, Divestment and Sanctions movement, for example.

My view, in sum, was that while sexual and physical abuse does occur on campuses, and prejudice and discrimination may be rampant in class, actual sexual and physical abuse do not usually take place in a classroom. So intellectual, educational settings are among the few places in life where these things can be analyzed and engaged with depth without threat of actual physical danger. Being reminded that one was once in danger has to be differentiated from whether or not one is currently in danger. Confusing the two is a situation that quickly becomes destructive. Being conscious about one's own traumatized past experiences, and how they manifest into current traumatized behavior, can be a force for awareness of one's own reactions, not a means of justifying the repression of information. Additionally, as a teacher, I opposed all restraints from administrations on classrooms.

In my subjective experience, some of the participants in the roundtable were so traumatized that they were unable to have this conversation. Ideas that they did not agree with were experienced as assaults. Instead of addressing the content of the idea, they would respond with their autobiographies of sexual assault and violence. Clearly, processed awareness of one's own experience of oppression and violation are crucial expressions that must be heard, and are essential contributions to public understanding. And expression of terrible experiences starts out unprocessed and raw. And pain must be heard. At the same time, unprocessed violation and pain cannot be at the helm of control of what information is allowed to be expressed by others, including teachers, and required to be engaged in a classroom. In that roundtable conversation, expression of difference was so intolerable to some that it was responded to, phenomenologically, with outraged accusation. The discussion itself was comprised primarily of buzz words. The fallout on social media was, frankly, hysterical. It reminded me of a microcosm reflection of the responses I get online for my support of Palestine. There were wild accusations, slander, and calls for punishment, banishment, and generalized condemnation, for ideas that were never addressed with substance.

Soon after, I received an email from one of the participants in typical accusatory style, stating that my approach had been "cruel." I responded that if he would send me his phone number, I would call him and we could discuss it. He replied again that I was "cruel." Again I suggested that he send me his phone number, as email is not an appropriate venue for substantive conversation. He then replied accusatorily that I had not sent him *my* phone number. I quickly sent my phone number and explained that I had offered to place the call to absorb the cost. He then phoned me, thereby automatically giving me his phone number, so that whole sub-struggle had been yet another unnecessary expression of pointless, circular control. Once we were in conversation, I listened to everything he had to say without interruption or comment and then asked him what he thought was "cruel." He then said that he "didn't understand" the ideas I had expressed. I told him that, in my view, there is a difference between not understanding and something being cruel. We discussed calmly for a while. Finally, I asked him sincerely why he thought I would be cruel to the people with whom I was engaging. In other words, what would be my motive for being cruel? He said he didn't know and that's why he didn't understand. In other words, there were emotional vulnerabilities, projections, and assumptions at play that kept us from exchanging meaningful ideas. And these were somewhat mitigated by direct human contact. This is not to say that we emerged from our discussion as friends, but certainly the level of accusation on his part diminished significantly.

My point here is that at the same time that pervasive abuse and violence remain unaddressed, in casual practice, once someone is established as a victim, and the other described as "abusive," "stalking," "violent," "policing," or "shaming," the conversation ends. Just as Catherine Hodes noted that perpetrators are increasingly the ones to initiate calling the police, or using the state apparatus as part of the harassment process, the accusation of Abuse itself can be a tactic of silencing. Once the Abuse charge is organized and launched, it becomes possible for large groups of people to dislike and even punish some targeted person without even knowing what it is, specifically, they have to say or how they understand what is happening, or even exactly what they are accused of having done. This approach denies the complexities of people's lives, the tensions we embody, and the ways we participate. There has to be a way to be clear that one person is too upset to responsibly face the terms of the Conflict without obscuring this by accusing the other of Abuse.

Calling the Police on Singular Incidents of Violence

In the entirety of my adult life I have not been involved with violence. When I was young, my mother hit me regularly and my father hit me once, significantly, and I also fought with my siblings. As an adult, however, I have never committed an act of violence, never been accused of committing an act of violence, and was only hit once, a story I will get to later. Some readers may feel that this lack of direct experience renders this section irrelevant. So, with that recognition, I proceed with offering my thoughts, feelings, and the revelations produced by the intellectual and emotional work I have committed to this project, understanding that some readers may not find it valuable or legitimate.

Putting the effort to end violence in the hands of perpetrators of state violence gave a new meaning to the term Abuse that was far from the intentions of the originating anti-violence activists. The antidote to violence at home was now officially the violence of the state. Words like Abuse took on double meaning. It retained the initial understanding of one person suffering from "Power Over" by another, but then added a second layer of meaning where the same words became excuses for the state to victimize individuals. "I'm going to call the police" becomes a call for help *from* violence in some cases, and conversely a call to cover up discomfort, disagreement, or implicating actions by invoking the threat of state violence in other cases. The same words and the same actions have dual use: to protect from harm, and to inflict harm. In this way, a confused overturning of meaning culturally enhances police access to people's personal lives. Grassroots desires to end violence are replaced by a normalization of permission and, in fact, a reliance on the police to arbitrate relationships.

Why do we call the police? I was discussing this with a room full of people at the Vulva Club in Berlin in 2015, as part of an early presentation of ideas from this book.

"If I was being stabbed and I saw a policeman, I would want him to make it stop," I said. "But if someone stole my cell phone? Why would I call the police? What would be my fantasy behind calling the police? So that a person who could not afford the phone that I can afford should be put in a cage. Why?"

One of the main reasons that people call the police, other than to stop ongoing violence, is because they are upset and they want someone else to be punished. But what is that going to give them? How many people call the police because they are angry and don't want to deal with their own actions, behaviors, or feelings? They just want the other person to be hurt. People often call the police to get their partners or children thrown out of their mutual homes or for other incidents in which there is no violence. It is punitive against the "crime" of opposition. You want someone to do something that they don't think is just, and so you call the police. Involved in this process is a fantasy that the police are going to take responsibility for problem-solving out of the hands of the caller. But time and time again, Americans are reminded of the fact that the people who become police officers in the United States are often absolutely incapable of problem solving. There are famous examples of parents calling the police to "scare" their children, and the children ending up being murdered by the police. In cases of Conflict, calling the police is the last thing any of us should be doing unless our only objective is to cause more pain.

During the writing of this book I had coffee with an old friend, Tina. I started describing the ideas that I was working with and she told me about an incident that had occurred in her own relationship. Her partner, Lillian, is an advocate for victims of domestic violence in the rural area in which they live. They spend a lot of time discussing cases. As part of Lillian's regular work responsibilities, she goes to court to try to get restraints, limitations, and punishment imposed on violent male partners. The job is frustrating because in their jurisdiction, courts usually refuse such requests. Lillian had recently finished a case where a man committed so much sustained violence over such a long period of time against his female partner that she had three separate incidents of hospitalization. That she was hurt three times so badly that she had to seek and receive extended care implies that there were many, many other violent events that occurred but did not produce such a dramatic outcome. Lillian went to court with all of the affidavits and hospital and police records necessary to inform the judge, but he dismissed her client's case and granted the man shared custody of their children. Such is Lillian's daily reality where actual, substantiated examples of sustained, damaging violence are disbelieved by the legal apparatus. And we know this is the case for many, many women and children in America.

Tina told me that seven years earlier, she had gone into treatment to overcome an addiction, and this caused enormous upheaval in their household. Tina was very self-aware and responsible about describing her own behavior, and conveyed to me clearly that she had been unstable and emotionally overwrought, had made bad decisions, and had projected onto, accused, and blamed her partner. The confusion and pain that this caused between them was significantly destructive. One day, Lillian acted out and punched Tina. This is an event that so many years later the two of them still refer to as "the incident." They made the decision to keep it to themselves and not to discuss it with other people. It never recurred. Through an intimate process of mutual taking of responsibility and Tina's progress into responsible sobriety, their conflicts were resolved. Tina explained to me that while what happened was undesirable and clearly an act of violence, it was produced by both of them. They understood that they both had to adjust their behaviors, and it was part of the transformation into a sober relationship. Tina was adamant that there would have been no point in calling the police.

Physical violence has many varied manifestations, and non-defensive violence is never justified or desirable, nor does it solve problems. The most common scenario is the regularly violent spouse who initiates violence as a control mechanism, where it is used to enforce behaviors in the victim. Then there is the couple who both lack problem-solving skills and resort to violence irregularly, or in a single incident, in ways that are equally undesirable but don't result in one person's domination. They do not endanger each other physically, although there are clearly signs of problems that need to be faced and dealt with. These are obviously different phenomena. And I think they should be treated differently even though they both involve physical violence. Once we stop being determined to produce a victim and are instead focused on learning the truth of what actually happened, we become willing to accept the discomfort of recognizing two people as being Conflicted and embrace a more humane and acknowledging vision of social relationships. This is essential if we want peace.

The one time, as an adult, that I was physically struck was at a residency at an artist's colony in the Northeast. As is sometimes a reality, in this session almost everyone given the privilege of the time and support was white. The one exception was Joanne, an artist from a Black community in the Deep South. She had never been to New England before, nor ever been in an all-white environment. She also had had very little personal experience with openly gay people. Most of the whites there were busy talking to each other about Northeastern white culture: they were discussing agents, MFA programs, commissions, theaters, publishers, writers, and teachers who were also white. Joanne was inherently excluded from many of these conversations. Very few of the white people knew anything about contemporary or historical Black literature or visual art, especially regional to the American south.

I watched Joanne become more and more isolated. I started sitting with her at dinner and trying to share my interest and knowledge of African-American artwork in an effort to connect with her and to support her. I brought up gay Black writers in conversation a few times and she seemed unfamiliar with them, so I dropped it, or repressed commentary on their queer content or perspectives. As we talked, she expressed discomfort with the food being served, which she found bland and depressing. She was always hungry. One day she learned that James Baldwin had once been in residence in her studio. This was at the tipping point of her stress, and she became convinced that since Baldwin had been in that studio, and she, the only Black person, was in that studio, it was where "they" put Black people. She started calling it "the slave shack." She'd come to dinner, and I'd ask, "How is your work going?" and she'd reply, "Another day in the slave shack." This in a very elite environment normally considered to be a privilege, so the structural racism of the selection process increased her anxiety and created isolation that produced distorted interpretations in a context that was pressured, inappropriate, and unequal.

One night there was an impromptu dance. The thirty or so residents brought out some tapes, moved the furniture around in the residency's library, and started dancing. She was standing outside alone, not dancing. I had considered that this might happen—a combination of alienating musical choices, discomfort, and a factual feeling of being out of context. I walked up to her, put my hand on her shoulder, and said something. I don't remember exactly what. It could have been "How are you doing?" or even "Do you want to dance?" At any rate, she pivoted around, gritted her teeth, and said, "Don't touch me," and then punched me in the head. She hit me so hard that I pirouetted and staggered back. I really didn't understand what had happened. And I don't remember what I said or did. In fact, the aftermath is a blank.

The next morning we all discovered that she had packed up her car in the middle of the night and left. The director called a gathering for any residents who wanted to discuss the situation, and a handful of us met in the common room. I knew that I had the power to hurt her. I could have further pathologized her, blamed her, and punished her. I could have painted myself as her victim, and ascribed homophobia to her action. I was informed by the director that I had the right to file a complaint. But wasn't I also to blame? Didn't I participate in benefitting from a racist admissions process? Wasn't I self-aggrandizing by substituting myself for, and therefore protecting, a just accounting with the authorities about how in the hell there could only be one Black resident? Making a complaint seemed beside the point. I rejected the offer of filing a complaint and submitted a list of forty artists of color to the admissions office, asking them to send each one an application. To my knowledge, none of those people were accepted. Yes, there was an act of physical violence, and yes, it was unjustified. But using it as an excuse to punish would have furthered the injustice.

In my own experience, I am also thinking of two other singular incidents of interpersonal acts of violence that I know of, where people acted on decisions that were the opposite of the choices Tina and I both made.

In one case, over twenty years ago, there was a lesbian couple named Mary and Beth, who are both white, although from different social classes. Mary grew up working-class and Beth grew up in the professional class. They both became professionals and worked in the same field. Being with them was beyond a drag. They bickered constantly in public. They taunted each other with cruelties. Beth openly had sex with men and used it in public to hurt Mary. Mary was long known as a psychological bully, and was also somewhat intimidating physically; on one occasion, she was angry and came up very close to me, invading my personal space. But neither had a history of hitting, pushing, slapping, or any kind of physical violence.

One night, after years of unresolved conflict, they had a fight. Beth picked up an object and threw it at Mary. It hit her hard and broke a bone.

Mary, obviously, was shaken up, angry, and hurt. She felt violated and she *was* violated, two things that often do not go together. When her friends did not respond to the event in the way that she wanted them to, she was even more hurt and angry and decided to seek a solution outside of the community. This event took place at a time, in the early 1990s, when the New York Police Department was just starting to develop awareness programs about gay and lesbian couples.

Most gay people my age, in that era, would never ever have considered calling the police about an incident of this nature. You called the police to prevent a crime, like if someone was breaking into your apartment. But no gay person that I knew would have called the police to solve a problem with another gay person by inflicting punishment after the fact. It was almost inconceivable. There was no expectation that the police would care or be helpful. In 1982, I had an argument with a girlfriend who locked me in my room. I called a friend, another gay girl, who came over and calmed everything down. But I never, ever, ever would have called the police. It was unimaginable. I do remember once when my girlfriend's apartment was robbed—this was probably around 1992—and we called the police. When they saw that we were lesbians, they were rude and cocky and insinuating. Their presence in the house was as bad as the robbery.

When Beth injured Mary, the New York City Council had just passed the Gay Rights Bill, and most of us had had experiences of legal exclusion and discrimination based on sexuality. Sodomy was still broadly illegal and would be until it was overturned by the US Supreme Court in 2003. The police were a sexist, frightening, hostile force. The AIDS crisis was in full swing, and people with AIDS were being arrested at demonstrations by an antagonistic city government. The police wore rubber gloves, and treated us with cruelty and disdain.

So I was a bit confused when Mary phoned me at five in the morning a few weeks after the incident and said, "I got that bitch locked up." She explained that she had filed a complaint against Beth who had been arrested for "assault with a weapon" and was now in a holding cell in a New York City jail. Being old school, I assumed that Mary called me because on some conscious or unconscious level she wanted me to get Beth out of jail. So I started calling lesbians I knew who were lawyers, and Beth was bailed out. Later we learned that she had been strip-searched and placed in a cell with people who had stabbed other people and a variety of prisoners in high states of distress and illogic.

Even though there had never been any indication of future violence, Mary got a restraining order against Beth weeks after the incident. At the same time, she would do provocative, bullying things, like sit near Beth at public gatherings. Obviously Mary was angry at having been physically hurt. But I think she also may have been angry about the collapse of the relationship. I think too that there was rage there from experiences earlier in her life that had been expressed all along in the couple's public display of conflict. When I really think about it so many years later, Mary might have also been enraged that her way of living was not successful, and was not producing the kind of emotional life that she wanted to have. There was the failure of the relationship and the failure of herself. But she insisted on pressing charges until finally Beth was found or pled guilty and was put on probation. Beth moved to another city, got a boyfriend, and I never saw or heard from her again.

I have been grappling with this event for decades now. I am still disturbed by it. Yes, what happened was violence. Yes, Mary was physically hurt, in a significant way. Yes, Beth's reaction was wrong, unjustified, and unnecessary. But how did calling the police, sending her to jail, and charging her with a crime after the fact address the problem? Enough time had passed that it was clear that they were separated and that there would be no repetition of assault. To me, it felt like overkill, the manipulation of a system that was put in place for other reasons, like protecting people from ongoing harm. But it was Mary's option. It was technically her legal "right," and many people would say that it was also emotionally her "right." But other factors come into play. Mary played a part in this interaction; everyone around them knew it. Of course, she was not the one who threw the object and it was not her fault that Beth threw the object. It was Beth's action to own. But I know that Mary was often mean, childish, and unfair. Those attributes are not illegal, and she should not have been physically assaulted. At the same time, she helped produce that moment, even if she did not cause it. What I want from her is this: some recognition that she also acted in a way that was unnecessary and did not help. But the system isn't set up for mutual acts of self-recognition. Unfortunately, because we are locked into a victim/perpetrator dichotomy, it becomes "blaming the victim" to say that the person who got hurt participated in the escalation without actually causing it, even though there is no true relationship between that acknowledgment and blame.

Decades later, a similar incident again occurred within my network. Two women, Jane and Sue, were in a relationship. Jane was a working-class white woman with marginal income, and Sue was an upper-class woman of color with good employment. Sue owned an apartment in an upscale neighborhood of an American city that she had paid for with family help. She and Jane decided that Jane would use her own life's savings to buy the apartment next door. Sue then got a job in a faraway place, and Jane went with her, creating more economic disparity. Sue started a relationship with a third party, Kathy, who joined her in this faraway place. Jane was aware of the new relationship, but was shocked when it supplanted and excluded her. She felt disposed of, disrespected, blamed, and found Jane's treatment of her to be callous and uncaring. Now Jane was not only on the outs emotionally and financially, she was isolated in a place where she had no purpose or support. It was painful, humiliating, displacing, and expensive. She felt manipulated, tricked, and lied to. She crawled home to her new apartment, having been set back in every significant way. One day, as was inevitable, she encountered Kathy in the hallway using the key to get into the apartment next door, the very apartment that Jane and Sue had once had as a love nest. Frustrated, angry, and hurt, Jane hit Kathy in the face.

Clearly, the way Jane acted was totally wrong. She had no justification for punching Kathy. Sue had done a lot of things that were hurtful, even cruel, but she had not used violence. And Kathy, with the bravado of being the replacement, had also been callous and cruel. As it stands, being dishonest, callous, and cruel are not illegal, and hitting someone is. Community standards of how to treat each other might have helped create some accountability and avoided this consequence. But perhaps not. People have the right to change partners, but there are many kinds of available paths to creating change. Taking responsibility, recognizing the other person's anguish, allowing for transitional indulgences, going through a process with third parties even if uncomfortable, can dissipate pain. Taking the time necessary to achieve a peaceful and kind separation is mandatory. Acknowledgment of what is good about the discarded partner, and acknowledgment of good experiences they shared and can continue to share, can make a difference. But Kathy and Sue did none of the above. They were not kind.

However, a few days later, they called the police and filed an assault complaint against Jane. It turns out that the building's security cameras had the assault on tape, and they submitted this to the police as evidence. Once again we are in the realm of what is literally and legally "assault." But, while indefensible, it is a singular event that is the outcome of a long period of cruelty and unkindness. That, to me, makes it different; not acceptable, but different. And again I question whether calling the police in a punitive, not preventative, way was justified. The further irony here is that Sue and Kathy are public prison abolitionists. They take public stances against the prison system, and call for its dismantling.

I believe that what these couples went through was mutual and therefore Conflict, not Abuse. There was unnecessary cruelty as a consequence of narcissism, an inability to self-critique, and lack of willingness to resolve Conflict or to recognize mutual responsibility. And if there had been a way to interrupt that runaway train of impulsive negative action through individual awareness and/or the community around them, these conflicts could have been resolved, or at least reduced. Neither of these situations needed to end in singular incidents of violence and certainly not in calling the police.

In both of these cases, lesbian partners used language, legal paradigms, and police consciousness to create punishment that had been established as legitimate by the political anti-violence movements. They used a mutant form of feminism to see themselves as "abused" and therefore entitled to call the police so that the other person would be punished. But the earlier anti-violence activists were responding to a very different kind of violence, a violence of "Power Over," a violence that was designed to control behavior and was sustained, not incidental, as a response to cruelty. The escalated claim, emphasizing the harm without recognition of the responsibility of participation, served as a smokescreen to keep these women from the personal work required to face and deal with the products of their lack of kindness.

I know, of course, that lesbians commit ongoing "Power Over" partner violence, and that there have been instances when they have murdered or maimed their partners. I am not saying that we are immune. That is far from my point. What I am observing is that there is a mimicking, or perhaps even an exploitation, of a discourse developed out of a very different kind of experience. In both cases, if there had been a way to parse out the emotional cruelties, to ask for awareness and accountability before one party exploded, perhaps these outcomes could have been eclipsed. But as Catherine Hodes points out, "Being 'abused' is currently what makes you 'eligible'" for compassion. Even though everyone deserves help and compassion.

Calling the Police on Your Partner, When It's Your Father Who Should Have Gone to Jail

Sometimes, of course, people call the police even when no violence has occurred. They may be enraged that they are not being obeyed, they may be escalating to avoid facing themselves, they may be in a power play where they refuse to speak to the other person and can't back down. They may not know how to negotiate. They may be angry that the neighbor's dog is barking. They may be hurt that the neighbor is having a party and they weren't invited. They may want their child or partner to unilaterally follow their orders. They may be too impatient or compulsive to go through a process of working out conflict. They may have negative friendships or a bad family relationship in which they are encouraged to blame and escalate. Overreacting in the present is often a consequence of unresolved anxiety from the past. We don't have to be professionals, geniuses, or scholars to understand this. It's common sense. And, as all novelists, playwrights, and screenwriters know, people do things for reasons, even if they don't know what those reasons are. Anxiety is best addressed by support and love in trying to understand those reasons, not the false "loyalty" of aggression to escalate unjust actions. When we are in community with people who are escalating, we have to ask the right questions in order to understand what past experiences the instigator is responding to in the present. That is the responsibility of real friendship, the true definition of love.

For example, a woman I know named Belize grew up with a violent stepfather. He beat her and her brothers and sisters, and regularly humiliated her, putting her down on a daily basis. Her immigrant mother was a very susceptible yet narcissistic person, in a difficult position of dependency. She stood by for years and did nothing except encourage her daughter to be "nice" to her stepfather. As the eldest, Belize's value was based on performing labor for others, especially household labor, and especially for men and children. To this day it is very difficult for her to turn down requests for errands and favors, even if she has things she wants or needs to do for herself. As children, she and her siblings threatened the father with the police, but no one ever called them. Later, after two marriages to passive men, she acknowledged her desire for women, and the wish to have a life-long relationship with a woman. But even though she had managed to separate herself from heterosexuality, she could not emerge from the control of male Supremacy. Whereas her expectations for men were very low, her standards for women were unachievably high. She wanted them to protect and serve her in every way that her mother never had. And Belize wanted them to submit, as she did, to male relatives in terms of time, attention, energy, expense, and household work in the same way that she submitted.

Finally, after a decade of being alone, Belize met Kelly, a woman she enjoyed and was enriched by. They started to build a relationship until, one day, Belize's adult son Vlad suddenly appeared, moving back into her house. He didn't work or go to school, didn't help around the house or even clean up after himself. He didn't respect the couple's privacy, and had no plans for his future. He would complain regularly to his mother about Kelly, triangulating her and playing on his mother's guilt for having left his father to come out when he was still a child. Whenever he did this, Belize became very anxious, and was unable to negotiate or problem-solve. She experienced sleeplessness and obsessive repetitive thinking, and provoked circular arguments with her partner about her son. Finally, Kelly exploded at Vlad, telling him to come to her directly if there were conflicts to be faced, rather than going through his mother. He was making it impossible for his mother to have the relationship that she wanted. When Belize discovered that her partner had confronted the adult son, she exploded in shame and rage, and began a series of cruel actions aimed at Kelly, including organizing her friends to "defend her family." She shut down Kelly's bank account, and shipped her bicycle back to Kelly's home city, against Kelly's will and at her expense. When Kelly had treated Vlad like an adult and asked him to sit down and work out their differences, Belize sent Kelly a lawyer letter saying that she was "harassing family members." Belize also organized a community petition threatening Kelly with the police, even though she hadn't broken any laws. None of the signatories ever spoke to Kelly, so they had no idea as to what was really going on. When Kelly insisted that Belize and her friends were overreacting and that the bullying should be replaced by communication so that they could face and deal with this normative conflict, Belize called the police and filed false charges (which the police dismissed immediately). She then organized a widespread group shunning of Kelly, including an email and whisper campaign that carried on for years. People were told that Kelly had "terrorized a mother and child," often having no idea that the "child" was an adult man. When Vlad's friends asked him why he was doing this, he responded that "Kelly hates men," reflecting Belize's own panic and shame about her homosexuality.

All of these actions were part of an "abuse scenario" that would have been appropriate to Belize's deceased stepfather, but had nothing to do with the normative conflict of a partner dealing with an adult son trying to control his mother's sexuality. Because she was shunning her partner, nothing could be worked through. Belize's friends fueled the runaway train instead of helping her to calm down. And in refusing to talk to Kelly, they simultaneously enforced the dramatic actions of shunning, scapegoating, and blame. When Kelly tried to communicate in order to diffuse the aggression, Belize called the police on the wrong person: forty years earlier, she should have called the police on her stepfather. Actually, her mother should have called the police on Belize's stepfather. But because the mother betrayed her, Belize was now betraying herself. She couldn't take care of herself in the face of male control, and she punished the partner who put her before the wishes of the men around her.

Kelly had committed the forbidden action of Belize's childhood: standing up to male exploitation. There was no violence, no inappropriate sex, no drugs, no cheating, no stealing, barely any fighting—none of the actions that are normally within the realm of what could be called "Abuse." Belize exploded because her sense of self-worth, which was rooted in the role of sacrificing for male relatives, was being challenged. Her guilt about her sexuality was being exploited by her son, and it was too painful to face without the help of her friends and family. And when Belize's mother discovered the situation, she praised the daughter she had allowed to be assaulted, in essence for destroying her own sexual and emotional life, rather than asking her son to make minor adjustments, which also would have helped him be a more responsible and accountable person.

I knew another woman whose family was in a similar situation of projecting the pain of the past onto an undeserving object in the present. A college professor named Diana had come from a family of intense violence and sexual abuse. At the point that we knew each other, Diana's mother, sister, and niece were all unemployed and living on welfare; the father had died over a decade earlier. The mother was depressed and watched TV all day in a dark room. The sister was working in the sex trade, and the niece wasn't doing much. The mother and sister had enormous fights on a regular basis, in which they would each escalate the conflict. The sister would yell, "You let Daddy rape me," referring to events involving her abusive father that had occurred twenty years earlier.

Instead of saying, "What your father did to you is wrong, and I regret that I didn't know how to handle it. I love you and I am sorry, how can we make things better between us?" the mother would yell back, "Get out of here. I never want to see you again." Neither the mother nor the sister knew how to negotiate, how to deal with conflict. They only knew how to escalate it.

Whenever the mother became louder and more agitated, the sister would escalate by storming out of the house. The time that I was there, she took the mother's cat with her.

"Give me back my cat!" the mother screamed, further escalating the situation when she should have said, "I'm sorry we're yelling at each other. I love you, let's calm down." She then escalated even further by calling the police.

As with Belize, I always felt that the mother called the police on the wrong person and at the wrong time. She should have called them twenty years earlier, when her daughter was fifteen and being raped by her father, but she didn't. The reasons, of course, are complicated, having to do with passivity, jealousy, immigration, rage, narcissism, and an inability to solve problems. Now, when all four women—Diana, her mother, her sister, and niece—were suffering the consequences of the long dead father's crime and the mother's inaction, only now were they calling the police. On each other. About a cat. No one could concede, acknowledge, negotiate. They couldn't work together to deal honestly with the obstacles in their lives. All they could do was act out in order to deflect their pain.

When I think about both of these situations, I think about these women living with lifelong fantasies of how much better their lives would have been if someone had called the police when they were children. Diana's father should have had an intervention and been separated from the children. I can't even guess how many hundreds of times Belize, and her sisters and brothers, and Diana, her sister, and their mother must have dreamed of calling the police on the fathers. But because of the mothers' character issues and socio-political vulnerabilities, it never happened, and as a result the daughters suffered all their lives. And because the communities around them—the friends, the extended family—were, like the mothers, unwilling to intervene and help them to redirect their rage, they were condemned to being angry with the wrong person, thereby depriving themselves of healing, love, and resolution that can only come from facing and dealing with Conflict.

One other thought to keep in mind when grappling with the concept of the police as the arbiters for relationship conflict is the behavior of police officers in their own households. The National Center for Women & Policing noted in its "Police and Family Violence Fact Sheet" that "at least forty percent of police officer families experience domestic violence." This is a rate higher than even that of National Football League players. So the police are often the least likely people to be able to solve problems, to think in nuanced ways about emotional pain and its projections, and as a result are not the people we need help from if we are interested in creating peace.

Chapter Four | **HIV Criminalization in Canada:** How the Richest Middle Class in the World Decided to Call the Police on HIV-Positive People in Order to Cover Up Their Racism, Guilt, and Anxiety about Sexuality and Their Supremacy-Based Investment in Punishment

I will try and account for what we might call the inflationary logics at stake; how these materials through amplification and distortion, work to create a profile that has little trace of any origin. The details of the situation were quickly discarded as the details did not matter. Reality did not matter.
—SARA AHMED, "A Campaign of Harassment"

BY THIS POINT in the narrative life of an idea, I have tried to show the difference between Conflict and Abuse. Then I discussed how overreaction to conflict is expressed by relying on the police as arbiters of normative disagreements that could, instead, be negotiated through self-criticism, supportive communities, and communication. In this chapter, I go to the next step: where in a self-advertised "progressive" nation, Canada, the state actively seeks to convince HIV-negative citizens that they have been Abused so that they will punitively overreact, thereby resulting in unreasonable incarceration, fear, and more power for the state. It is a perfect example of how overstating harm can be presented as "moderate" or "sensible" and how the exaggerated response masquerades as "responsible."

Tim McCaskell is the handsome, white-bearded, slightly grizzled iconic Canadian AIDS activist. We're eating lunch on an extremely cold February day at a Toronto Ethiopian restaurant where the retired schoolteacher always has the vegetarian platter. A martial artist, McCaskell is usually on his bike, even in winter, but this time he's just coming off five days of IV antibiotics for a medical issue common to long-term survivors and he is temporarily fatigued. He is telling me about the latest wave of HIV prosecutions in Canada, and the uphill struggle that activists face after some severe legal setbacks. McCaskell's organization, Toronto AIDS Action Now!, was founded in 1987, the same year as ACT UP New York, but the contexts couldn't have been more different.

Privileges and Problem-Solving in the Canadian and US Contexts

Canada has long had a coherent government-provided health care system, and the US has not. Although the pharmaceutical industry is significantly present in the Canadian economy, the vast majority of research arenas that produced the meds that keep everyone with HIV alive in North America came from the US. Since the US government was not accountable to people with HIV, forcing pharma to change became the responsibility of American civilians. So the conditions and obligations of People With AIDS in Canada and the US were profoundly and irrevocably different. While the US is more powerful, has more military might, and globalizes its culture, Canada now has the richest middle-class in the world. Despite a decade of right-wing government austerity politics and severe cuts to social services before the Liberal Party's victory in 2015, the remaining Canadian safety net seems cushy by American standards. Yet Canadians find its diminishment severe and dramatic. Every wealthy democracy provides more of a safety net for its citizens than the United States, so Canada only seems extraordinary in direct comparison. While the US 1 percent has far more global power, the average Canadian's life is more protected and comfortable than their American counterpart.

When AIDS emerged in 1981 as GRID (Gay Related Immune Deficiency), gay sex was illegal in the United States and would remain so until a Supreme Court decision overturned sodomy laws in 2003. In Canada, however, the 1969 omnibus crime bill made anal sex legal for people over twenty-one, which was the age of majority at the time "provided no more than two people are present." So while the US was punitive, Canada provided a kind of moralistic, controlling, and judgmental freedom based on an early prescriptive articulation of gay "normalcy" rooted in the couple. Beyond the specificities of sodomy laws and health care, it is the relationship between citizens and government in Canada and the US that are quite different. Even under right-wing administrations, the Canadian government is more responsive to the voices of its citizens than the US government. Partially due to the small population, partially due to a culture of overlap between government and society, and partially due to their structure of campaign financing, Canadians have easier access to their government than Americans have to theirs.

Montreal's Josh Valentine Pavan is half Tim McCaskell's age, and emerges from a new, bold, young, and ingenious community of queer HIV and Prison activists. Pavan believes that Canadians have a more "omnipresent" state than Americans and therefore have to problem-solve through their government more regularly than Americans do, which would explain what seems to me to be more of an identification with the state. They are more likely to know their representatives, to expect their government to respond to protest, and to have more access to government officials than Americans do. What movements like AIDS Action Now! and ACT UP do share is that both were the source of social transformations in their respective countries of how people with AIDS were acknowledged, viewed, respected, and treated. Interestingly, even with these profound cultural differences, perhaps because of shared radical political identities, both ACT UP and AIDS Action Now! never asked for government funding, even though for Canadians this is a more radical act, since they are more accustomed to such funding. Both conceptualize themselves as political movements, not social service agencies. Both are still here.

Think Twice Before Calling the Police

Today Tim McCaskell and I are talking about "Think Twice," the new campaign of AIDS Action Now! aimed at HIV criminalization in Canada. "Think Twice" *about calling the police* is the plea of the HIV-positive who have been newly pushed into rogue status. Since a Supreme Court of Canada decision in 2012, it has been illegal for some HIV positive Canadians to have sex without disclosing their status, in some cases even if they use a condom and no one gets infected. In the US, thirty-eight out of fifty states have a range of laws against people with HIV, from non-disclosure to spitting, with punishments ranging from fines to a thirty-year sentence in Arkansas. Michael Johnson, a Black college athlete in Missouri, was sentenced to thirty years in jail in 2015 for infecting two white male partners with HIV. Nonetheless, there has yet to be an American high court confirmation or any nationally imposed standard. Canada is now one of the top ten countries in the world for HIV-related arrests and prosecutions per capita, leaving their 70,000 (including undiagnosed) HIV-positive residents in a state of threat and confusion. As of the spring of 2015, according to another of the new young breed of AIDS activists, Alex McClelland, 170 people have been charged; half are in in the province of Ontario, where Toronto is located. Most cases involve men who did not disclose their status to their female partners. Seventy-eight percent of all charges have resulted in convictions, of which almost all have gone to jail. Some of those have faced lengthy prison terms, even when the partner did not become infected. As of spring 2014, thirty men who had sex with other men were facing these charges. Having frustrated all legal appeals, activists have been trying to work with the "Crown" (prosecutors and solicitor generals) to establish prosecutorial guidelines, but have been unable to achieve significant progress. This is why AIDS Action Now! has no other options but to run a consciousness campaign aimed at potentially upset or anxious partners who may want to get back at their lovers by calling the police, even if they were not infected.

The Racial Roots of Canadian HIV Criminalization

The Canadian campaign for criminalization began in 1990 when a Ugandan immigrant, Charles Ssenyonga, was ordered by Toronto Public Heath to stop having sex after having infected three women. He died in 1993 before being fully charged. Then in 1998, the Supreme Court of Canada ruled that Henry Cuerrier, a white man, had committed a crime when he had unprotected sex with two women who did not become infected. The Cuerrier conviction was upheld by the Supreme Court and produced a ruling that in the context of sex posing a "significant risk," HIV nondisclosure can be considered an "assault." Of course, "risk" was not defined. Another significant case was that of Johnson Aziga, also a Ugandan immigrant, who received sensational press. Diagnosed in 1996 and charged in 2008, Johnson acknowledged having had unprotected sex with eleven different women without disclosing his status; seven of them became infected and two died of AIDS. In 2011 Aziga became the first person in the world to be convicted of murder for infecting someone with HIV. He was then jailed "indefinitely" under the Dangerous Offender act, because he was said to be at a high risk to again have unsafe sex. According to the *Canadian Journal of Law and Society*, Black men make up fifty-two percent of the heterosexual males who have been charged but only six percent of HIV-infected men in Canada. The overrepresentation of Black male defendants is significant in a country where only 2.5 percent of its population is Black. According to McCaskell, "the trope of the sexually predatory, diseased Black immigrant helped marshal racism to harden public opinion behind HIV criminalization."

Viral Load and the State

One of the most significant elements of Canadian HIV criminalization is the emphasis on viral load. The Supreme Court of Canada ruled that people who use condoms are required by law to disclose their HIV status unless they have a low viral load. This 9-0 decision reverses decades of global policy defining "safe sex" principally by condom use. "Of course," says Josh Pavan, "safe sex is relational and viral load presents as individual." For the first few decades of AIDS, health and illness were marked by "T-cells," a type of white blood cell that is central to immunity. As people neared death, their T-cells plummeted, and as sick people responded to new medications, the T-cells replicated.

However, now that compound treatments are in general use, the new marker of sickness and health is "viral load," literally how much HIV virus is in the person's body. The current standard treatments repress viral load, and the goal for people with HIV is to test "undetectable," that is to say that the viral load is so successfully suppressed by medication that it can't be detected. The "undetectable" person has to maintain their medication to keep the virus suppressed, but the less virus, the less infectious. Low viral load is so effective in preventing HIV transmission that the US Center for Disease Control announced in January 2014 that since sex with low viral load without a condom is no longer necessarily "unsafe," it will now officially be called "condomless sex." So the new shape of AIDS is the binary between suppressed and unsuppressed, not positive and negative. So a positive person on medication who is virally surpressed is actually a safer sexual partner for someone wanting to remain negative than a person who does not know their status, and therefore could be positive and virally infectious.

In the United States, because of our lack of health care, only 35 percent of Americans who are HIV-positive are undetectable. So the US government could not criminalize viral load in the same manner because it does not provide most HIV-positive Americans with a way of becoming undetectable. In Canada, however, health care is nationalized, so the government can theoretically make policy based on a requirement that all HIV-positive people reach an undetectable viral load. Yet Pavan, a bright and serious young man with a mop of Black curls, knows from his wide range of activist work that envious Americans should not overestimate the reach of Canadian health care.

> Nationalized healthcare or the myth thereof allows the failure to reach an undetectable viral load to be recast as personal irresponsibility rather than a social problem or policy gap and sets the stage for prosecution. And I don't think it's just a national quirk, it's pretty central to HIV criminalization around the world, the other countries that lead in per capita prosecution are Sweden, Norway, Denmark, New Zealand.

So the reality of access to health care for HIV-positive people in Canada is more elusive than deprived Americans would imagine. In British Columbia, for example, percentages equal those in the US; only half of positive people are on treatment, and only a third of those are undetectable. Canadian anti-immigrant sentiment also contributes to obstacles to treatment. During the reign of Conservative Prime Minister Stephen Harper, 72,000 asylum seekers were placed in detention. And, until 2014, illegal immigrants were denied Canadian health care, so they too would not be eligible to reach this protected status.

Being "Abused" Instead of Responsible as State Policy

The Aziga case focused on the punishment of men who actually infect their partners, only one aspect of HIV criminalization. Implicit in the court rulings is the idea that negative people are not legally responsible to protect themselves from HIV, and that, in fact, the responsibility lies only with the positive partner. This is consistent with other manifestations of the conflation of anxiety/conflict with abuse. Instead of seeing a negative person who has unprotected sex as a participant in the problem, the law recasts them as victims. This interpretation runs counter to the global message of the last three decades of AIDS prevention work emphasizing the role of HIV-negatives in protecting themselves. The status quo for years has been that negative men and women stay negative by insisting on "safe sex," a concept built around the use of condoms, and more recently PrEP (Pre-exposure prophylaxis). In this way, communication between sexual partners has been the mainstay strategy of HIV prevention. With criminalization, the responsibility of negatives is ignored, with all emphasis on either disclosing or calling the police. Instead of encouraging more open communication between lovers, the government is imposing itself as a substitute for learning how to problem-solve. As a result, charges in these cases are denunciation-based, a disturbing role for the government to play inside individuals' sexual relationships.

"In order to make a police complaint," write Canadian legal scholars Glenn Betteridge and Eric Mykhalovskiy, "people must understand themselves to have experienced a potential *criminal* wrong." Their observation is key to the Conflict versus Abuse debate. Negative people were self-conceptualized, especially in a queer context, as individuals who had the responsibility to keep themselves negative. But at the same time, given the recognition of each other's experiences in an interactive community, we do have a mature, nuanced, and sophisticated understanding that people get infected because they are human. And we should not isolate, denounce, and punish people for being human. But now, as Betteridge and Mykhalovskiy underline, this state of being HIV-negative has been recast by the Canadian courts as one of potential victimhood. Once the responsibility to protect one's self is removed, the negative can re-conceptualize their experience as that of being "criminally wronged," even if they were never at risk for being infected, simply because their condom-using positive sex partner did not disclose. Even though lack of disclosure is an action with no material consequence on the negative's HIV status, it still, unjustly, qualifies as Abuse. And the solution of this formally normal, now newly criminalized definition of Abuse? To denounce the sexual partner to the police, even though infection did not take place. While the absence of infection is notable in these cases, Pavan warns against emphasizing them.

> There's a pretty heated debate among activists as to how much to emphasize the no-risk cases. If you build a campaign around the no-risk cases, then you get a result where they get decriminalized but nothing else, because you haven't actually contested the root issue of criminalization, just argued for a more perfect application of the law. Especially in light of Ruthie Gilmore's recent piece on the state of the anti-prison movement and the call to refuse the focus on the relatively innocent.

"The discursive structuring of their experience has a number of likely sources," Betteridge and Mykhalovskiy continue. "Extensive media coverage has created high profile criminal cases in which reporting focuses on the 'moral failings' of criminal defendants." In this way, the deliberate but unjustified branding of non-disclosure as anti-social, even with condoms, is central to the consciousness of people who call the police when they feel anxious. Edwin J Bernard, the Coordinator of the HIV Justice

Network, a London-based criminalization watchdog, confirms that "Canada is definitely a world leader in terms of the police and the media collaborating to ensure that every arrest is covered in the media as a public health warning, especially because it also does double duty as a fishing expedition for further potential complainants to come forward." It is a nation mired in overstating harm in a manner in which people are isolated and punished for no reason, and the power of the state is enhanced.

What are the alternatives? Well, if we treat sexual partners as "the conflicted" rather than the monster HIV-positive and the criminally wronged HIV-negative, we can produce a kind of solution that my friend Matt Brim enacted in his life. Matt was infected in his thirties, in the contemporary era, because he had anal sex without a condom. He tested positive and began treatment at a clinic at New York University Hospital. He told the man who had infected him that he should get tested. The man said he hadn't known he was positive, but Matt didn't care if that was true or not. Matt knew it was his own decision to have unsafe sex, and that he was a participant in this Conflict. Instead of shunning, denouncing, or punishing his sexual partner, instead of organizing group shunning, calling the police, or bullying the man, Matt simply helped him make an appointment at the same HIV medical service. Then Matt went with him to the examination. Why can't that be state policy?

Criminalizing Human Experience

In the Canadian case, the ideology of Abuse/punishment over Conflict/mutual responsibility is prevailing. But, as always, despite the victimology of insisting on "Abuse" as an objective neutral value, we actually have choices about how to understand this. There are currently 34 million people in the world who are HIV-positive, every one of whom was directly or indirectly infected by someone. If the world followed Canada, each HIV-positive person with an infectious viral load who had sex without revealing their status would be put into prison. That could be tens of millions of people. Believing that arresting and incarcerating people is going to change the behavior of every infectious

HIV-positive person who ever has sex is a grand aim in intent, but supremely questionable in terms of effectiveness. Very few people behave perfectly around that special combination of sexuality and feelings, and even fewer can withstand being blamed and scapegoated. But when the state focuses negative attention on the individual instead of on the source of their demonization, a painful outcome is guaranteed. The numbers alone show us that unsafe sex is a common human experience; so common, in fact, that we could start to understand unsafe sex as part of the normal conflicts and contradictions that signify being flawed and mortal, i.e., a person. Much as we understand that unwanted pregnancy is an undeniably human part of life, so is HIV infection, but we don't incarcerate men whose female partners become pregnant when they don't want to be, even though they didn't use condoms. Yet despite its "progressive" reputation for affordable higher education, significant arts funding, health care, and widespread recycling programs, Canada has decided to respond to this common human experience with punishment.

Ian Salt Bradley-Perrin, another one of the smart young AIDS activists rooted in Montreal, disagrees with my take here. He says that the point of this law is not to change people's behavior, but only to punish them. Judges don't conceptualize themselves as being part of a larger public health endeavor. That is why all of the testimonies of public health experts have gone unheeded in these criminal cases. Because, Bradley-Perrin believes, that was never the point of these laws in the first place. I am open to his interpretation because I am no longer surprised by how many people are motivated to punish others in order to feel better about themselves, rather than addressing, understanding, and resolving conflicts.

Of course, thinking this impulse through to its logical conclusion, prison is the worst place for a person who is HIV-positive; appropriate treatments are not accessible, stress is high, and condoms and clean needles are not as available as needed. Incarceration creates more death and more infection. So while what criminalization succeeds at is stigmatizing and punishing people, the outcome of criminalization is counter to its stated intent, unless prisoners are not included in the category of "people" that the state says it wishes to protect. More interesting is the examination of the question systematically. While Aziga, an extreme example, was responsible for the infection of seven people, HIV criminalization in Canada targets individuals while ignoring governmental, media, and religious institutions whose policies facilitate infections through maintaining stigma, sexual repression, and obstacles to safe sex and medication. According to some service providers, the criminalization itself creates more infections.

"Laws criminalizing HIV non-disclosure make people at risk fear getting tested," says Morgan Page, former Trans Community Services Coordinator at the 519 Church Street Community Centre in Toronto. "They know that if they test positive, they can face not only stigma and sexual exclusion, but also criminal charges whether or not they use condoms or actually do disclose."

Once people are given the right to punish or to threaten punishment by the state, they are no longer required to interrogate themselves and can fall back on convenient dehumanized views of the people they want to hurt. This is what Supremacy Ideology does: it provides the empowered with delusions of superiority, as the ideology itself masquerades as reality. This is why some people feel righteous in calling the police instead of facing their own anxieties, and why others reinforce them in this terrible decision, or even worse: they stand by and do nothing. For example, in the US, the racist assumption for years has been that the reasons for such astronomically high rates of HIV infection among men who have sex with men is because Black men don't have safe sex. A great deal of theorizing and planning has been done rooted in this assumption. There was an assumed lack of information, an assumed lack of self-esteem, clichés about Black masculinity, and an assumed impact of alcoholism and substance abuse, all leading to the presumption of unsafe sex. However, Greg Millett, the White House's senior policy advisor on AIDS, released a report in 2015 revealing that, in fact, Black gay men have safe sex three times as often as white gay men. In other words, Black gay men are three times more accountable, aware, and proactive around safe sex than white gay men. So why the high rates? Because Black men are much more likely to have HIV-positive partners than white men. If they want to have sex with other Black men, their partner pools are more limited and their risk of exposure is overwhelmingly higher. Laws against people who are HIV-positive would affect higher percentages of Black men, even though Black men are more responsible. It took until thirty years into the AIDS pandemic to actually ask Black queer men enough questions about the realities of their lives in order to understand what is really happening to them. Lesson: never, ever decide that you know who someone is, what they did, their objective, context or goal, how they feel or what they know, until you ask them. And not asking means a direct investment in not understanding the truth.

Women as Monsters

Women are a particularly murky part of the punishment puzzle. Most HIV-positive women in Canada already live in deprived and stigmatized communities. Aboriginal women, who represent about four percent of the Canadian female population, accounted for forty-five percent of positive HIV tests among women in 2007. Black women, who represent a little more than two percent of women in Canada, accounted for about twenty percent of all positive tests among women in 2007. Trans women have the highest HIV infection rates of any group, generally estimated at fifty percent. A report published in 2010 suggested that 7.9 percent of the female population in Canadian federal prisons was HIV positive.

"Laws based on viral load hit women particularly hard," Tim McCaskell says. "If I want to know my viral load, I can just go to my doctor. But an Aboriginal woman up north may not have access to getting her blood work done."

HIV-positive women have lower viral loads than men, but have a harder time repressing those viral loads. While the reason for these differences is as yet undetermined, it could be because the drugs were mostly tested on men and may not be as effective with women.

By spring 2014, Canada had accused sixteen women of non-disclosure, and fourteen have been charged, including one who was charged three times. But prosecuting women raises an even thornier question. Do women in North America actually transmit

HIV to anyone? In 2006, Canada became the first country in the world to prosecute a woman for transmitting HIV to her child. Now, with the drug Truvada available to women during pregnancy, this too has become an unlikely outcome. So how many Canadian women have actually infected anyone? Twenty-three percent of HIV positive Canadian men say that they were infected by women. But according to the Canadian HIV Justice Network, the risks for men contracting HIV through vaginal penetration is only 1 in 2,500.

This figure brings us into a conceptual territory that statistics cannot address. Given that there are presumably many more men having sex with women than there are men having sex with men and/or sharing needles, wouldn't the female-to-male transmission rates be much higher? Any thoughtful person can understand that at least a large percentage of these men are falsely reporting in order to cover up gay sex and drug use.

It has been known since 2007 that circumcision reduces male susceptibility to heterosexual AIDS transmission by at least 60 percent (based on male self-reporting), explaining why female-to-male transmission in Sub-Saharan Africa, for example, is more significant than America. Only two of the women convicted of HIV criminalization in Canada were accused of actually infecting someone. In both cases, it was women of color: Suwalee Iamkhong, a Thai immigrant, and June Tippeneskum, an Aboriginal woman, were both convicted of having infected their husbands. One was deported and the other imprisoned for three-and-a-half years. The husbands' histories with needles or sex with men was not determined. No phylogenic testing was done to see if their HIV was the same strain, and there was no investigation into whether or not the men were sharing needles with these convicted women or with others. If women could sexually transmit HIV, wouldn't there be an epidemic for heterosexual men and lesbians as well?

Statistics are coy on the matter of whether female-to-male transmission is real, for no sources in Canada cite heterosexual men as a significant risk group, even while reporting the numbers of men who say they were infected by women. The silence of service organizations speaks volumes. For despite pro forma warnings that women *can* infect men, few in the Canadian AIDS "business" feel compelled by on-the-ground reality to address it.

And when was the last time that heterosexual men's real needs were ignored? Never? In the meantime, as we culturally sort out this question, female sex workers are consistently targeted by HIV criminalization as "vectors of infection" to men who then "bring it home" to their wives, when actually female sex workers are overwhelmingly the more likely party to get infected. According to the Canadian HIV/AIDS Legal Network, "There is no epidemiological evidence in Canada to show that transmission of HIV from sex workers to their clients regularly takes place." From the most intimate realm of romance and desire to that of public policy: the state victimizes to avoid facing its own internal instabilities and contradictions. Instead of public health menaces, HIV-positive women are just people in need of services and care.

It is safe to say that most, if not all, of the Canadian men claiming to have been infected by women are not telling the truth. So, you have almost one-fourth of HIV-positive men in Canada telling a false story about themselves in order to be eligible for compassion, a compassion that is only available if they were infected by women, an illogical conclusion that cannot possibly exist. This extraordinarily stark situation gives us all a chance to learn from the HIV example. How would we understand our responsibilities to our friends, family members, and co-nationals if we could extrapolate that perhaps at least a quarter of the people we know are misrepresenting themselves as Abused in order to gain our compassion? Would we ask ourselves why we so readily endorse victimology without gathering more information? Or would we question the very construction of compassion, how we practice it, and who we offer it to? And what we expect back in return?

Crimes that Can't Occur

A second falsely implicated group is comprised of those whose specific sex acts do not transmit virus; for example, bottoms, people who are exclusively anally receptive during a specific encounter. While men or women who are anally receptive run a 1-in-122 risk of infection, men who are penetrators in anal sex run only a 1-in-1,666 risk of transmission. And these statistics have to take into account men and women who falsely report in order to obscure the stigma of being anally receptive, so the differential in risk may be even more dramatic. Yet, as is the case with women, men who are anally receptive and HIV-positive and who do not disclose their status can also be charged with aggravated sexual assault or attempted murder, incarcerated, and sentenced to spending the rest of their lives labeled as sexual offenders, even though their partners were at low risk. As well, infected people who perform oral sex are not putting partners at risk, and many feel that receiving oral sex is similarly not a risky transaction for the generous partner.

So if HIV criminalization dissuades people from getting tested, further stigmatizes the HIV-positive, and makes them afraid to disclose; incarcerates people who are made more ill by being in prison; blames individuals instead of institutions; overly targets immigrants and Aboriginal people; and jeopardizes women and others who are biologically unable to infect anyone, then what purpose does it serve? Clearly laws like these are ideological, but in service to which values? As Theodore Kerr notes, instead of focusing on protecting and helping the HIV-positive who are actually endangered, HIV criminalization is designed to promote the Supremacy ideology of being HIV-Negative. As he told me in a personal correspondence:

> The privileged are often good at articulating injury but not always able to identify if they are actually experiencing it. There is a difference in being able to recognize the conditions under which injury has or is happening, and actually living, or having lived through it.

Claiming Abuse as an Excuse for Government Control

Dr. Marilou Gagnon, Associate Professor of Nursing at the University of Ottawa, sits on a number of governmental committees related to Canadian HIV. "There is a paradigm shift," she says, "from *Treatment as Treatment* to *Treatment as Prevention*, using the same pills, but with different goals." Gagnon says that the state now believes that "social approaches" like condom use have failed, "which positions biomedical approaches as the new solution." Dr. Gagnon, who did her post-doctoral work with ACT UP Paris, warns that "side effects, complications, and resistance are individual, but now treatment means elimination of transmission so testing is now an entry point into the system of surveillance." Those who can't or don't comply become anti-social. The individual disappears.

"It's a broad generalization," Tim McCaskell says. "But Canada's history of public health care and a social safety net strengthens the logic of social intervention to 'protect' a supposedly vulnerable public." This wouldn't be the first time that a bullying entity inflicted unjustified harm in the name of "protecting" someone, rather than helping them solve their internal and social conflicts.

According to Gagnon, "The groups that we are interested in are the unsuppressed, the non-compliant, resistant, and risky. In Canada, we are championing the idea that the unsuppressed are in need of intervention." She adds, "The continued employment of counselors and service providers depends on them agreeing to these changes."

Mikiki, an "HIV/AIDS Harm Reduction Outreach Educator," has to walk this line between helping clients and serving the government agenda of gathering data for enforcement every day. They speak to clients about criminalization *before* testing at the Central Toronto Community Health Centre. "I've had conversations with folks about what kinds of information we need to collect and how we do contact tracing and I try to keep my language of the process as transparent as possible so that people know what they're getting into and can navigate with a little more autonomy."

In 2011, Canadian courts upheld that there is "no freestanding right to dignity or privacy" which makes revealing HIV status legal. Mikiki informs clients that "anonymous hook-ups" can't be traced, both to inform clients as well as to suggest legal strategies so that they are prepared when asked for the names of people they've had sex with, should they test positive.

In the spring of 2015, a Canadian document surfaced on Tumblr called "How to Have Sex in a Police State," issued by "an anonymous collective of people living with HIV ... We have no leaders, no spokespeople and no meetings." The collective wrote:

We face a new type of emergency here in Canada. State neglect in the response supporting people with HIV is now coupled with intensified forms of state control, surveillance and criminalization. Canada is among the most punitive countries in the world for HIV-positive people, where the state is turning towards criminalization instead of public education and support.

Anyone who doesn't disclose their HIV positive status when having sex with a condom OR low viral load can be arrested and prosecuted. Since this decision at the Supreme Court prosecutions are on the rise. The risk of being labeled a criminal is now biologically marked—we are infected with criminal potential.

Charges can range from assault to attempted murder and do not require HIV transmission to occur. A majority of people in these cases are charged with aggravated sexual assault, one of the most serious offences in the Criminal Code reserved for violent sexual assaults. Those prosecuted can face long sentences, are registered as sex offenders and held in segregation units. One accusation from an angry or upset former lover can result in lengthy court battles, incarceration and sensationalized media exposure. Even if the person decides to drop the charges, the state can pursue criminal prosecution in the "public interest." Within this context of intensified criminalization we see the reversals of hard-fought protections for our privacy and rights.

The names and HIV-status of people who test positive can end up on government databases for life. Also, through increased public health oversight, community-based organizations have now become an arm of state surveillance, discipline and control. Many of them now fully endorse and implement new coercive testing approaches in the community.

Today, in order to prevent intervention from the criminal justice system and public health officials it could technically be in your best interest not to know your HIV status.

Avoid all HIV or STI tests at clinics where your real name is recorded.

MAKE THIS AN ISSUE IN YOUR COMMUNITY
We are in a dangerous moment under the watch of a hostile regime and we urgently need to take back control of our lives, our health and our freedom. When possible, talk about HIV and talk about the potential impacts of HIV criminalization with friends, sex partners, colleagues, family and with communities that you are part of. Make it known that you are a person that other people can talk to about these issues. Work in your communities to build consensus at a grass-roots level to end the criminalization of HIV.

"Paradigm shifts usually come with intellectual battles," Dr. Gagnon says. "But these have happened very quickly."

Claims of Abuse as Assertions of Normativity

It may seem strange to see such enthusiastic persecution of HIV-positive Canadians in the contemporary moment. After all, today HIV disease is not the worst thing that can happen to someone in North America who has health insurance. Many HIV-positive people can live full lifespans. One could argue that certain kinds of cancer resulting from industrial waste or degenerative diseases without known treatments are far more dangerous to civilians than HIV. Aren't we supposed to be living in an enlightened age of tolerance with anti-discrimination laws protecting the HIV-positive firmly in place? It's not like the early days when AIDS hysteria and lack of treatment fueled campaigns to quarantine or even tattoo people with the virus. So asking "why now?" is a natural and valid question. Of course, it cannot be denied that HIV will always carry a particular stigma of fear and contempt because it was initially associated with homosexuality, especially anal sex. No matter how many heterosexuals are infected, HIV has been "queered," which facilitates easy scapegoating.

In addition to a national health system that allows the conceptualization of coordinated health and legal strategies, Canada has something else that the US has yet to fully realize: homonationalism. First identified by Rutgers University Professor Jasbir Puar, "homonationalism" describes the phenomena of dominant-culture gay people who achieve full legal equity, identifying with the state and being welcomed into social categories of Supremacy that they, or their predecessors, had been previously excluded from because of homophobia. It is the switch for some members of the LGBT community from disenfranchisement to dominant cultural advantages, which are always accorded to some at the expense of others. The classic example of homonationalism is the Netherlands where white gay people have the exact same legal standing as white straight people, and so are increasingly present in emerging racist anti-immigrant arguments and movements that are heavily prejudiced against Muslims. The early Gay Liberation movement, which argued for social revolution in gender, sexuality, and relationships, was overwhelmed by the AIDS crisis and re-emerged as the Gay Rights movement, focusing on relationship recognition. While the pro-family ideology surrounding the modern gay rights agenda is opposed by right-wing religious fundamentalists around the world, gay marriage, privatized nuclear families, and the consequential consumerism is compatible with nationalism and the racial, religious, gender, and sexual ideologies that accompany it. Josh Pavan has a different take on the "why now?" question:

> What if homonationalism is actually slowing the number of criminalization cases because cute gay boys on a date at the drive-in who got a little frisky but were too shy to disclose are seen as empathetic citizens worthy of state protection?

At the same time he does acknowledge that homonationalism in Canada

> split and demobilized the organizations and soft activists and independent funding sources that had been the frontlines of defending the rights of people living with HIV.

Clearly, from my American perspective, with widespread gay adoption and anti-discrimination laws, homonationalism is far more advanced in Canada than it is in the US. It divides the former queer community. Today some enjoy special social approval and recognition for being in traditional family structures that straight people can understand and identify with. Not only does this make them more comfortable, but it can also make them feel superior. After all, homonationalist queers have the power to use the state to hurt other gay, bi, and trans people who are not enfranchised. Canadian homonationalism goes beyond mere access, as the legitimization transforms the LGBT self-concept as well. Unlike American leftists, left-wing Canadians are quite patriotic by US standards. From rooting for Canadian teams to a sense of civic pride in relationship to the US, there is a nationalist concept of Supremacy that American leftists work hard to deprogram. When I was US coordinator of the campaign to free imprisoned Canadians John Greyson and Tarek Loubani from incarceration in Egypt, I was surprised to see "Free Tarek and John" buttons embedded on a maple leaf. No American movement that I work with would use the US stars and stripes without irony. Of course, there are profound differences between French-speaking Quebec and other provinces, and Quebec "nationalism" is even more accute nationalism. But still, it's a bit contradictory: on one hand they reject a depiction of themselves as enjoying privileges, yet they also are nationalistically reactive when it comes to criticism. The publication of a shorter version of this chapter on Slate provoked over 280 comments, most of which were by Canadians either blaming HIV-positive people or criticizing me, as an American, for discussing the implications of their social policies. Canadians often complain, rightfully, about US cultural domination, but are very thin-skinned about the kind of self-criticism that US leftists learn to integrate. And while they want to be seen by Americans, they don't want to be criticized, so outside acknowledgment of flaws in cultural tropes provokes lashing out and defensiveness.

Now that Canada has surpassed the US by hosting the richest middle class in the world, the combination of privilege, the accompanying entitlement, and gay rights can be truly obnoxious. The impact of this nationalist, pro-family ideology on the queer community of friends in Canada is worth examining by Americans, because this is where we are neoliberally headed. Gay rights produces new insiders, and it also produces new outsiders. On one hand the newly enfranchised include LGBT citizens, family members, and the HIV-negatives who are now separated through their access to state protection from non-citizens, those not in families, and the HIV-positive. This new Other—what T.L. Cowan calls "the abject object" queer who can't access the state—becomes newly differentiated from the recently acceptable in a number of ways. Implied in the public's support for same-sex marriage is a fantasy that gay marriage is a mirror of straight marriage. And even though we don't really know what the reality of straight marriage is, there is an ideal that involves an aspiration towards monogamy or some kind of sexual constraint. It's fair to say that many straight people support gay marriage because they see it as normalizing, and do so with an undercurrent of expectation that gay marriage will tame gay male sexual culture and produce approximate monogamy among gay men. In this way, gay marriage is unconsciously understood as an antidote to AIDS, thereby separating "gay" and "AIDS" in the public imagination.

Once gay marriage is available, people who refuse it are, in a sense, refusing the offer of normalcy, which means refusing clean, approved, and controlled sexuality. They are offered "good" homosexuality, but may choose "bad" homosexuality, making them even more deviant, different, and socially dangerous than they were before. Even though most people in Canada who have been victimized by HIV criminalization are straight, there are more and more gay cases. And for all concerned, AIDS will always be queer. The stigma of the "gay disease" has historical reach that demographics cannot undo. Also, as legal scholars Betteridge and Isabel Grant's article points out: "There may be a different ethic in the gay community around laying complaints for non-disclosure, there may be a higher level of acceptance for mutual responsibility for preventing HIV transmission." But as LGBT people identify more and more with the state apparatus of punishment as a substitute for self investigation, this knowledge of the nuance of human experience may dissipate, since privilege has always been a dulling factor in one's comprehension of human difference. The Canadian government's rejection of condom use, communication between partners, solving problems through negotiation and in community, and the responsibility of HIV-negatives may make these grassroots ethics a thing of the past.

In Conflict: Real Friends Don't Let Friends Call the Police

This leaves AIDS Action Now! and Tim McCaskell with no choice but the moral obligation imposed by the uncomfortable task of carefully, patiently, thoughtfully, sitting down and trying to help others, one by one, to "Think Twice" rather than call the police. Just as a group of bad friends reinforces unilateral supremacist thinking by encouraging group punishment and shunning of the conflicted other, good friends insist that people *think twice*, to look to their own participation in conflict instead of calling the police. Good groups help their family, friends, and community members recognize and dissipate anxiety rather than joining them in acting out cruelly against others. Asking people to be ethical is the only strategy left for HIV-positive Canadians. After all, once people are given the right of dominance, that is the right to punish or to threaten punishment by the state, they are no longer required to examine themselves.

It has never been shown that punishment works. Punishment, denouncing, excluding, threatening, and shunning often create a worse society. It divides people, causes great pain, compromises individual integrity, and obscures truths in the name of falsely shoring up group reputation. Similarly, there is no correlation between having the ability to punish and being right. More often than not, the wrong people get punished. And the punishers use their power to keep from being accountable. So creating new classes of people who can threaten someone with the state, or who can call the police, does not produce more justice, and is more likely to produce more injustice. Creating HIV-negative people as a new class who can punish others by calling the police may reduce their ability to negotiate, nuance, problem-solve, communicate, and take responsibility for their own actions.

HIV criminalization assumes that society itself is negative, and that the threat to society is positive. HIV criminalization is making it easier for the negative person to avoid communication and instead call on the state to punish the positive person. It encourages the HIV negative person to see themselves as victimized instead of as an equally conflicted party in a human relationship, with mutual responsibilities, feelings, and accountability. It is a governmental privileging of anxiety and punishment over communication, thereby dividing people between those who claim to be good and clean and normal and therefore deserving of state protection, and those whom the first group wish to separate from and hurt whether it is justified or not; whether it makes things better or not.

On a freezing day in Canada's long winter, one of America's most revered academics, Professor Judith Butler, is lecturing at the University of Toronto. As in all her appearances, the place is packed floor to rafters and many are turned away. Her subject is "Public Assembly and Public Sovereignty." Butler cites Hannah Arendt on "The right to appear." She goes on to acknowledge that, "politics requires a space of appearance." Her discussion couldn't be more relevant. She's talking about the Turkish rebellion in Gezi Park, but when she says the words "suspended citizenship," I think of the shunning that is happening in Canada. How people are being removed from society, from the conversation, unjustly threatened with the police, with disappearance. She raises the question of "Controlling who can pass into the public" and some of the other four hundred people present ask ourselves, Why does one group of people need to turn against another in order to feel good about themselves? And how it is our moral obligation as human beings who share this time and this place to not punish, but rather to remain calm, to open up communication, and to place our hands gently on each other's shoulders and say, "Think twice."

PART TWO | The Impulse to Escalate

Chapter Five | **On Escalation**

Everyone is the other, and no one is himself.
—MARTIN HEIDEGGER, *Being and Time*

THE FORCE THAT TAKES Conflict and misrepresents it as Abuse is called Escalation. Escalation is a kind of smokescreen to cover up the agent's own influence on events, their own contributions to the Conflict. By escalating in the face of nothing, normative conflict, or resistance and acting as if it is Abuse, we avoid having to confront ourselves, or our family, our clique, our HIV status, our country, our own individual and group shortcomings, our anxieties from an unresolved past. Instead, we use accusation to create an artificial furor to override or distract from our own responsibility. As I showed in Part One, escalating Conflict to the status of Abuse obscures our desires, our own contributions to problems in relationships, our own anxieties about sex, love, and HIV, our own projections from our pasts onto the non-deserving present, and it disavows our agency in a manner that enhances the power of the state. Escalation under these circumstances is a resistance to self-knowledge.

Certainly I am not a practitioner of doing nothing. There is little more destructive than the passive bystander allowing cruelty to be freely imposed. I'm the opposite of a Buddhist, as I believe in action. But there are all kinds of actions: some are designed to acknowledge and reveal the sources of conflict and pain in order to resolve them, and some are designed to obscure those sources so that resolution/change can never occur. Which one we choose, of course, is related to how we see ourselves and others, and what we don't see about ourselves and others. There is no evidence that time heals all wounds, or even most wounds; instead, it freezes unnecessary enmity and makes it harder to overcome. Time allows perpetrators to forget the pain they have imposed. As Bertolt Brecht said, "As crimes pile up, they become invisible." And so I don't believe in an ideology of non-response. Therefore, this is no argument for silence. Silence can itself be an escalation. Little children give their parents "the silent treatment" because they don't know how to negotiate: how to listen, to respond in a way that is transformed by having listened, to change in order to meet the other. Ideally the parent does know how to negotiate, and so they help the child learn how to express and how to listen. But we all know now that many parents are the source of the problem. They either impose the pain from their own lack of resolution, or they employ the tactics of shut-down, refusal, and punishment instead of trying the radical openness that produces positive change.

In thinking and working on this escalation process, I have come to understand that the same action of unjustified escalation most often comes from one of two positions: Supremacy, or Trauma. And in realizing this, I am surprised by the similar behaviors expressed by these two divergent experiences.

Supremacy Ideology as a Refusal of Knowledge

Of course, there are many things about each of us that we wish were not true, and because their revelation may subject us to criticism, we want to hide them. But in the case of Supremacy, the social structures of power in which we live often do that work for us. For example, we all know about "Driving While Black," where

Black people get pulled over because they are Black. But we don't have a concept called "Driving While White" where white people don't get pulled over because of our skin color. Yet not being pulled over is as significant an experience as being pulled over. But it is obscured. In not being pulled over, our Supremacy keeps us from the information that we are protected from being unjustly pulled over. This Supremacy keeps us from knowledge about ourselves and how we are living. We may think, absurdly, that we are simply good drivers, or more likely, not think anything at all. We have no idea that we are inhabiting the benefits of white Supremacy when we don't get pulled over. We pretend that this injustice is neutral, and in fact is not happening.

When the Black person is pulled over for no reason, they understand what is occurring. They know that their lives could be in danger from police violence. Sometimes the cumulative pressure of repeated experiences of being pulled over for no reason can make a Black person explode, like Sandra Bland ("Say Her Name"), who was found hanged in a jail cell after being falsely arrested by a Texas state trooper. A dashcam video recording of her arrest shows that she got angry at being violated, despite the knowledge that she ran a high risk of being punished for resistance to injustice; that the rebellion itself would be constituted as the crime. In this way, the explosion is the cumulative expression of being treated unjustly with repetition. But when the white person is pulled over for no reason, they may have no understanding at all as to what is happening, because it is not systemic, simply an annoyance. Supremacy tells us that not being pulled over means that nothing is happening when, in fact, enormous events are taking place, and we come to experience this kind of protection from information as a "right." We become distorted in our expectations that the objective, neutral, and normal condition is to not be confronted with our Supremacy, i.e., the consequences of our actions and experiences on others. And when we are informed against our will, we experience this shift in privilege falsely, as a violation, something to be repelled and punished.

In the spring of 2015, WikiLeaks posted thousands of emails from the Sony entertainment corporation that had been hacked by North Korea. Among the revelations: Sony executives were involved with right-wing Israeli movements (no surprise), and

Ben Affleck, the working-class hero from Boston, had slave-owning ancestors. Actually, it wasn't that fact that made the news, but rather that he and Sony and Harvard Professor Henry Louis Gates had colluded to hide this fact by excluding the information from Gates' PBS geneology-focused television series, *Finding Your Roots*. It seemed possible that Affleck was understandably ashamed of his ancestors. Some white people fought against slavery, others owned slaves. There was a choice. In a later statement, he described himself as "embarrassed" to have it be known that he had slave-owning family members.

We all have an ideal imagined self and a real self, and there is always a gap between the two. I've never met a person who was exempt from this. The process of moving forward in life requires, I guess, constant adjustment on both sides. We each come closer to a more mature understanding of who we really are, some kind of acceptance, while at the same time working to change the things we can in order to get closer to our desired self. In this way, that gap narrows from both sides: acceptance, and change. But it never goes away. When we can't move forward and the gap widens, many of us become paralyzed. The breach between the real self and the imagined self is unbearable, and the reality of our lives becomes unacceptable, undoable, and we become stuck: we can't move out of our parents' house, we can't take a job that compromises our entitlement, we can't actually fulfill our dreams and, finally, we can't adjust those dreams.

Of course, there is a specificity to hiding one's slave-owning ancestors: African-Americans are assumed to have slavery pasts and so become (correctly or incorrectly) its reminder to the world. But white people are assumed not to have slavery pasts, and so those of us who do, pass incognito. As a result, slavery becomes something that was done to Black people by no one. When I teach Frederick Douglass to my class, I always point out that one of his owners was named Gore, as in Al Gore and Gore Vidal, because we all have to remember where that money came from. So hiding the reality creates the broad harm of obscuring power. On the other hand, it is hard to know who our distant ancestors actually are to us. At the same time that some of us are ashamed of them, others use their suffering, or their accomplishments, to enhance their own meaning, and that can also be absurd. Now, of course, the actions of our ancestors can be irrelevant or significant to our contemporary lives. To hold up their misdeeds, misfortune, or heroics as any reflection on our own meaning may be entirely without merit. Or it could be of overriding significance. Was the murder of my mother's aunts and uncles during the Holocaust significant in my value, the meaning of my life, the justification for my actions? Unclear. Did it affect the emotional life of my family? Of course. But how, exactly? That can only be speculation. Did it influence the delay in my coming to express support for Palestine? Of course! But how, exactly? Affleck was embarrassed, but it may have been without cause. Or then again, he may be an absolute product of his ancestors' decisions. This, we cannot know. Our ancestors are not us, and even our own past actions may not represent who we really are in the present moment.

Now, I don't know Ben Affleck and I have no idea how that real human being makes decisions or experiences events. But, according to the leaked documents, Gates tried at first to resist Sony's request by protesting that, "Once we open the door to censorship, we lose control of the brand." But despite his desire to be branded with integrity, he did capitulate to the corporation eventually, and that "bad" information about Affleck was deleted from the broadcast. His ideal self overrode his real self. Now, these men may have been personally traumatized in all kinds of ways that are invisible to the general public. Gates, we know, was arrested by a white police officer, and accused of breaking into his own house because a passing civilian couldn't imagine a Black person living in an expensive home in Cambridge, Massachusetts. And that, I am sure, is just an emblematic iceberg tip. Affleck, for his own reasons, felt that the truth would hurt his public image, his self-image, his ability to make money, his ability to be loved, or some other kind of related currency. So he revved up the apparatus (in this case of the corporate state, not the governmental state) in order to not have to deal with the consequences of reality. This event illustrates one element of Supremacy that is crucial to the question of escalation: the feeling that a person or a group is entitled to obscure information about harm they may be associated with. That the telling of the truth is more significant than the horrible truth itself. And so they feel that the repression of information, regardless of its long-term consequence, is necessary and justified.

But let's turn away from movie stars. In our own realms—families, cliques, communities, workplaces—we have all experienced the patriarch, the male supremacist, the nationalist, the racist, or just the local provincial big man who will not tolerate any opposition. He can never be wrong. He can never apologize. He explodes in rage whenever there is another experience being presented. He belittles others but can't stand any criticism of himself. He may use sarcasm or cruelty to tear others apart, but his understanding of emotional life is shallow. He won't allow people to talk to him about what is going on. He doesn't seek resolution, which means to him that he would have to acknowledge having made a mistake, which is an impossibility. He is petty, the kind of person who sends an attacking email and then, when the recipient phones to discuss the conflict, won't take the call. He denies complexity, and the people around him do not challenge him directly. His partner, his friends, the people who feel protected by, elevated by, or who benefit from his power, organize other people to not oppose him. They deflect criticism from him. They are careful around him, and are rewarded. He doesn't ask other people, "What are you feeling?"; never says, "I don't understand what is going on. How do you see it?" He acts as though others should follow his orders, and when they refuse he punishes, bullies, shuns, makes false accusations, organizes group exclusion, distorts narratives, and may threaten and use the law or even violence. He expects that once he asserts his position, everyone else will obey, fall in line, and that this is how the moment is resolved: through obedience.

Traumatized Behavior: When Knowledge Becomes Unbearable

Obviously I am not a clinician, but I have lived, loved, listened, felt, expressed, and observed. I have looked within and without. So without authority beyond my own experiences and how I understand them, I have observed that people living in unrecovered trauma often behave in very similar ways to the people who traumatized them. Over and over I have seen traumatized people refuse to hear or engage information that would alter their self-concepts, even in ways that could bring them more happiness and integrity. For the Supremacist, this refusal comes from a sense of entitlement; that they have an inherent "right" not to question themselves. Conversely, the unrecovered traumatized person's refusal is rooted in a panic that their fragile self cannot bear interrogation; that whatever is keeping them together is not flexible. Perhaps because Supremacy in some produces Trauma in others, they can become mirror images. And of course, many perpetrators were/are victims themselves.

There is an extensive literature of Trauma easily available and I am not going to summarize it or repeat its discoveries here. But we know that usually a traumatized person has been profoundly violated by someone else's cruelty, overreaction, and/or lack of accountability. The experience could be incident-based (rape by a stranger or being hit by a drunken driver), or it could be ongoing over a long period of time (being constantly demeaned and beaten by a stepfather, paternal sexual invasion, alcoholic or mentally ill parents), or systematic (intense and constant experiences of prejudice, denial of one's humanity, deprivation, violence, occupation, genocide). The traumatized person's sense of their ability to protect themselves has been damaged or destroyed. They feel endangered, even if there is no actual danger in the present, because in the past they have experienced profoundly invasive cruelty and they know it is possible. Or in the case of ongoing systemic oppression, they receive cruelty from one place, and project it onto another.

But one key difference in the projection and anxiety of supremacy behavior vs traumatized behavior is that what feels to the supremacist as a "right" often feels to the traumatized as "shame." The actions may be the same, they may both shun, blame, project, refuse to repair. But the feeling inside is very different. There is a strong element of shame in Trauma that makes thinking and behavior so inflexible. The person cannot accept adjustment, an altering of their self-concept; they won't bear it and they won't live with it. And if their group, clique, family, community, religion, or country also doesn't support self-criticism, they ultimately *can't* live with it.

In my own life, I have found that the most dangerous response to shame is recognition. Those of us who have lived lives of shared public space like a city, or who study history, know that people suffer. We know that people's lives are complex, filled with contradiction and obstacles. So when someone tells us that their mother allowed their stepfather to beat them, or their son cannot take care of himself, or their father was sexually invasive, or their parents are alcoholics, or they were projected onto by a trusted lover so that they no longer allow themselves relationships, or that they themselves suffer from anxiety and mental illness, it can play out in different ways. The offering of honest information can be a test to see what it is like to tell the truth, to see if real experience will be met with rejection. But I find that if the information is received with consequential recognition, i.e., "Now that we know this, our relationship is elevated," there is a possibility of a backlash, because that means the experience is real; the awful thing is no longer a repressed secret but a recognized reality. And this can provoke an explosion of regression. The recognition itself is now called a harm. The pain of the original violation is projected onto the person who knows about it. "What you are doing to me is worse than anything my father ever did to me," becomes the accusation. Because, unlike the father, we are not pretending it away. Often the words "privacy" or "boundaries" are used to deflect recognitions of Shame. Privacy, or rather invasion of, is when the government collects data on you without your consent. Shame, to me, is hiding information that reveals common human experiences, contradictions, and mistakes. Sometimes this is imposed from the outside through stigma. For example, being HIV positive is a common human experience, but some people hide it because they fear unjustified cruelties imposed by others. But for many, shame-based hiding is often imposed from within. They want to conceal their experience because they don't understand that it is widely shared. There is a narcissism in trauma-based shame: a belief that one is special and different and that others can't possibly feel the same way, understand, or need understanding.

This partially explains why the strategy of political organizations like Jewish Voice for Peace, the largest international grouping of Jews opposed to the Israeli Occupation, has been so inspiring. They take responsibility to acknowledge the injustices towards

Palestinians that we (as Jews) have both committed and allowed to take place. We don't claim "privacy," we don't hide the "dirty laundry." We model the experience of showing publicly what we have done wrong, and we say and act in accordance with a vision of what we could do right. In this way, we are the good friends, saying to our fellow Jews (family members, friends) that they don't have to be afraid of facing how wrong we have been. We are facing our own actions so that the cruelty can end. The oppression cannot end unless we (a critical mass of we's) do this, and the outcome is much more important than the pretense of perfection. The is the good group, the positive community, the healthy family, the truly loving friends.

This question of shame seems important in escalation. Why does one person approach a situation and want reconciliation and peace, while another approaches the same situation and needs to shun, destroy, and thereby feel victorious? The business of psychological studies is a messy one. There are so many and they contradict each other, but like poetry, they can stimulate thought. I read a study by June Price Tangey and Patricia E. Wagner published in 1996, and another by Hadar Behrendt and Rachel Ben Ari written sixteen years later that pointed to a similar answer. Both teams felt that people who come at conflict from guilt approach it very differently than people who come at it from shame. In fact, both studies found that people who come from guilt very much want to negotiate, are able to apologize and admit fault, can make concessions, and are invested in positive resolution. People coming from shame, on the other hand, direct anger, aggression, and blame towards the other party. This difference was explained by the assessment that people who feel guilt experience less emotional stress and anxiety than those who feel shame. And guilty people can therefore focus more on the implications of their own actions on others. They found that those who feel shame also feel more threatened and are deeply concerned about what other people think of them. Behrendt and Ben Ami write in the *Journal of Conflict Resolution*:

> Guilt plays a pro-social function in strengthening relationships; it encourages taking responsibility, motivates amendatory behaviors such as apology or confession, leads to higher quality solutions to crises and is associated with more

constructive anger management ... Guilt is also associated with positive empathy and the ability to acknowledge and understand others' points of view. In contrast shame is associated with responses that are injurious to social relationships.

It is commonly understood and a frequent social trope in popular culture and casual discourse that as an adult, normative conflict can be very frightening for someone who is already traumatized and has not been in a recovery process long enough to be able to identify their own distorted perceptions. If a person's sense of self has been punctured, and they have not been willing or able to repair it, they may become intolerant of difference. They may confuse anxiety and vulnerability. They may exaggerate threat, overreact, seek the protection of bullies and shun others, and thereby become bullies themselves. They may lash out particularly cruelly at people they love and desire, as the feeling of loving can remind them of the abusive parent that they once loved. They may never feel safe unless they have an unreasonable amount of control over others, as in shunning. Shame, too, seems to be a driving force in traumatized behavior. Negotiation feels like a defeat, a reminder of the earlier violation. Giving in, adjusting, and changing feel life-threatening. Difference, as to the Supremacist, becomes a threat.

Supremacists and the traumatized can be through-the-looking-glass, employing similar tactics for opposing reasons. The people they can't control become cast as monsters, dehumanized specters that both the Supremacist and the Traumatized collude to create as manifestations of their own projected anxieties: the anxiety of being faced with difference. This monster can be a person with HIV, a Palestinian, or even just someone we know, have loved, desired, or shared space with, who has a challenging or merely different perspective and therefore becomes unbearable. They become a dehumanized object to be destroyed because of what they reveal about us; that there might be something in us that needs to be adjusted. The unrecovered traumatized person cannot or does not negotiate because creating peace means altering one's position and acknowledging the other person's experience. A destroyed self feels such shifting as endangering, even though it is the only road toward repair and progressive growth.

Interrupting Escalation Before It Produces Tragedy

As both supremacists and the traumatized refuse information and communication that could alter their concepts of themselves, escalation is created. Up to this point I have thought about how overstating harm and overreaction to conflict give more power to the state. The state in turn entices some of us into a place of reward while scapegoating the more vulnerable as a smokescreen to avoid facing the conflicts inherent in the social structure itself. In all cases, this destructive involvement with the state takes place *after* the explosion of overreaction. The police are called *after* actual violence has occurred. Or someone calls the police unnecessarily *after* imagining or claiming that Conflict is instead Abuse. But unfortunately, there is no one to call *before*. Who do we call when it matters, when it's the moment to inhibit escalation, before the explosion becomes inevitable?

Ideally, the people to call *before* are the healthy, fair, and self-critical group—family, friends, community—who have the love and awareness to see what the conflicted cannot see, and who can help the anxious calm down and seek communication and negotiation, and in this way create reconciliation. But because we misunderstand what real loyalty means, we often do the opposite within our groups: exacerbate escalation rather than relieve it.

So that moment before the cataclysm is the most important: the moment of initial, unnecessary escalation. This is when someone's anxiety, fear, immaturity, self-inflation, racism, inexperience with problem-solving, or submission to distorted thinking kicks in, and the escalation towards overreaction begins. This, as Dudley Saunders says, is the time when overreaction is "internally logical," but not an accurate response to the external. It seems obvious that if we can create a social norm that encourages de-escalation, we can save a lot of relationships, communities, and lives. But that means looking deeply at overreaction itself. And that includes the difficult recognition that for some, unjust escalation is a choice, and for others, it is a compulsion.

It's true that my discussion is "undisciplined," as it is not rooted in traditional academic research or controlled studies with live subjects. But it's civilians who will have to find solutions to escalation, and in this spirit I am looking within, thinking, feeling, observing, listening to eclectic sources and other people's stories, to try to think of ways to help myself and others to not escalate Conflict so that it becomes Abuse; to face and deal with it, instead of avoiding it. When I think about moving forward, in mutual recognition, towards resolution, I think about the word *agreement*. Not that we would hold the same views, but rather that we would communicate enough to agree on what each of our different views actually are. That I could tell you what you think and you would recognize my rendition as accurate, and you could do the same for me. And in this way, we would at least agree on what we each understand differently. This could, in turn, facilitate some insight into this difference. And, as radical as it sounds in the era of a norm of hiding behind technology, this requires talking to each other and listening.

One problem here is how to intervene with a person who is overstating harm, hiding behind technology, shunning or otherwise escalating. In some cultures we are trained not to assist directly, saying we are "non-confrontational," that indifference is polite. Instead we can learn to be accountable, to ask, "How can I help you and X to sit down and talk?" Perhaps the person invested in maintaining victimology in order to avoid their own issues will say, "No, I will never talk to X again. In fact, *I am terrified for my life*. You should have nothing to do with her." In other words, now that they are facing community responsibility, they escalate even further, their claims are even more inflated, and the cloak of self-righteousness is drawn even tighter. Unfortunately, at this point, most interveners will back off. *Hey, I tried*, they can tell themselves. In the end, it's not their life being harmed by this escalating person. And if they engage any further, they could become a target too. So they call it quits. Almost nothing could be more painful to the person being projected onto. The only thing worse than not getting help is asking for it and still being denied. Now the stakes are even higher, the falsely accused is even more isolated, and the interveners feel self-satisfied while being entirely ineffective. The next step is to come as a group. "Hey, now there are five of us here together, with you. We want to help you and X sit down and talk. We find what you're doing to be very disturbing. We won't shun you, we won't punish you, but we also won't be co-opted into silence. How can we find an alternative?" This is the structure behind every successful piece of non-violent progressive political action:

1. Scapegoated people cannot be made to stand alone.
2. Community needs to move towards negotiation.
3. More and more people have to join in together to create change.
4. The conversation is not over just because an escalator insists that it is.

Human life, being mortal, is inherently filled with risk, and one of the greatest dangers is other people's escalation. It can hasten the inevitable end before we've had a chance to really begin. It can be a terrible waste of life and potential. Being the object of overreaction means being treated in a way that one does not deserve, which is the centerpiece of injustice. Yet, protesting that overreaction is often the excuse for even more injustice. There is a continuum of pathology in blame, cold-shouldering, shunning, scapegoating, group bullying, incarcerating, occupying, assaulting, and killing. These actions are substitutions for our better selves, and avoid the work of self-acknowledgment required for resolution and positive change. Refusing to resolve conflict is a negative action, yet many families, cliques, communities, religions, governments, and nations choose this option all the time.

We know that people get killed over nothing, and by extension people get scapegoated, shunned, demeaned, excluded, threatened with the police, locked up, and assaulted without justification every day. The mere fact that someone has been the recipient of group cruelty has no relationship to whether or not they have done anything to merit it. Without talking to them in person and fully understanding what has occurred from their point of view, being punished is no measure of anyone's innocence or guilt. But the person being shunned by being excluded, silenced, or incarcerated will not be listened to by others, so the terms of their punishment cannot be contested. In this way, shunning is a trap. Escalation can take many forms:

- Escalation can be a smokescreen, a way to deflect attention from the real problem at hand because the person acting out doesn't know how to approach the conflict and doesn't have support to do the work to make that possible. The only support they have is to blame and assume the role of the "Abused."

- Escalation can be an expression of distorted thinking or mental illness, and can be rooted in earlier experience, some of which may have a biological consequence. These projections from the past onto the present can be expressions of anxiety. They can also be a compulsion, a hyper-vigilant automatic action with no room for thought or consideration of motive, justification, or consequence.
- Escalation is almost always exacerbated when parties are members of shallow communities like dysfunctional families and bad friends. Religious/racial/national Supremacy concepts are at the basis of destructive groups, bound together by negative values.
- Escalation can be a tactic of the state.

In the case of this book's subject, *overreaction to conflict*, the patterns are often familiar. Someone says or does or *is* something that the reacting individual or group doesn't like. Perhaps the offending person objects to a negative situation, they respond to an unjust structure, or by just being themselves they illustrate difference. In other words, they say or do or are something that requires an individual or a community to examine itself, something they don't want to do, or are not supported to do.

Control is at the Center of Supremacy and Traumatized Behavior

Again I turn to Beth Richie's illuminating book *Arrested Justice: Black Women, Violence, and America's Prison Nation.* She offers a definition of "control" in relationships that is very pertinent to this discussion. She describes scenarios in which one partner "creates a hostile social environment in the shared intimate sphere of their lives." She describes this as "power exercised by one person's extreme and persistent tension, dominance of their needs over others, chronic irritability and irrational agitation." They don't say *this is what I need, what do you need?* Negotiation or adjustment are deemed unreasonable. Subjects become unapproachable. Interestingly, this behavior, describing intimate relationships, is also an accurate description of how the US state treats poor women, showing again how intimate constructions become social dynamics. The dominance of white, wealthy, and male "needs" over the needs of poor, immigrant, and non-white women is a pervasive quality of the state. "Irrational agitation" is certainly another, as the renewed focus on police violence reveals.

I would certainly also agree that in expressions of narcissism, an entitled and arrogant person can create that environment in a relationship, community, family, or household. They can bring the ideology of their Supremacy, especially White Supremacy or Male Supremacy, into other people's lives through the integrated conviction that they should not have to be aware of others, negotiate with others, take other people into consideration. This is an ideology that men often bring to their relationships with whomever is serving them, whether it is a mother, a female or male partner or child, or another female adult. The objective is that the woman's independent needs, or the subordinate man's actual experience, should be subservient to keeping the supremacist male on track with his goals, even if those goals are dependency or self-aggrandizement. That this is common in sexual relationships is so well known it doesn't even need to be illustrated. As well, it is common for adult men to expect women in their circle, including the workplace, to drop everything in order to perform favors for them that usually involve compensating for some task they didn't bother to take care of or complete themselves. Certainly I have seen adult males feel confident and secure in living off their mothers, controlling their mother's sexual and emotional lives, and having their mothers cook, shop, clean, and earn money for them. That daughters and sisters absurdly have to serve their male relatives is beyond the everyday.

But Richie's definition helped me to expand my own thinking by recognizing that these control elements of Male Supremacy, White Supremacy, and governmental apparatus also can describe the behavior of women and others who were violated in their youth by fathers or others. Just as supremacists may control what their partners say and do, people traumatized in childhood may consequently live with a fragile self as well as insecure boundaries with their partners that also produce control. Many discourses, both popular and clinical, exist to address how those who have survived violence, sexual abuse, and psychological assault during their childhood may behave, depending on where they are in their developmental process of awareness in order to "feel safe."

Feeling "safe" of course is already a problematic endeavor since there is little guarantee of safety in our world, and the promise of it is a false one, as the effort to enforce this is often at the expense of other people. Both Supremacists and the Traumatized may conceptualize themselves as "weak" or "endangered" unless others around them are controlled, repressed, punished, or destroyed. The concept of "safe space" can also be a projection in the present based on dangers that occurred in the past. It may have once been used for those living in illegality, like gay people, Jews, immigrants, or adults who now have agency but were oppressed as children. But now those of us who have become dominant continue to use this trope to repress otherness. It is used by the dominant to defend against the discomfort of hearing other people's realities, to repress nuance, ignore multiple experiences, and reject the inherent human right to be heard. Instead, it may even be considered victimizing by the supremacist/traumatized person to not simply follow their orders when they "feel" or say that they "feel" endangered, even if that feeling is retrospective.

As Christina B. Hanhardt illustrates in her book *Safe Space: Gay Neighborhood History and the Politics of Violence*, safety is an acquisition of power, often dependent on unjust structures of subjugation to satisfy the threatened person or group's need for control. Normativity itself is dependent on the diminishment of others. We know now that determining punishment by the feelings of one party is the essence of injustice. Philosopher Sara Ahmed made a similar point earlier in her book *The Promise of Happiness*, showing that happiness is something that may be predicated on the oppression of others, and may in fact only be obtainable by controlling others, to their detriment. In my book *The Gentrification of the Mind: Witness to a Lost Imagination*, I expanded on Ahmed's theme by discussing "gentrified happiness" in which people exploit others to avoid feeling uncomfortable.

When one party has been significantly hurt by the violent behaviors of parents, long before becoming half of a couple in adulthood, sometimes the partner is made to take responsibility for the damage done by the parents. The partner is then charged with creating the fantastical "safe space," and that experience can feel very much like being subjected to what Richie describes as "one person's extreme and persistent tension, dominance of their needs over others, chronic irritability and irrational agitation." It can involve a lot of control.

Self-help books for partners of survivors of childhood abuse repeatedly warn partners not to challenge the survivor's concept of themselves. The classic text in this genre is *Allies In Healing: When the Person You Love Was Sexually Abused as a Child* by Laura Davis, co-author of the multi-million seller *The Courage to Heal.* In the introduction, Davis writes, "Survivors frequently have difficulties with trust, commitment, sex and intimacy." Yet what happens when the survivor herself is not aware of this? She may attribute the difficulties to others with whom she is interacting, instead of recognizing that such responses are normative consequences of earlier violations. Or perhaps she won't internalize this information because in her social circle, the acknowledgment makes her feel ashamed and anxious. What if her friends and family members are anti-psychological and refuse to make those connections? That instead of helping to recognize that the anxieties she is projecting onto her partner may be rooted in her earlier trauma experiences, they collude in blaming the partner/co-worker/friend? The partner is then placed in an untenable situation where overreaction occurs, but no one will take the responsibility to acknowledge it.

This is what makes the group surrounding the overreacting person so essential, according to Dudley Saunders:

> [Overreaction] can only be discussed as an observable phenomenon, not an experiential one. But looked at that way, it offers a clear mandate to the reader who witnesses overreaction: they must refuse to validate overreaction simply out of "loyalty" or to avoid getting too engaged with the emotional issues of the individual. There is, in other words, a social responsibility to provide scale when we witness overreaction. Truly, an adult who would react this way to a child getting hysterical because he was refused a second dessert would be seen as parenting badly, as, in some sense, committing a kind of de-socializing child abuse: it is the parent's

> responsibility to provide scale and set limits for children who do not yet have the capacity to experience reality accurately. And we, as friends, owe each other the same when our issues destabilize us if we don't tell the truth and help each other get our sense of scale back, we are actually refusing to help when it is most needed. (private correspondence)

In some places, there is an ideology that undue control of others is inherent to the recovery of an abused person. Because the child's real needs were violated and disregarded, adulthood can produce an inability to tolerate difference, or confusion between vulnerability and danger. Inadequacy, failure, or even discreet incidents in which the partner does not repress all signs of difference can be experienced by an unprocessed hurt person as threat or Abuse. Interestingly, in this way, Male Supremacy, in which a man controls his partner, his mother, his community or nation, may resemble *exactly* the behavior of a hurt and suffering traumatized person who cannot tolerate difference, confuses vulnerability with danger, and interprets some signs of other people's independence as "unsafe." Obviously there are reasons for overreaction. If someone is upset but thinks that it is Abuse, the focus could instead be on understanding what it is about them that creates their overreaction; it could be Supremacy, or it could be unprocessed Trauma. For this reason, Conflict must be discussable. Accusations of Abuse cannot be substitutions for talking things through. Very little is automatically clear. As Sara Ahmed says, learning from Audre Lorde: while actually dealing with the substance of Conflict may initially feel more upsetting than repressing it, the response to high levels of distress should sometimes be to create even higher levels of distress. In this way, internal and external domination systems are revealed, and ultimately dismantled.

My conclusion from this experience of noticing the similarity of behavior between the projecting traumatized person and the entitled self-aggrandized supremacist person is that both need and want dominance in order to feel comfortable. And yet the sources of this need are so different. Underlying all of this is the fact that traumatized behavior is most often caused by Supremacy. Most sexual and physical abuse in a family is caused by Male Supremacy. Oppression from the state is often rooted in both Male and White Supremacy, or in the case of Israel, Jewish Supremacy. Racism, colonialism, and occupation are all Supremacy-based systems. These two entirely different entities, Trauma and Supremacy, operate with resonance and similarity under the same system. And, of course, these two impulses can co-exist in the one body.

The Making of Monsters as Delusional Thinking

At the base of the demand to refuse information/knowledge/communication in order to maintain rigid control is the belief in one's self as human, and of the other as not-human: a specter or monster. Inherent in the insistence on a refusing party's righteousness and the other's blame is the illusion that the control is value-free, neutral, natural, and simply the way things are. But we are all, in fact, human. Because Trauma and Supremacy are ideological but also emotional and perhaps biological, they are compounded obstacles to peace. They are systems. These systems live within, and are expressed without. These are inabilities, limitations from the soul, and expressed through the active body; therefore they represent, as Mary Daly might say, "dis-ease." The dehumanization involved in overstatement of harm as a justification of cruelty is a form of illness, a systemic malfunction that is produced by our humanity, mortality, and literal vulnerability compounded with levels of protection, societal placement, and reward. Unfortunately social convention that either denies the existence of mental illness in one's own ranks or uses it as an excuse for shunning others, makes it difficult to call the Supremacy/Trauma mirror what it is: delusional, i.e., rooted in untruth. And if you can't name something honestly, it cannot be acknowledged, addressed, and healed.

This takes us back to the traumatized person who is suffering the consequences of her physical or emotional abuse as a child. She wants to blame her internal pain on her partner. If the traumatized person is a member of a bad group rooted in shallow relationships, they will agree and gang up on the partner, calling this "loyalty." The partner not only suffers from false accusation, but also simultaneously loves her girlfriend and wants the suffering to be faced honestly in a manner that both begins the healing process and ends the injury of false blame. But the bad group won't allow it. They use distorted thinking to punish the telling of the truth, the resistance to projection, instead of marshaling their resources to help their friend/family member face and deal with the consequences of her earlier abuse. They use their group relationship to keep the truth from being spoken, and in this way, healing, i.e., change, cannot begin. If it did, the dynamics of the bad group itself would be questioned. The role of the bully that the traumatized person turns to for "protection" would be interrogated. The bad group is invested in keeping the woman projecting and dependent. And so, to keep the group together, anyone telling these truths is shunned.

Kaspar Saxena, the Canadian artist and intellectual, works on historical monsters. In his 2014 monograph, "Tiqqun's Young-Girl and Other Monsters in the Middle," he describes the phenomenon clearly:

> An image of the most pervasive evil of our modern age appears where one might least expect it ... she appears to be alive but exists without humanity or soul. She appears innocuously in plain sight, but is really a vast oceanic Vagina Dentata ... She is a super-villain ... her purpose is to destroy Empire with its poisons from within.

Sara Ahmed has famously called this person the "feminist killjoy," the woman who ruins everyone's fun by telling the truth. She must be silenced, shunned, punished, and destroyed so that business can continue as usual, unopposed. Ahmed's articulation has so resonated with people, that the term "feminist killjoy" has become an underground popular cultural phenomenon, appearing as homemade bling, tattoos, and even in the form of a large-scale haunted house, created by artist Allyson Mitchel.

The Cultural Habit of Acknowledging Distorted Thinking

Maybe it's because I'm an old-school New Yorker. After all, pre-gentrification, post-World War II New York was the haven for pioneer psychoanalysts, refugees from Fascist Europe. So many of them came here, trained others here, opened institutes, taught, staffed hospitals, wrote, lectured, and had private and public practices with many patients and students. During that vulnerable period, our city welcomed people whose life calling was to understand and heal suffering as they emerged from mass killings by fascists. I've always been moved by the photograph of Sigmund Freud's home at Berggasse in Vienna, after he was in exile in London and Nazis had taken it over. The photo depicts the former site of his offices covered in swastikas. It's a cogent representation of the desire for understanding covered with shit. Many of these Nazis and collaborators were individuals whom the refugees knew personally and so had to be dealt with on very personal as well as socio-psychological terms. It is stunning to read over and over how psychoanalyst refugees from fascism tried to understand the fascist psychology. Many had the desire or the fantasy to engage fascists in treatment, to help them understand that feelings do not need to be acted on. I find a great beauty in their desire to understand cruelty, even when it was aimed at them. Perhaps in this way their influence, as refugees, had permeated late-twentieth-century New York City.

Partially as a result of this influx of scapegoated people trying to understand the cruelty of their accusers as a means to collective healing, the idea that we all have conflicts that are worth acknowledging for the collective good became a contributing factor to post-World War II New York culture. It became normal and natural for many New Yorkers to unabashedly, eagerly, openly, excitedly, and entirely without shame, be in therapy. It is less common in New York than many other places to hear bravado or bragging after a trauma about not needing to talk it over. But even more importantly, the fundamentals of psychological thinking were integrated into daily life. The idea that people do things for reasons, and that these reasons are worth trying to understand, can be a normative assumption. It certainly is mine. That this understanding process is productive and generous becomes implied. Asking *why* becomes understood as socially and interpersonally beneficial. That there is a conflict between the conscious and unconscious mind becomes broadly understood and casually recognized in this context, and is not a matter of stigma. And, most importantly, the information that these reasons and conflicts are rooted in early experiences was like mother's milk to us.

Importantly, New York is a walking city, and a city of apartment buildings. So instead of waking up in private homes, getting into cars, and parking at the job, we share buildings, walk on the street, take public transportation, and are exposed to each other in real ways many times a day. As a result, the information that people suffer, make mistakes, and express themselves is not news. Nor is it shocking, or wrong to say so. Everyone who lives in New York and rides the subway knows that people have problems and get upset. It's not a secret and we don't pretend it's not happening.

Given all this exposure and knowledge and lack of shame, in the context of the mid-twentieth-century city of difference, to think therapeutically was the definition of being an adult. Now, in the age of gentrification, the city's culture changes. As I explored in my book *The Gentrification of the Mind*, the influx of people reared in privatized and stratified suburbanization, who prefer homogeneity to difference, counters these attitudes. Homogenization breeds Supremacy ideology and difference becomes re-conflated with blame. But the mid-twentieth century desire to understand rather than to conform was a recognition of the existence of Catherine Hodes' instructive touchstones for young social workers to engage: "context, objective, impact."

To say, *She did that cruel thing because she was so anxious and guilty that her anxiety overwhelmed her and she couldn't think clearly*, is, in reality, an act of compassion and even love. It is not an insult; it is an insight. It is not mean; it is kind. It shows an awareness that the other person is suffering, we are suffering, and if we could all acknowledge that suffering has content, we could all understand, as a community, somewhat better how to help each other. While some would rather say, *She's evil and a monster and she did that on purpose so we are going to punish her with shunning and condemnation*, there is instead a legitimate cultural option to try to *understand*. As Will Burton says, "pain has a story, a narrative," and knowing it reveals human complexity which is an invitation to decency. When we try to understand, we discover causes, origins, and consequences about each other and our selves.

The Denial of Mental Illness

Unfortunately, groups that rely on perfection, the good/evil dichotomy, and are motivated by a paralyzing fear of ever being wrong, often deny that mental illness/distorted thinking is in play. Bad families, bad friends, negative communities, and supremacist identities hide and deny contradictions, and rely on the projection of blame onto others to maintain their cohesion as perfect. Pervasive depression gets called *sadness*. Anxiety that is so severe as to control one's life gets called *upset* or *difficult* or *sensitive*. And no one is allowed to talk about why any of it is happening.

I had a friend, C., with whom I was discussing someone we both love. I told her that I was concerned that our friend was suffering from an anxiety so severe that she could not think clearly enough to solve problems. C. rejected any explanation that implied a lack of access to the unconscious, saying that her own mother had been confined to a psychiatric hospital and that "there was nothing wrong with her except that she needed to be listened to." While C. was willing to acknowledge that our common friend was acting badly, I immediately saw that she was hostile to any way of understanding behavior as being caused by emotional illness. That because she believed that her own mother was not mentally ill, and that in fact she was invested in this belief, she couldn't identify thought disorders in anyone that she loved. C. couldn't bear it, believing that the refusal to recognize distorted thinking was equal to love and loyalty. But her approach offered no way out for our friend. Under C.'s ideology, our common friend had no way to change. Years later, C. herself had a mental health crisis and committed suicide. Perhaps if she'd been open to the existence of mental illness and had not defended against her mother's illness, she would have been able to see her own, even perhaps in biological terms of inheritance. It could have saved her life. At C.'s funeral, our common friend eulogized her as "too sensitive for this world," which is itself a defended position. Suicide is often a failure of community, and claiming it as inevitable is a defense against that failure. If C. had been able to understand and accept her own condition, she may have been able to develop an approach to treatment that would have allowed her to live. And our friend also could have a better life if she didn't view mental illness as euphemistically otherworldly. In this way, that clique's inability to recognize and confront mental illness was a factor in a series of events that resulted in permanent tragedy.

In January 2016, a *New York Times* report, "Scientists Move Closer to Understanding Schizophrenia's Cause," revealed new evidence showing that the biological roots of schizophrenia did not reveal any different approaches to treatment. Separating evidence of biological causes to some forms of mental illness from any specific treatment allows us to acknowledge and recognize people's experiences without tying that recognition to a particular medical response. This can remove fear of medication or institutionalization from the separate process of accepting that we or a person we love have a biologically-based mental illness not related to will, character, or lifestyle. Obviously, there are abuses in the identification of mental illness, and this is widely believed and acknowledged. These abuses compound with the denial of mental illness because of fears of stigma, and attachments to perfection and Supremacy. This combination of known abuses and refusal of recognition creates a crisis in which distorted thinking cannot be transformed. In my view, the recognition that a person has distorted thinking that comes from or produces suffering is important, but it has no inherent implication for action. It doesn't imply medication, incarceration, or any particular brand of treatment. It just means stating openly that an internal conflict is not being resolved, is instead being expressed externally, and that those who did not cause the pain will be the ones to be blamed and to pay for it.

To understand, compassionately, that someone is suffering from distorted thinking to the extent that they are hurting themselves and/or others is not an attack. It is the honest, loving truth. Yet in false loyalty systems, saying that someone is suffering is considered worse than the suffering itself, which everyone pretends isn't occurring. Ironically, bullying, shunning, scapegoating, threatening, violence, occupation, racism, and other forms of cruelty are not only created by instability, they produce instability. When they overreact, both the supremacist and the traumatized person insist that others not resist or object to their orders. They expect complete control, but in reality they produce instability in others in the form of unnecessary pain.

"You make her sound unstable" is an accusation that has much greater weight than the fact that she is suffering from instability, as many of us do, and as many of our life experiences justify. So we are not allowed to understand or say openly that our friend's instability is rooted in pain, fear of being inadequate, shame about her sexuality, or an unresolved wound from childhood. We are supposed to pretend it's simultaneously reasonable, undiscussable, and not happening, and simply obey. As a result we cannot say that the conflict is a consequence of that pain. If the person lives in a Supremacy-based community, naming the pain and discussing the source is simply not allowed. Lying is considered loyalty. As is often the case in cultural frameworks of defended people in states of denial, the telling of the truth is considered far worse than the unmentionable truth itself.

Let me put it this way. The supremacist, who blames others because they have to be perfect, and the traumatized person, who will fall apart entirely if they understand any flaw, both say, "*You* need help." The responsible person who understands that all parties participate in conflict, says, "*We* need help." If we really think that someone "needs help," we help them. The claim "you need help, therefore I will compound your problems by shunning and bullying you," obviously is entirely unethical, hypocritical, and socially detrimental. The accusation then becomes just another excuse to escalate by aggrandizing ourselves.

Shunning and punishing does not help them and it does not help us. Shunning by family, cliques, or governments is an active form of harassment, and is consistently detrimental to all parties, even as it becomes normalized and status quo. Our friend, family member, co-worker, fellow HIV-negative, fellow citizen, or co-religionist may suffer from mental illness manifesting as Supremacy or Trauma. Consequently, they may be calling Abuse as an apparatus to absolve themselves of responsibility that they do not have the support to face. Our complicity with ignoring their suffering and our complicity with falsely placing the blame on the other party is not only not loyalty, it hurts them. It makes them worse. This is the opposite of friendship. The denial is dishonest and it prolongs the torture. It sucks. And it's shallow, and desperately needs to be dismantled.

Chapter Six | **Manic Flight Reaction:** Trigger + Shunning

It is one matter to suffer violence and quite another to use that fact to ground a framework in which one's injury authorizes limitless aggression against targets that may or may not be related to the sources of one's own suffering.
—JUDITH BUTLER, *Precarious Life: The Powers of Mourning and Violence*

IN THIS PART of the discussion of the causes, meaning, and consequences of escalation, I return to the Trigger, which we visited briefly in Chapter Three as part of "trigger warnings." "Trigger" is a common word in queer discourse and "trigger warnings" are a common theme in queer academia, provoking public commentary from well-known LGBT writers and academics including Patricia White, Elizabeth Freeman, Tavia N'Yongo, Jack Halberstam, and Aishah Shahidah Simmons.

A "trigger" is a form of overreaction crucial to the conflation of Conflict with Abuse. We react constantly through life. Breathing, noticing, thinking, swallowing, feeling, and moving are all reactions. Most reactions are not really observed because they are commensurate with their stimuli, but a triggered reaction stands out because it is out of sync with what is actually taking place. When we are triggered, we have unresolved pain from the past that is expressed in the present. The present is not seen on its own terms. The real experience of the present is denied. Although reacting to the past in the present may make sense within the triggered person's logic system, it can have detrimental effects on those around them who are not the source of the pain being expressed, but are being punished nonetheless. They are acting in the present, but are being made accountable for past events they did not cause and cannot heal. The one being falsely blamed is also a person, and this burden may hurt their life. The person being triggered is suffering, but they often make other people suffer as well. There is narcissism to Supremacy, but there is also a narcissism to Trauma, when a person cannot see how others are being affected. Although the triggered person may be made narcissistic and self-involved by the enormity of their pain, both parties are in fact equally important. And it is the job of the surrounding communities to insist on this.

In Chapter Three, I discussed this chain of events with regard to people who have carried a conscious or unconscious wish that the police would have intercepted their parents' violence, cruelty, or sexual abuse. As adults, when confronted with a new Conflict, they become triggered, overreact, and call on the police or bond with bullies or other authority figures when in fact the Conflict could be negotiated fairly with the help of accountable communities. Because of the similarity between Supremacy and Traumatized behavior explored in Chapter Five, it may be unclear in which of these paradigms the overreaction is based. As we know, both can exist in the same body. And since these experiences are so connected to and reflective of the state apparatus, these emotional reactions can have geopolitical expressions.

Shunning, interestingly, often accompanies the trigger reaction. Rather than talk openly to the other person, exchanging reasoned, self-critical ideas or feelings, the triggered person eliminates the other, hiding from them while lashing out. The new technologies like email and social media make this very easy. You can attack while hiding. You can articulate threats, misperceptions, and false accusations, and make sure that you never, ever hear information that could alter those perceptions. Certain character types send criticizing, hurtful emails, with misconceptions and false information concluding with, "I consider this matter closed" or "Do not respond." They may ignore clarifications or even block their email, or defriend or block them on Facebook or Twitter, when what they should do is have a conversation. I was recently blocked by someone on Facebook because I named a Black artist who had died of AIDS. They did not allow a conversation in which I would have discussed that having had AIDS is not something to be ashamed of, and saying that the person had AIDS is not an attack on their character. On another occasion, I was one of five people who received letters from a colleague who told each of us that he no longer wanted to be in communication with us because we were "losers." His concluding line was, "Do not contact me." Years later, when he was very ill, one of us rose to the occasion to help him, even though he never apologized. If someone wishes to alter a relationship, they must discuss it with the other person, negotiate the change, and listen to the other person's account. There is no ethical way around it.

Sending condemning emails, or taking hurtful actions and then hiding behind technology, is either a Supremacy action or Traumatized action. It insists on unilateral reality, the removal of difference. It deifies the inability to negotiate and enshrines the imagined victimized status as a desired position to reinforce and maintain.

Shunning, an active form of harassment, is never useful in resolving problems; in most cases it is petty and primarily a way to avoid an adjustment of the self that is required for accountability. If it has no terms for resolution, it is simply a form of asserting supremacy and imposing punishment, and punishment, as we know, rarely does anything but produce more pain. Deciding not to speak to someone who murdered your mother makes sense. But so does deciding to speak to them, as a movement of victims for reconciliation makes clear. Shunning someone you know or loved or shared space with because there was a misunderstanding caused by email, or because they said something you don't want to face, is one of the centerpieces of injustice. Having reasonable and achievable terms for reconciliation is different. If someone scabs your job when you are unjustifiably fired, you may not want to interact with them, but positing terms for reconciliation, such as that they lead a movement to return your employment, is necessary. Otherwise no reconciliation is imaginable. But shunning as an end-point to normative conflict is the definition of absurdity. Shunning is not only a punitive silencing, but it is a removal from humanity, and therefore reliant on the Making of Monsters. After all, no one owns humanity and humans cannot be removed from themselves. It's a delusion.

AIDS Action Now!'s "Think Twice" campaign ("Think twice before you call the police") is a recognition of the triggered moment when a person overreacts, lashes out, then escalates and shuns by attempting to isolate the other through incarceration. "Think Twice" is really a simple plea for people to wait before deciding that punishment will actually resolve Conflict, which it almost never will. And if they can't make the decision alone, their true friends have a responsibility to help them have some restraint so that they can move forward towards negotiation. Moved by the humanity and recognition behind this campaign, I started looking at other configurations and cultural/political movements that also recognize this triggered moment and, like AIDS Action Now!, address it and propose a solution.

So here I want to briefly look at examples from four systems of thought, all vastly different from one another: Historical Psychoanalysis; Contemporary Psychiatry and its pop psychology filter; Modern American Buddhism through "Mindfulness"; and Al-Anon, a 12-step program. All four of these divergent methods understand the combination of triggering followed by shunning as significantly destructive enough to be critically addressed. And interestingly, they draw similar conclusions.

Trigger + Shunning #1: Manic Flight Reaction (Historical Psychoanalysis)

Edith Weigert was a German psychiatrist of the classical generation. She was trained in Germany, and worked at Tegel as an associate of Sigmund Freud. After the Nazis came to power, she fled to Turkey in 1935, where she practiced until she went to America in 1938, where she joined the Washington, DC psychoanalytic circle that included Harry Stack Sullivan and Frieda Fromm-Reichman. In her book *The Courage to Love*, Weigert discussed treating patients "without restraint," just as her colleague and friend Fromm-Reichman was able to treat even hospitalized schizophrenics without medication. With the

American introduction of anti-depressants in 1955, there was a discourse early on between the refugees and the Americans about drug treatment versus the concept that patients can heal in the context of a therapeutic relationship.

In *The Courage to Love*, Weigert identified something she called "manic flight reaction," a capitulation to anxiety that "denies the tragedy of human existence." "Manic" implies compulsion, acting without being able to think through the consequences, the desired goal, or possible alternatives. Manic action not only involves not being able to think through, but a companion lack of awareness of what is happening. Instead, unreasonable answers that escalate problems are experienced as reasonable and successful. "Flight" is the shunning part, the refusal to negotiate, to separate one's self from the person we actually have to partner with in order to resolve conflict. "Flight" is really the inability to problem-solve or work for peace. "Reaction" implies the trigger, when one person is operating out of what Dudley Saunders calls "an interior logic." Translated into the language and content of this book, "manic flight reaction" is an overreaction to conflict, in which conflict is not understood as a difficult but normal part of life. When anxiety is at the wheel, we tragically project, blame, and then separate. We flee reality, which is the fact of conflict as part of life, rather than confront difference and expand our understanding of ourselves.

Weigert, as a victim of Nazism, understood political oppression by groups as expressions of personal conflict, thereby establishing the continuum. This compassionate, psychological approach to understanding fascism was widespread among psychoanalysts. Wilhelm Reich, one of my heroes, wrote many books with titles like *The Mass Psychology of Fascism* (1933), theorizing fascism as an emotional and psychological expression with the implication that it is treatable through the therapeutic relationship. In her book, Weigert described the rise of Nazism, for example, as "vindictiveness directed by transference to the Jews, the socialists and the communists." Here she made the crucial link between personal behavior and group cruelty. Using the word "transference," she implied an attachment of an emotion to people who are not the source of that emotion. In this way, we externalize internal conflict. She wrote that "the disasters of mass hysteria and intranational and international power struggles need deeper psychological study." Again, as was consistent for her generation of refugee psychoanalysts, she saw personal psychology as a component of the political phenomena of group cruelty, instead of religious-based concepts of Satan or evil, or racially-based concepts of inherent group moral corruption.

These ideas play out most clearly in Weigert's descriptions of being an analyst in Germany at the time of the rise of Nazism, and they are absolutely fascinating. At one point, she recounted a single representative day of seeing patients in Berlin:

> In the course of a morning I saw a patient who pondered whether he should join the party to save his career and his family. He was followed by a Jewish student who was struggling against great odds to prepare himself for agricultural work and immigration to Israel. The next patient was a social worker who tried to abreact the shock of abuse and humiliation by storm troopers. She was followed by a Communist who doubted whether he could trust me enough to reveal, via free association, plans of revolt and destruction.

Her observations reveal the wide range of choices available to the bourgeois citizenry in response to the rise of the bad group; in this case, fascism. No one response was inevitable. Each of these people lived in an environment where some individual or group was being victimized, through projection, because of difference. Some recognized themselves as the objects of this group projection. They knew they were the "monsters" intended for blame. Others identified with the bullies and strategized how to win their protection. Others opposed them openly, and others witnessed their cruelty disapprovingly but did not take action to intervene. The lesson here? There are options, and even though anxiety may make the reality of choices elusive, they still exist. Recognize the existence of the anxiety, then strive to overcome it in order to perceive other options. Again, the component ideas of "manic flight reaction" are illustrated. The mania is the triggered response, the compulsion that makes recognizing and assessing options impossible. Then the trigger is followed by the "flight," the shunning, avoidance, the separation that fixes the person being blamed as the irredeemable other, as the inherent object of anger. In the case of Nazism, literal shunning through legal separation came first; refusing to socialize, work, marry, or study with Jews was followed by deportation, then extermination.

"At that time," Weigert wrote, "I wondered how we could possibly work towards the goals of mental health in an insane society." She described these patients as "involved in an unmanageable external situation," much like HIV-positive people facing criminalization, Palestinians under occupation and military assault, or individuals being group bullied, blamed, and shunned in a family or community. But like most of her peers, Weigert persisted in her belief that through the therapeutic relationship, healing can occur. In other words, that in the embodiment of the good group, through the therapist, a person can be helped to understand their own motivations, reactions, and choices, to achieve an ongoing desire for awareness.

In reading her work, I was surprised to find a mid-twentieth-century parallel to my own understanding of Supremacy and Traumatized behavior as mirrors. She referred to Harry Stack Sullivan's observation that "the greatest harm" that people do to each other is to damage self-esteem in children by "overstrictness or overindulgence and other deprivations." In other words, here she presented the roots of both Supremacy and Trauma discussed in the same breath; spoiling your son or demeaning your daughter can produce the male supremacist son, and the victimized, traumatized daughter. These

> mobilize automatic defenses against the painful experience of anxiety. These defenses become habits of character formations, more or less incapacitating not only emotions, but also perception, cognition and will. We find the deepest degree of fragmentation of the ego and alienation from interpersonal relations.

"Overindulgence" is a deprivation of constructive attention, a refusal to teach social/life skills, a refusal to teach self-regulation in social situations, a refusal to teach how to distinguish between wants and needs. Desires are indulged at the place where needs are starved. This is the abandonment of the child, and the responsibility to parent, disguised.

But gorgeously, Weigert, a psychiatrist, posed a solution to "manic flight reaction" that is not necessarily rooted in medication, hospitalization or even treatment in and of itself. Instead Weigert called on "the courage to love" as the antidote. She writes:

> The courage to love is inexhaustible in its resources of genuine repentance, repair and reconciliation.

She underscored the necessity of the willingness to repair, and the power of relationship. This is the recognition that the separations are delusional, that they are artificially imposed blame for normative difference, which is no one's fault. It is understanding, over all, that heals "manic flight reaction." Weigert's solution, in the end, has to do with Supremacy and Trauma's common enemy: the desire to know and understand.

Trigger + Shunning #2: Borderline Episode (Psychiatry and Pop Psychology)

Dr. Weigert made the connection between personal projection, overstatement of harm, and political injustice. She treated people whose problems were both fascism and neurosis, with the underlying understanding that fascism is an expression of neurosis. Contemporary psychiatry and its public face, pop psychology, are less inclined towards articulating those relationships politically. Yet they also define the problematic sequencing of being triggered followed by shunning as a denial by one person of the other's complexity, followed by the object's transformation into a monster or specter to be silenced and isolated. In this case the psychiatric category of "borderline personality disorder" or the experience of "borderline episodes" closely resembles the trigger + shunning sequencing of "manic flight reaction."

I am not endorsing this terminology, but use it to show that very divergent ideologies recognize the same problem, i.e., the trigger + shunning sequence. Psychiatrists call it different things and interpret it in different ways, but they all recognize it as an overly reactive expression of pain that has negative consequences on other people's lives. Showing this commonality across ideologies is my larger objective.

There are a lot of operative definitions of "borderline," but the updated DSM-5, the most mainstream diagnostic standard, describes it as including

> markedly impoverished, poorly developed, or unstable self-image, often associated with excessive self-criticism; chronic feelings of emptiness; dissociative states under stress.

This is an equivalent of the Supremacy/Traumatized behavior dichotomy, where the aggressor's self cannot stand any kind of opposition. Whether through Supremacy or Trauma, we are unable to question ourselves. Perhaps because the person has been so belittled and violated by an authority figure or an oppressive system, they don't have enough stability of self to face the conflict created by difference. The refusal that Hodes points to, of looking at the order of events, or actually investigating *what happened*, is a kind of "dissociative" state, a level of anxiety about being challenged that is so high that they can't even remember what the actual conflict is about, and don't want to be reminded either. All they know is that they feel threatened. What really happened becomes unreachable. In other words, it is a state of being unaccountable.

The DSM-5 also points to a

> compromised ability to recognize the feelings and needs of others associated with interpersonal hypersensitivity (i.e., prone to feel slighted or insulted).

Lack of empathy, of course, is central to conflating Conflict and Abuse. Inherent in the sequence is an absence of thought as to the consequences of the false accusations on others. This is followed by feelings of shock and rage when others resist their unjust treatment. All this, of course, is rooted in a childish but pervasive expectation that their orders will be followed. And if that obedience is not in place, huge feelings emerge of being threatened by the others who express disagreement.

And here is the classic "trigger," the "manic" according to the DSM-5:

> Impulsivity: Acting on the spur of the moment in response to immediate stimuli; acting on a momentary basis without a plan or consideration of outcomes; difficulty establishing or following plans.
>
> Close relationships often viewed in extremes of idealization and devaluation and alternating between over-involvement and withdrawal.

These elements address the behaviors central to this book: overreaction, overstatement of harm, intolerance of difference, "triggers," or sudden changes in attitude and behavior expressed as impulsive lashing out and then shunning. Here we see some of the same elements that were identified earlier in the process of refusing the responsibilities of Conflict and transforming it into overstated claims of Abuse: blame, scapegoating, one-dimensional explanations of people as purely good or exclusively bad that prohibit complex understandings of Conflict (not Abuse) as being mutually produced. It is an inability to self-criticize or to see one's self as one reason for the conflict. There is lashing out in punishment, acting out in blame; calling the police on an HIV-positive sexual partner, organizing a community to shun and isolate a lover or friend, dehumanizing of Palestinians or other entire peoples or races. These attributes of official definitions of "borderline" reveal both intense fear of difference and overreactions to difference as a projected threat to one's safety. At their root is a refusal to alter one's self-perception of a threatened perfectionism.

What makes "borderline" different than the other theories of trigger + shunning that I explore here is that those who use the theory of "borderline" understand it, in part, as a product of chemical shifts and brain changes produced by trauma. *The Journal of Psychiatry and Neuroscience*, in May of 2007, published an article with five co-authors, titled "Neuroimaging and Genetics of Borderline Personality Disorder (BPD)." Their research revealed that "[d]ifferences in the volume and activity in brain structures related to emotion and impulsivity have been observed between individuals who have BPD and those who do not." They showed that borderline behavior has been linked to the amygdala and limbic systems of the brain, the centers that control emotion and, importantly, rage, fear, and impulsive automatic reactions. The hippocampus and amygdala may be as much as 16 percent smaller in people with borderline personality disorder and "experiences of trauma may lead to these neuroanatomical changes." Positron emission tomography (PET) scans have generally indicated that people with BPD show hypometabolism of glucose in their prefrontal cortex and limbic system relative to people who don't have BPD, suggesting that the disorder may result from a failure of the "rational" prefrontal cortex to regulate the "impulsive" limbic system. In this way, people who are borderline "have impeded maturation of higher-order consciousness." Studies repeatedly show that people who meet borderline definitions and were abused as children had significantly smaller volume in significant areas of the brain. In other words, parts of the brain, especially those associated with "impulsivity," i.e., "triggering" and extreme emotions like rage, are literally scarred and shrunken due to abuse.

Obviously there are pros and cons to this approach. And the idea that experiences change biology is one that some people resist. But to my mind, the advantage of this information is that people who have been severely abused as children and who act out against others later can consider the possibility that their reactions may not mean that the other person is hurting them. Rather, the theory gives them an opportunity to understand that there may be a biological reason that is propelling their behavior. So instead of "I have a headache because you put a curse on me," they can be confident in stating, "I have a headache because my blood vessels are constricting." In other words, the biological explanation relieves them of the pain of falsely believing that they are being persecuted, or of the shame in the acknowledgement that the conflict may be caused in part by their misdeed. It is "simply" biology, a system they have not designed and that, in some ways, has its own objective beyond their control. The obstacle to this option for understanding arises if the person is part of a group that is invested in the denial of mental illness. If the person and those around them are pretending that their reactions are justifiable, then they will not accept that they may be acting out of biologically-based overreaction. This refusal, and the construction of false loyalties in which bad friends or bad family structures resist complex understandings of why people are overreacting, makes real healing impossible.

In the summer of 2015, the *Guardian* reported on Dr. Rachel Yehuda's study at Mount Sinai Hospital revealing that Holocaust survivors' children show genetic consequences of their parents' suffering. If we recognize that severe trauma produces biological changes in offspring, how can children of traumatized people further understand their own fears and anxieties?

Can we develop broad recognition that children of traumatized people might overreact to normative conflict or difference and have trouble problem-solving and handling anxiety? Would this produce compassionate self-understanding and changes in how our groups respond to an individual member's fears? Also, could the biological consequences be the result of their traumatized parents' behavior, as opposed to passive genetic inheritance?

One of the greatest obstacles to being on the receiving end of distorted thinking or mental illness is that the person or group involved will not acknowledge that this is what is happening because they are subject to culturally based stigma. But biological explanations may help people come to terms with delusional thinking more easily than more reductive theories that "something" is "wrong" with the person. Imagine a general recognition in the culture that the reason you loved her yesterday but are calling her a monster today may be because of brain scarring from when your father beat you and demeaned you throughout your childhood. So, as a result, your demand that your friends send her cruel emails and shun her is not what good friends should do. If taking this biological information to heart, instead of carrying out instructions for punishment, was considered an act of love rather than an attack, then the kind of group bullying that currently accompanies overreaction could be redeemed. And I mean this on a geopolitical as well as intimate scale.

These ideas around "borderline" also have a mass-market version. The pop psychology book *Stop Walking on Eggshells*, by Paul Mason and Randi Kreger, like many of its ilk, can be found in the "Recovery" section of large bookstores and is designed for people who "care about someone who has borderline personality disorder." Their "checklist" for partners, close friends, and family members includes the following:

- *Are you blamed and criticized for everything wrong in the relationship—even when it makes no logical sense?*
- *Do you feel like the person you care about sees you as either all good or all bad, with nothing in between?*
- *Are you accused of doing things you never did or saying things you never said?*

The overall theme for "borderline" is rapid and unpredictable changes in a person's thoughts, moods, behaviors, relationships, and beliefs. They are *triggered* by the nuances of other people that feel like criticism, such as normative disagreements. Adding to the bewilderment, those struggling with borderline personality disorder might sometimes dissociate, or feel as though they can't recall what happened, whether they acknowledge that or not. When looking at the qualities of these mainstream definitions of borderline personality, their traits also resemble very closely what I have been calling both Supremacy and Traumatized behavior patterns. The absolute intolerance of difference and insistence on obedience is clear. The lack of recognition of mutual contribution to conflict replaced by blame and scapegoating is central. The absence of an order of events makes it all a blur of impulsive reaction. The creation of the other as a non-human "monster" in this pop framework is called "splitting." When the other seems to be meeting their needs, they're cast in the role of goodness, but when the person challenges them, their intimate becomes the villain. The inability to hold simultaneity, nuance, and shades of mutual weakness and strength is, in fact, the centerpiece of "borderline."

Interestingly, one issue that the pop psychology approach addresses that the psychiatric DSM-5 version ignores is the act of calling the police unnecessarily, which is common enough to merit its own chapter.

Under the heading "Lies, Rumors and Accusations," Mason and Kreger write that some partners of people who had borderline episodes

> told us they had been falsely accused of harassment and abuse by the Borderline Personalities in their lives, had been the subjects of damaging rumors and even faced legal actions brought against them by borderlines without legitimate cause.

Returning to the theme of perfectionism as a tenet of both Supremacy and Traumatized behavior, the authors note that

> The fragile self-esteem depends on keeping all sense of failure outside the self. So they present themselves with a self-righteous air of angry superiority and entitlement and accuse the ex-spouse of being psychologically and morally inferior. The

> spouse is viewed as dangerous and aggressive. Having been wronged these people feel justified in seeking retaliation. Or more urgently, they believe in launching a preemptive strike.

Now this is an insight that can illuminate the apparatus behind HIV criminalization in Canada, the efforts by the state to encourage people to denounce their lovers to the police. In the same vein, Catherine Hodes pointed out that perpetrators do better in forensics than victims; that victims are often the ones arrested on the scene if the perpetrator calls the police. She also noted, importantly, that perpetrators increasingly are the first to initiate legal actions like seeking or threatening restraining orders. The authors of *Eggshells* note that "Borderlines often possess the ability to appear calm, logical and persuasive under certain circumstances." However, when alone with their partners they "appear to lose contact with reality or become paranoid," something that their friends and family may not know, as they may handle superficial relationships with more ease and grace than intimate ones. This presents yet another reason to *ask* the person being accused what their experience has been.

Mason and Kreger point out that the falsely accused partner may hold memories of the happy times they shared and the essential positive qualities of the relationship, combined with empathy for the suffering borderline. But they need to understand that the borderline doesn't feel the same way, as the disease, by its very nature, denies simultaneity and involves dissociation or loss of emotional memory. "Splitting may keep the borderline from" seeing their partner "as a whole person with good and bad qualities." All of which contribute to organizing group bullying, calling the police, or initiating shunning as a form of punishment.

Trigger + Shunning #3: Fight, Flight, Freeze (Mindfulness, American Buddhism)

Mindfulness is a popular and increasingly expanding movement rooted in the subculture of American Buddhism and based on the concept of conscious attention and awareness of the present moment. It is thought to cultivate greater tolerance and compassion for what is real and actually happening.

Mindfulness employs a form of meditation in which breath is used as a focal point for attention or awareness. It also emphasizes *compassion*, a positive regard and well-wishing for one's self and all beings. It is a desire for the lessening of suffering for all beings, including one's self. Adherents of mindfulness theorize that discomfort with the self is the starting point for treating others in unjust and destructive ways; it is a construct built around improving one's own life, instead of being motivated only by the creation of social justice for others. There is an underlying ideology that bettering one's own life improves the lives of others, a kind of spiritual trickle-down. A central tenet of mindfulness is what they call "*acceptance*," which is theorized as the beginning of "real change." Mindfulness also includes a concept called "allowing," which is a kind of recognition that one does not know everything, and that there are realities, experiences, and understandings that reside in other people and other expressions of life which is in contrast with the perfectionism of Supremacy and Trauma-based behaviors.

Like the other systems for understanding behavior discussed earlier, mindfulness practice recognizes the trigger + shunning sequence as a significant place in human interaction where pain is produced. They call their version of it *fight, flight, freeze*. In the language of this book's themes, *fight, flight, freeze* is when someone feels endangered by something that is not actually dangerous in the present, but they don't have any awareness of what is really happening beyond their own sensation. The reason they can't differentiate between their own projection of danger and normal conflict may be because they have Supremacy feelings and won't put up with opposition, or that they have been Traumatized and feel threatened by difference. Because they don't have awareness, or are part of a bad group that doesn't allow for self-criticism, they can't take a step back to understand why they feel the way they do. Instead, they register the triggered reaction as though it were an objective reality. The trigger + shunning combination here that some call *manic flight reaction* or *borderline episode* follows a sequence. First, the person will *fight* (assault, attack, demean, etc.), then experience *flight* (cut-off, shun, dehumanize), and then finally *freeze* (dissociate or become rigidly fixed in an intractable and unjustified position).

One of mindfulness's most visible teachers is Tara Brach. Her official biography states that she was an undergraduate at Clark College, a tenants' rights organizer, and that she lived in an ashram for ten years teaching and practicing yoga and concentrative meditation. She then attended a Buddhist Insight Meditation retreat led by Joseph Goldstein which is when she "realized I was home." Brach earned her Ph.D. in Clinical Psychology working on meditation as a modality for treating addiction. She did a five-year Buddhist teacher training with Jack Kornfeld and worked as a psychotherapist and meditation teacher. In 1998 she founded the Insight Meditation Community of Washington, DC and today regularly gives lectures, teaches classes, conducts workshops, and leads silent meditation retreats. Her self-identified "themes" focus on emotional healing and spiritual awakening through mindful, loving awareness as well as alleviating suffering by practicing compassion. Her most popular book is called *Radical Acceptance*.

I watched video of two lectures by Brach on Conflict that she gave in the spring of 2014. The first, "Awakening Through Conflict," is a general talk designed for people who have not experienced profound trauma. The second, "From Fight-Flight-Freeze to Attend-Befriend" is explicitly designed for people who have experienced trauma, including racial oppression and war.

I'm not going to pretend to be able to contextualize Brach within American Buddhism; instead I look at the ideas in her presentation that directly address the concerns of this book, namely the trigger + shunning sequence. I want to understand the specific ways that yet another thought/belief system sees the dynamics of trigger + shunning, or attacking people in the present for events that originated with others, often long gone, in the past. How, I wondered, would Brach's framework address that problem?

Brach is an attractive, healthy, but somewhat bland woman in early middle-age. In one of her lectures she wears a sparkly blue high-end hippie shawl and in the other a shiny metallic blouse, and is surrounded by flowers and a Buddha. It's contemporary upscale, tasteful, educated, and intellectual New Age. She uses very simple language, but has a sophisticated presentation. She uses words like "unstuckness." She often asks rhetorically, "Does that make sense?" and then looks to her audience, who presumably nods.

In the first lecture, "Awakening Through Conflict," Brach starts with the clear assertion that "It's not our needs that produce conflict. It is our strategies for meeting them." These "maladaptive strategies" include "to constantly justify ourselves, to rationalize, to pretend that we are different than we are, to put up a front."

Her number one focus is on what she calls "blame." Now, in my understanding of that word, *blame* is when the reasons behind conflict, the order of events, are not allowed to be addressed, where the understanding that could reveal how both parties contribute is blatantly denied. For me, it is not the understanding itself that is the *blame*; it's what fills the void left by refusal to understand. In Brach's terms, however, the word takes on a different meaning, one that to me feels more like *anxiety*. Her *blame* is the obstacle that keeps people from being able to face and deal with conflict, to think things through honestly. It's the "stuckness."

"Blame gives an initial sense of control," she says. "But it's a false refuge because it creates more division."

Instead Brach favors a process she calls "Awakening Through Conflict." Interestingly, she acknowledges that this is "hard and uncomfortable" because it requires "commitment and intention." What this implies to me is that in order to stop *fight, flight, freeze*, one has to be in a community that provides support to face and deal with problems, which is difficult and uncomfortable. Bad groups that encourage or passively allow bullying and Supremacy thinking would make this almost impossible.

"The beginning of awakening through conflict is very consciously being committed to presence, not holding on to being right and not holding on to blame," Brach says. The sentiment would be very unlikely in a group committed to being right. "This is what keeps wars going," she asserts, not speaking metaphorically. On shunning, Brach quotes Adrienne Rich, saying that two people "telling each other the truth breaks down human self-delusion and isolation." In other words, she opposes shunning, and recognizes that truth lies in hearing difference.

Quite a bit of her rhetoric uses words that gesture towards science, especially biology. For example, she often refers to *evolution* and *evolutionary potential*. She characterizes refusing the freeze, or interacting, as "offering attention" which she describes, in biological terms, as "part of our evolutionary unfolding." And she poses *blame* as an obstacle to evolution.

Over and over she uses different language and employs different values to point to the same places that interest me. For example, the question of what I call *smokescreens*, i.e., creating false accusation to hide real problems. She calls this a "cover." "Vengeance," Brach says, "is a lazy form of grief ... It's a cover for the place that really needs attention ... If you put aside the blame, what would you have to feel that is difficult to feel?"

But it is her lecture organized for people who have been profoundly traumatized that resonated the most for me. In "From Fight, Flight, Freeze to Attend-Befriend," her emphasis is on how reconciliation takes place. Interestingly, in her conversation with more traumatized people, she includes biological language about the science of the brain, a kind of popularization of the neuropsychiatric theories around borderline. She often speaks about the brain literally, such as, "the brain has the capacity for compassion." She will make a fist and point to it as a model of the brain, indicating sections as areas of brain function. She refers to the experience of being triggered as a biological reality, which she calls "flip your lid," at which point she opens her hand as if the brain was actually turning over. In fact, Brach uses the word "neuropsychiatry" and says things like "relationships activate the pre-frontal cortex."

Throughout, Brach's focus is on the action of "making someone else the bad other," the *making of monsters*. "If we are stuck in conflict with another person, that means that the emotion inside us is stuck. Let go of that idea of blame," she says. "And come back here." She points to her chest. "The gift of mindfulness is that it unsticks emotion." She illustrates how, through delay, we move from the angry, aggrieved person to a shift in identity that allows reconciliation. She argues that dismantling the monster is desirable because it is better for the person originating the blame. Her focus is less on the object of the overstatement of harm, and more on how detrimental false accusations are to the accuser. So while she hits many of the same points as these other companion ideologies, mindfulness is less an appeal to justice than a plea to the accuser to "step out of imprisoning beliefs" in order to improve their own life.

Finally, she overtly discusses *the group*, the person's surrounding influences. "When we are stuck," she says, "we need a reminder of belonging to reconnect ... Groups can move us if they are conscious, meditative, communicating groups. Being in a group can move us from fight, flight, freeze, where there is hostility, to attend-befriend." She then points to Truth and Reconciliation processes in South Africa. "Blame and hatred is released," she says, "as we come into contact with a larger field of compassion." So what is not going to be helpful is a group that "couldn't reach out" to the person being blamed "and do the empathetic response." This kind of negative group reenforces people in their own negative reactivity. "We need something larger that allows us to reintegrate."

Since this process is meditation-based, Brach's main focus is on delay. Meditation is a kind of waiting and postponing of reaction. She has many stories and examples of how arousal levels can be calmed down, always coming back to the biology of the brain. "If we pause and start bringing our attention inward ... then we can start accessing our frontal cortex, our compassion networks and we can start accessing mindfulness. Does this still make sense?" She looks again at her audience, who presumably nod. "Okay."

Trigger + Shunning #4: Detaching with an Axe (Al-Anon)

Most people are familiar with Alcoholics Anonymous, the movement founded in 1935 by Bill Wilson in which alcoholics help each other stop drinking, and face the causes, triggers, and consequences of their drinking through a program called the 12 Steps. Al-Anon, the companion program for people whose lives are affected by someone else's drinking, was founded in 1951 by Wilson's wife Lois. Their central concept is that by applying the 12 Steps in a peer-organized setting, without leaders or counselors, the person affected by someone else's drinking can improve their own life even if the qualifier (an Al-Anon term for the alcohol-abusing person whose behavior is affecting others) continues to drink. Al-Anon literature focuses not on the alcoholic, but on the Al-Anon member.

At its core, Al-Anon addresses the experience of loving and trusting someone who is not reliable because they have the disease of alcoholism. Although Al-Anon is about alcoholism, in the contemporary world, people also attend because their friend or family member is not reliable for a range of reasons: e.g. drugs, gambling, sex addiction, mental illness, or distorted thinking. Or the other person may not be reliable because of their own investment in someone who is not accountable. It's an interesting situation because loving someone who can't be counted on to be present, fair, empathetic, reciprocal, honest, or dependable is a very particular experience. It means loving someone for reasons other than for what they can do *for* you. It means loving them because they move you, not because they provide for you. While on one hand, this generosity and open-heartedness is a kind of release, it also creates its own problems. The assumption of Al-Anon is that there is no mechanism to help that other person become accountable or honest unless they decide to enter "The Program" or some other form of treatment. There is only the 12 Step group itself to help *you* improve your life. And the method by which these improvements take place is based in listening and sharing. So Al-Anon is inherently the opposite of shunning. Not only is there no gatekeeping, but everyone is allowed to speak. Further, there is no cross-talk, no countering, and no criticism. The method works by simply listening, and then talking openly about one's self. Since it is the opposite of shunning, all are welcome.

One of the main focuses of Al-Anon is the inability of the Al-Anon member to help the alcoholic become more integrated in their own life. This is a source of great pain and disappointment to many. They want to help the loved one resolve their conflicts, not only because they want that person to have a more balanced life, but also because they long to have someone to rely on in the way that they are themselves reliable. The qualifier is often very demanding of the Al-Anon member, maintaining expectations that they will take responsibility for things, fix things, and pay for things, as well as cover up problems, create positive environments, accept unequal conditions, and live with inconsiderate situations without protest. This kind of expectation is called "alcoholic behavior." Or, if you are using the mental illness model, "distorted thinking." Denial is at the center of alcoholic behavior and reflexively at the center of behavior that brings people to Al-Anon. The Al-Anon member is in denial that they cannot make the alcoholic/distorted thinker become aware, honest, and responsible because only that person can decide to go into recovery. Al-Anon is constructed on the idea that by telling and hearing the truth in 12 Step meetings, the person can continue to love and even live with the active alcoholic happily, without expecting or demanding that they also become someone who can tell and hear and act on the truth about their own situation.

Being triggered, in a way, is a component of alcoholic behavior. When someone is drunk, or fixed in some other system of distorted thinking or projection, they act out on their friend or partner or family member, not in appropriate measure to how that person deserves to be treated, but as a propulsion by other forces such as alcohol. Normally, if a person is kind, they should be treated kindly. But if you're drunk, or sick with anxiety or other thought disorders, you may unleash rage, childish expectations of perfection, intolerance to difference, or punishment for truth-telling, because the alcohol releases inhibitions. This impulsivity, the *fight* element of *fight*, *flight*, *freeze*, or of borderline, the *mania* of *manic flight reaction*, is part of the Al-Anon member's general experience. They are blamed for problems they have not caused, and treated in ways that are not merited by their own actions. Their assertion of their experience, or resistance to the alcoholic behavior, while being only Conflict, may cause the alcoholic to overreact with outrageous defiance, i.e., Abuse. One of the challenges to the Al-Anon member is to not engage alcoholic behavior, because it does not respond to reason, facts, order of events, or general fairness.

The shunning that follows the trigger, or the *flight* of both *fight*, *flight*, *freeze* and *manic flight reaction*, is what Al-Anon calls, ironically, "Detaching with an axe." This is considered undesirable and something to avoid doing to other people. They instead advocate "detachment," a recognition that the other person has a disease (alcoholism or some kind of distorted thinking) and therefore a withdrawal of investment in how the other behaves when impaired is advised. But they do not advocate shunning (the *with an axe* part) because it is also impulsive. And like mindfulness, Al-Anon proposes delay. Instead of meditation as the delay tactic, they suggest going to meetings, calling sponsors, reading literature, and any kind of contemplative and focused use of time to distance one's self from the alcoholic event. The purpose of this delay, in Al-Anon, is for the person to think through their choices: to examine what kinds of responses are available, to consider what their outcomes could be, and to deliberately and consciously choose actions, if they are going to act, that are in concert with their own values and goals.

The problem of the "bad" group of friends, community, and family is overtly addressed by Al-Anon, which considers alcoholism to be "a family disease." The good group is the meeting itself, "the fellowship" where people listen to whatever you have to say without interruption while sharing the value of accountability and resistance to compulsion. And you, in turn, listen to them. But Al-Anon warns about the "bad" group which they call "people, places and things": the stuff to be avoided when you want to refuse compulsivity and think things through enough to take some responsibility. Al-Anon, because it preaches humane detachment (i.e., not reacting impulsively), not shunning, is by definition a program of reconciliation. And they try to provide each member the tools with which to proceed sanely on their own, with plenty of supporters around who are there to encourage self-criticism, empathy for others, and actions that create serenity.

They All Agree: Delay and Accountable Community

Despite the extremely divergent values, concepts, and histories of these four categories of thought about human behavior, there are two conclusions about which classic psychoanalysis, modern psychiatry and its stepsister pop psychology, Al-Anon, and mindfulness agree. The sudden, *triggered* reaction a) without consideration of choices; b) without looking at the order of events, motives, justifications, contexts, or outcomes; c) without taking responsibility for consequences on others and the escalation of

Conflict; and d) without self-criticism, is the source of social and personal cruelty and the cause of great pain. Lashing out by over-reaction, as has been demonstrated, deepens the problem. All of these systems recommend the same tactic: *delay*.

And in order to delay, they all agree, one needs to be in a community: a relationship, friendship circle, family, identity group, nation, or people who encourage us to be self-critical and look for alternatives to blame, punishment, and attack. We need to be in groups that are willing to be uncomfortable and take the time to fully talk through the order of events, take all parties into account, and facilitate repair.

Chapter Seven | **Queer Families, Compensatory Motherhood, and the Political Culture of Escalation**

Opposition is true friendship.
—WILLIAM BLAKE, "The Marriage of Heaven and Hell"

LIKE ANY GROUP, a family could be a positive example of a community designed to help its members treat others fairly, to avoid scapegoating and instead be self-critical. Yet in some ways the family is the prototype for the "bad" group. Often a family mythologizes itself as perfection, as the social ideal, in which outsiders are dangerous. And much of the family's work is about maintaining a strange kind of anti-social version of "loyalty" in which we prove our love to family members by upholding any wrongdoing they commit on others. In some ways, racism, class oppression, nationalism, and religious Supremacy are all family-based systems. They are rooted in identification with others theoretically by genetics, reproduction, or some culturally constructed simulacra of biology. Family systems are a model for the "us" vs "them" mentality. And as families adhere to governments, nationalist ideology and the state, they extend their institutional reach of punishment.

As the increasingly normative queer family gains access to this machine of Supremacy, separation, and the arm of the law, it too risks becoming or does become a force for reaction. The mother role remains firmly fixed in both society and media representation as a place of guilt and martyrdom, and for women this may become replicated internally. The bonds may or may not be as precisely genetic or biological as most heterosexual couplings that produce children. But, psychologically, the emerging legally constituted or recognized queer family can be constructed on lines that are derivative of and gesture towards biological kinship. This is one reason the problems inherent in heterosexual families get reproduced, often without much renovation: nationalism, group identification, racial and religious exclusivity, false loyalty, male Supremacy, but with male relatives, peers, gay fathers, or sons of queer mothers occupying the spot formally reserved for heterosexual male partners. Of course the greatest challenge to feminism has always been and continues to be the family itself, and the Queer Family may not be the exception. The social imperative that women become married and mothers now also affects women who are queer and is more and more the expected norm. There's no way out.

We already know that the family is dangerous, especially for women. But this is only quantifiable in terms of physical violence, and remains immeasurable in terms of emotional consequences. The US government admits to 1.5 million women being physically assaulted by an intimate partner every year. Other estimates are much higher. The National Violence Against Women Survey, sponsored by the National Institute of Justice and the Centers for Disease Control, interestingly asserts that 52 percent of all women have been physically assaulted at some point in their lives, but only 22 percent of all women have experienced that violence from an intimate partner. Who hurt the other 30 percent? I find this gap quite startling. What happened to them? Almost 60 percent, that is to say the *majority*, of women who have been physically assaulted in their lives were hurt by someone who was not their intimate partner. Who was it? It seems unlikely that all of that violence came from random street assaults, since most violence takes place between people who know each other. That leaves another suspect outstanding: the family. Is the family the place where most women experience violence and sexual abuse for the first time?

Family-based violence, sexual abuse, and its threat surely have an influence on the ways that many women understand their intimate relationships as adults. Depending on levels of awareness and recovery, violence and violation in childhood would influence how we behave as an adult. Growing up with chaos can make it harder to know how to create order as an adult. We may be more likely to make things worse, or initiate and escalate conflict as adults if that was the model with which we were raised. Repeating these behaviors does not mean that problems in relationships are our fault, if we—as Catherine Hodes suggests—step out of the victim/perpetrator model and focus instead on what happened, why it happened, and how to make things better. It is our job as conscious adults to overcome blaming-the-victim scenarios, confusing *fault* with ***participation***, so that the reality of this connection between childhood and adult conflict can be faced and honestly understood. This conceit: confusing participation in conflict with blame—forces us into steadfast refusal to confront our own contributions and responsibilities and to punish instead.

It would be dishonest, and grossly unhelpful, to deny that previous family-based abuse heavily influences how traumatized people experience intimate relationships. If we can't make these connections, then the abusive family becomes romanticized instead of understood. It becomes the prototypical "bad" group as its silencing and demands for obedience become the model for a destructive "loyalty." This produces a reliance on the familiarity of "bad" groups that keep their members from being self-critical and therefore unknowing about how to create repair. Given the need for control that some traumatized people feel as adults, *difference* in combination with love and desire can *feel* abusive because difference, by definition, is out of our control. If instead, these experiences were detailed and talked through in a chronology of events, the place of this projected Abuse would become elusive. Other sources of discomfort would have to be considered. In other words, the charge of Abuse can shut down a conversation that could reveal or elucidate earlier violations—especially by family—that the claimant does not know how to face without being disloyal or cast adrift. This is what Ilana Eloit calls

> a genealogy of conflict as a collective political practice for conflict resolution that is exterior to the State apparatus and that invests in the transformative power of the community.

Good Families Don't Hurt Other People

Today, a "good" family model is based on an ideology called "loyalty" or, more neo-liberally, "being supportive." Often this is one in which the members reinforce each other regardless of the content of their lives and the consequence of their actions on others. They are "always there for you." They overpraise in a broad sense. George W. Bush may be a war criminal, but his family is always there for him. As Edith Weigert recalled about Harry Stack Sullivan's observation, families can create a "deprivation of indulgence." No standard for how to treat others is forged. They can reproduce class and gender Supremacy systems by not expecting their members to face and deal with conflict, to learn how to take care of themselves or others, to literally and spiritually clean up after themselves, or to be self-critical. As a result, family members learn how to be exploitative, expectant, and entitled. They learn to view some jobs as beneath them or some paths as above them; they understand that accountability is beyond them because they always have the family and its emotional resources to fall back on. They can come to expect a level of gender, class, or race Supremacy without having to work or earn their comforts. From the family's perspective, this is considered "love."

Some "good" bourgeois families build their strength at the expense of others, especially others in need or who don't have a family. It's inherent to the construction of the bourgeois classes. The family says "no" to others in order to enhance their own status. The family puts its own privileges first, positioning the rest of the world as a threat to their time and resources, or even their double standard. Bizarrely, we have deceived ourselves into believing this is responsible behavior, even though it only serves the state and its embedded classes, not the broad community. It defines itself by in-group silence about each other's cruelties to outsiders and preservation of its resources for its own exclusive use. Of course, no one is being asked to purposely disable their children's futures by restricting them from enjoying superior education, health care, or living conditions. But rather, I am asking for some reality about the meaning and values and consequences of entitling our bourgeois children to dominate, even if the entitled don't know how to best implement alternatives. And I am suggesting that some of this is inherent to social definitions of the mother role, particularly as it adheres to state systems of dominance.

Of course, I know that gay men are fathers, and that heterosexual men can be invested fathers, single fathers, and all the rest. But women still earn less than men, have less social currency than men, and internalize guilt and sacrifice as a national and international pastime. Options for action are not always evident, and no one has more excruciating decisions to make than parents. But real engagement about doubts and social recognition of the consequences of male or class entitlements are always available, albeit uncomfortable for all parties. And they are not just individual actions. These are also the responsibilities of the surrounding community: teachers, doctors, social workers, bus drivers, neighbors, and others outside the family who can and do offer balance. Sometimes, as a teacher, my number one job is to counter what students have been told about themselves by their families, whether demeaned by gender, sexuality, or interest, or elevated by race, gender, religion, or nationality.

The "bad" family, as we understand it, is the opposite of this Supremacy model. Instead of bonding with each other to the detriment of outsiders, the family turns on its own members directly, demeaning them, beating them, fucking them, conditioning them towards self-destructive and socially detrimental behaviors. As my father once told me, "Families do worse things to their own members than they do to other people. They kill them, they rape them, they burn them in boiling oil." And he was right.

The problem with this pathological dichotomy is that when "bad" families destroy their own members, they produce people so traumatized that they can't problem-solve with others and become the source of impulsive, triggered acting out: e.g., blaming others, committing violence, overstating harm, bringing in the police or the state in lieu of problem-solving. The problem with "good" families is that they do the same thing, but from a place of over-privilege and Supremacy, so that when they are cruel and unfair, their family members "stand by" them, and create no consequences for their actions. Both of these systems hurt other people's lives and produce new adults who don't know how to be responsible and to problem-solve, who are entitled to a level that is detrimental to the rest of the world. And the rest of us have to live with these people. Even if we also are them, taking into account our earlier recognition that Supremacy and Trauma can exist in the same body.

I believe that a truly "good" family is one that is deeply and in fact primarily concerned with the behavior of its members towards other people. That instead of reinforcing indifference, exploitative behavior, arrogance about class, race or gender, blind allegiance to the state, and cruelty towards sexual partners, they systematize methods of accountability. In this way, each family member would grow up with a loving practice of opposition, with the commitment to psychological insight, individuation, and a means of discussion that emphasizes context, objective, and the order of events. Blind adherence would be the definition of "disloyalty," as it is detrimental to peace and justice. Our model for relationships within groups can be transformed from obedience to biology, biological assumption, or simulacra of biology, emphasizing instead the ethics of each individual's actions, cumulative consequence, and the necessity of self-criticism. In other words: accountability.

Rethinking the Family Ethic as a Form of Harm Reduction

Before we continue, let us pause for a moment to engage this concept of the politics of "fear" where a family operates as a privileged group—and it has to be a group, because individuals cannot punish in the way that bullying groups can. A familial group can say they are *afraid* in order to gang up on or punish people who are actually, themselves, in danger. Families can unite unjustly to shun a wide range of people, like the residents of a proposed homeless shelter across the street or the group of Syrian refugees who want to move in next door. In the more intimate version, families can condemn a teacher who claims that their child doesn't know how to share, or a sexual/romantic partner who thinks an adult son should clean up after himself, or a colleague who accuses a family member of theft, sexual abuse, violence. We are trained to deny, defend, and deflect anything that would make us identify with someone outside the family structure regarding a transgression by a family member; in other words, we externalize problems that exist within a family and pin them on people outside of the family organization. I'm thinking, for example, of the neighbors who fire-bombed the home of children with AIDS in Florida in the 1980s, who justified the act with the delusional logic that they were "protecting" themselves, even though they were at no risk. Of course, the opposite also exists. There is still that classic "bad" family which builds its internal legitimacy around maintaining one of its own members as the constant scapegoat. But the "good" family blames the outsider. It fears them because of what they can reveal about the family and its members, that the family may be human and have flaws.

Since racism, nationalism, class oppression, and religious Supremacy are all family-based systems, traditionally constructed hetero-normative family "loyalty" is a primary tactic of scapegoating, shunning, blaming, bringing in the state, and other projections destructive to human relationships. These elements are about elevating those who have some kind of assumed or assigned genetic similarity or reproduction-based connection, including HIV negativity, ahead of other human beings. This opposes the previously held value of liberation that all human beings, by virtue of being born, deserve care, recognition, protection, fairness, and opportunity. It replaces group care with privatization both emotional and material. These processes, as Nan Alamilla Boyd writes in her article, "Sex and Tourism: The Economic Implications of the Gay Marriage Movement" in *Radical History Review*, "reward docile (gay and lesbian) bodies with citizenship."

The biological basis for inclusion is interestingly replicated in the contemporary state-approved version of the queer family. In these cases, often love creates the interest in having children together, or having children together is an external marker proving love. But in many of these families, sex and reproduction have no relationship. And yet, a kind of simulacra of reproductive sexuality is prevalent when lesbian parents look for donors with biological markers that stand in for a fantasy sexual reproduction between the women. This is most noticeable in cross-racial or cross-cultural female couples in which the women look for donors representing the non-birth parent's race or close to it, so that the child will resemble an imagined biological melding of the two. Everyone knows that child was not produced by the two women having sex, and yet they choose a biological mix that imagines that it does. This does a lot of complicated things, but one is to allow the families of each mother to integrate the child based on race or physicality into their concept of tribe. The racial element stands in for a kind of resemblance. And it allows the broader categories of group stratification to also admit the child into their insider/outsider system. If that particular group implies any kind of Supremacy, insiderness, currency, or special tenderness, the racial signification of the donor will support it because it gives the illusion of heterosexual biology and its inherent group identities.

In order to avoid the overstatement of harm in defense of negative family structures, it is our responsibility to understand what dynamics constitute actual threats to human decency, not threats to Supremacy systems. Our job is harm reduction in the broadest sense. Inherent in this objective is the knowledge that all human beings deserve to be heard and considered. On the governmental level, empathetic people reject the insider/outsider dichotomy that *citizens* are superior, to whom non-citizens or residents of weaker nations should serve. We reject this because it hurts those who are outside and privileges those who are inside. Similarly, we should ask the same of families. The separation between traditionally constructed family members and non-family members in terms of an ideology based on the "right" to resources, kindness, access, and accountability is at the heart of most of our systems of injustice.

Queer Families and Supremacy Ideology

The fact that a family is queer doesn't exempt it from this truth. As pro-family ideology has come to dominate queer communities, we are quickly forgetting everything we ever learned about family when we were still feminists and looking at how all social institutions affect women.

What are the most amplified group values in an environment where the queer community is dominated by pro-family/pro-natalist politics, and at the same time has more access to and comfort with the state, the law, and official modes of enforcement and punishment? With this shift towards dominance comes a new relationship for white and economically functional queer people with the government, for the family enjoys a relationship with the state that an individual does not have. Increasingly queer families within entitled racial, citizenship, and class groups access governmental powers of enforcement that individuals and disenfranchised communities cannot reach. As some queers feel increasingly "normal," they identify more with the state, and are more willing to call on the state to punish others on their behalf. The discourse of safety, danger, and protection can become a place of intersection of the state and the family against the individual, including the queer individual.

Interestingly, this plays out most dramatically in the category of whiteness. After the Civil War, the reconstituted Union had to reorganize its hostilities in order to maintain white Supremacy. What began then was a period of "White Reconciliation." Gatherings or joint reunions of white soldiers from the Confederacy and the Union were organized as annual unity events. Blacks who had been slaves or soldiers were excluded. The white race had to be reunited. Since the family is, for many, the root of racial identity, we can see that legalized gay marriage plays a similar role in unifying the white race. Heterosexuals have long shown interest in supporting ways of life that reflect their own and reject difference. Prior to the US Supreme Court decision in the spring of 2015, more US states had legalized gay marriage than had anti-discrimination protection for LGBT people or Medicaid funding for abortion. By that summer, same-sex marriage was upheld nationally while abortion, birth control, and voting rights for Black Americans continued to be impeded. So queer families are doing a lot better than queer people who are not in families, and better than women in general, and white queers have the favor of the courts over every Black person. There is reward when straight people see themselves in our lives, and lack of protection when the factor is Difference. And of course, pro-natalism is encouraged for gay women, while refusing motherhood is continually obstructed for women who have sex with men.

Before queer people won legal recognition, organizing in the same structures that heterosexuals used, identified with, and reinforced, the separation of white queer people from their familial/racial group was more common. Familial homophobia pushed some queer people out of their white families and white towns, and cut them off from the money stemming from their white family's class acquisition. In this way, some white and bourgeois queers moved to urban centers and became centrally located in queer communities, which were more interracial and cross-class than their straight cultures of origin. Today, with gay marriage and parenthood prevalent, and the advent of gay nuclear families and normalized queer childbirth, a kind of white reconciliation is taking place. Inside this movement, white gays who assemble into nuclear families are readmitted into their birth families and resume their positions in their race and class formations. This not only breaks up the mixed queer community of friends, but also withdraws resources and access from those friends. These white queer families realign with the state that held them in pervasive illegality less than a generation ago. And this, of course, produces an investment in unjust social structures that once rejected but now enhance white queer families. Accompanying this is a paradigm shift in values from the protest-from-below rooted in a freedom vision, to an investment in inequality and corruption.

The ideology of familial Supremacy and untouchability poses all kinds of dilemmas when individuals come into conflict with family members who call on the "bad" group formation to avoid problem-solving. These symptoms are internal as well as external. What happens when families are destructive to outsiders? What happens when family systems inflate the power of some members and destroy the lives of others, for example through sexism? Who is responsible then? Who is accountable? Whose job is it to intervene? The more power and centrality the family has in queer life, the greater the consequences that dysfunctional family systems have on the broader community. It is now time for an overt conversation about the responsibility of queer friends in response to family systems that are corrupt, or as we politely call it, "dysfunctional." It is a hugely complex conversation that I can only introduce in a preliminary way here, because the coming together of the queer family, the state, and the politics of false loyalty bring us truly crucial questions about anxiety, fear, trauma, projection, and all the emotional issues behind family, dominance, and safety. We have an enormous challenge now that the community of queer friends is facing profound transformation by queer pro-family ideology, an ideology that constructs the idea that people are bound together as a central legal and social structure of "protection" against outsiders, who are a "threat." This is the very same construction that victimized many of us in fundamental ways in relationship to our own families. Lest we forget.

The pro-family politic in the queer community has overwhelmed a lot of things that we once understood but no longer remember. Childcare is privatized instead of collectivized. Interestingly (and I leave it to historians to chart this one), lesbians in the feminist movement of the 1970s and '80s, before the dawning of the pro natalist mentality, were more overtly active for quality child care, which was considered to be one of a number of issues that were grouped together as "reproductive rights" ("Abortion rights, affordable and safe birth control, an end to Sterilization Abuse, Lesbian Rights and Quality Child Care"). But in our contemporary, queer pro-family ideology, there is no visible gay or lesbian movement for childcare rights. Our understandings about the consumerism of privatized living are forgotten. We've lost a lot of imaginative ground and also emotional complexity in how we talk about and understand relationships. Most importantly artificial ideas about perfect parents, ideal children, and storybook romance do great harm to many of us. How does the earning differential between women and men play out in queer families? Increasingly I see young gay women gaining acceptance from their families based on an expectation that they will gay-marry and have children. Isn't any ideology that pushes young women into marriage and motherhood reactionary? What about gay male parents and surrogacy? Hiring women to provide childcare? There are all kinds of anxieties, projections, and distorted thinking involved in our concepts of parenting.

Single motherhood, which is significant among queer women, has its own specific emotional pitfalls. One's self-perception as a romantic failure or as a failed partner may be erased by the kind of normativity produced by motherhood. Queer women without partners are particularly vulnerable to the promise of legitimacy and social worth if they subsume sex and love into parenting, especially with male children. Their uncontrollable lesbian sexualities may have proven to be failures, and their desire to mimic heterosexual normalcy may also have failed. Yet the one thing they did right was to have children. It's painful to see my beautiful generation, whom I love so much and value so deeply, be scarred by these defeats and reconstructed only by their social role as mothers. The fact that it's queer people initiating, instead of being on the receiving end of, familial dysfunction doesn't make these things less difficult.

As the queer community becomes more and more saturated with "family values" and familial imperatives, we see an increased privileging of "family," even if it is corrupt and detrimental, over the community of friends. The privileging of destructive family relationships by friends is emotionally and psychologically damaging within the queer community, just as it is within straight society. I know it is difficult, but in order to address this, we have to incorporate some method of talking realistically and humanely about psychic pain, anxiety, projection, and trauma into the ways we understand families. We can't understand family politics if the emotional issues are ignored.

Compensatory Motherhood and the Need to Blame

In the construction of motherhood and the idea of a "good mother," the model of self-sacrifice predominates. Sacrifice to the "child" is symbolic of good citizenship: in service to the values of the society, the state, the group. Motherhood, as it is conceptualized in both gay and straight contexts, is supposed to be compensatory. Mothers are supposed to make up to their children for the pain and inequity in the world. But if we are really feminists then we know that the mother is also a person. She has a body, she has a sexuality, she has dreams for her own life. She has things she wants and needs. Up until a certain point, these desires cannot be priorities over protecting and developing her children. But this information has to be integrated into the children's world views so that they don't grow up to become adults, especially adult men, who expect and believe that women are in the world to serve them for the remainder of those women's lives. And, just as importantly, the experience of the middle-aged single mother who is deprived of equal adult intimacy as a place to learn about herself and her sexuality is widespread, while its root causes are underexplored, and its impact on her peers is undiscussed.

In 2011, *The Chronicle of Higher Education* reported that almost a fifth of men between the ages of twenty-five and thirty-four still lived with their parents. And this number does not include men who live outside the home but are financially supported by their parents or female partners. For women, it's only 10 percent who live at home at the same age. Even though men earn more than women for the same work, twice as many women leave the family to take care of themselves and others. There could be a number of reasons for this. Women may experience more domination within family structures, while men have more freedom. Women may be expected to work for and take care of men in the family while men get to make their own decisions about how to behave. Whatever the causes, adult men stay home and often that means that their mothers take care of them. Often, with single mothers, or emotionally absent fathers, this leaves the adult son as the mother's primary partner in domestic intimacy—the person she talks to at the end of the day, the person around whom she financially and emotionally organizes her life. Just as this kind of man has trouble being an equal caretaker for the rest of the world, it is also distorting for the mother.

Taking race and class into account, educated white men are the most employable people in America, Canada, and Europe. For some adult men of color or those who are undereducated, unemployment keeps them home, and for some adult men who are white and well-educated, staying home keeps them unemployed. While the oppression or demeaning of women inside the family makes women individuate and leave, it is the diminishment of women in the family that keeps men infantilized. Homophobia in families may also have produced more independent thinking and drive to express for queer family members while more normative assimilation into family structures may produce more conformity to gender roles. In households where brothers, sons, male community members, fathers, and exes are exploiting the mothers, mothers are supposed to *compensate* for the burden of normative and reasonable expectations of responsibility and accountability. What emotional rights do queer mothers have in the face of adult children? Especially adult male children? Are they expected to sacrifice everything forever? Writing about white families in the bourgeois class, *The Atlantic* columnist Hanna Rosin wrote in "The Overprotected Kid" in March 2014:

> One common concern of parents these days is that children grow up too fast. But sometimes it seems as if children don't get the space to grow up at all; they just become adept at mimicking the habits of adulthood. As Hart's research shows, children used to gradually take on responsibilities, year by year. They crossed the road, went to the store; eventually some of them got small neighborhood jobs. Their pride was wrapped up in competence and independence, which grew as they tried and mastered activities they hadn't known how to do the previous year. But these days, middle-class children, at least, skip these milestones. They spend a lot of time in the company of adults, so they can talk and think like them, but they never build up the confidence to be truly independent and self-reliant.

Rosin's piece goes on to offer some provocative new ideas. Despite how enriching it may be for a child to learn from their parents, school should be starting them on the journey of learning how to individuate, how to develop their own world, their own habits, responsibilities, and relationships; how to live on their own, support themselves, and help others. They need to have their own secrets, dreams, private experiences, and independence. And so do their mothers, unless we think it is all right for a woman's emotional life to be over at age fifty. As Rosin's article makes clear, children who spend too much time with their parents and do not individuate may mimic adults and carry adult affect, vocabulary, and mannerisms, but it is a façade. They haven't truly grown up—i.e., learned how to take care of themselves and others. They become fearful and uncreative adults, even if they imitate adult gestures that signify boldness and creativity. "How lives unfold in a society reveals a tremendous amount about a society," Rosin writes.

The idea that mothers must distort their own lives in order to compensate for the world in the lives of their children is paramount. But many, many mothers also imagine that they are compensating for their own deprivations as a child. No one ever listened to her, so she produces a monologueing, "mansplaining" son. No one ever helped her, so she infantilizes her children throughout adulthood. She wanted to be a writer and had no parental encouragement, so she supports her child financially for years so he can write a book that he has no ability to create. Or she may labor long hours to provide a life in the private sector for her child that she never had, producing a privileged, entitled child with no idea how to do the labor that he is accustomed to receiving.

This mother/child relationship that attempts to compensate for the mother's own deprived childhood is also a projected substitute for the work of correcting, retrospectively, one's own pain. One of the fallacies in a queer context is the assumption that queer mothers are somehow inherently feminist because they managed to separate themselves from heterosexuality. Being attracted to or even loving a woman has no relationship to treating her, and by extension one's self, as a person who matters. On one hand, lesbians give each other meaning in private, and yet this requires a transcendence of lifelong messages about women's lack of worth. Treating another women with decency, care, forgiveness, and flexibility is certainly not an automatic impulse.

There is also the adjacent idea, comforting but false, that the sons and daughters of lesbians are inherently feminist. Because they don't have models of intimate male power at home, somehow they are supposed to extrapolate a connection about refusing male privilege in the world. But feminism, or full and complete personhood for women, is an idea. And each human being has to do the work to explore it, build a relationship to it, and understand what their own changes must be in order to be part of it. "*On ne nait pas feminist, on le deviant*" (one is not born a feminist, but becomes it), said Simone de Beauvoir. I know a man who advertises himself as an "eco-feminist," but he expects his mother and her female partner to clean up after him. So actually he is neither eco nor a feminist. His mother thinks he is because in her birth family, women shopped, prepped, cooked, served, and cleaned up after men at every meal. Her son cooks his own eggs in the morning and sometimes makes them for her. So she believes he is a feminist, even though he often leaves the dirty pan in the sink.

Politics is a consequence of how a person understands their experience. In that way, the son of a feminist is not a feminist. He may become one, but he would have to learn how not to exploit women, including his mother. And in this world, it is the responsibility of his peers to make sure he understands what that actually means. His friends have to parent him as well as his actual parents, because that is where real values are established, in the conflict between what our families tell us and the reality of the world. We have to be separate from our families in order to come to this evaluation, in which we build our own understandings and values, taken as much from critical understandings of what we have experienced as what we haven't.

On the news, as I am writing this, a man in Romania stole some masterwork paintings (Monet, etc.) and hid them in his mother's home as part of a fantasy that somehow he would figure out how to sell these paintings to pay off his debts. His mother was afraid that he would get caught, so she destroyed the paintings by burning them in her oven. This woman decided that she should punish all of civilization present and future, as well as herself, rather than let her son be responsible for the consequences of his actions. There is something in the cultural apparatus that has imbued this woman with the self-perception that if she hurts the world and herself and maintains her son in a state of dependency, then she is a "good mother."

Every person needs to be parented. By this I mean that every person needs to be helped, encouraged, and supported in becoming accountable to themselves and others. To not be threatened by taking other people into account. To not be frightened of difference.

Now, we have known for a long time that the state aligns with families based on class and race. Families that need financial help and support, or that face the consequences of oppression and social assault, are often defeated by the state. Queer families that also fit the Supremacy class and race profile are increasingly invited into this nationalist deal with the devil. Today, the family is a new queer nation-state, the thing to be positioned as the center of the culture, the civilizing force, the most important.

As the writer Dudley Saunders told me:

> We're training our families that they are not part of a world, they don't have responsibilities to others. That they are superior and trump all other human relationships. It's almost like royalty. You train the family that only people within the structure exist. In this way the family structure is something that actually makes society impossible.

The phrase "chosen family" makes me quake with fear. I prefer the far more valuable term, "friend." A true friend can be a blood or legal relation. They can be in the same clique or neighborhood or workplace. They can belong to the same racial, cultural, religious, or national group. But a true "friend" asks the right questions about category itself, and thereby transcends it. A true friend has the conversation.

PART THREE | Supremacy/Trauma and the Justification of Injustice: The Israeli War on Gaza

Chapter Eight | **Watching Genocide Unfold in Real Time:** Gaza through Facebook and Twitter, June 2-July 23, 2014

My rights cannot be subject to your feelings.
—SA'ED ATSHAN

IN OUR CONTEMPORARY MOMENT, one human disaster rooted in over-identification with the "bad" group or unself-critical family that blatantly violates human decency is the Occupation of Palestine and the suppression and murder of Palestinians by Israelis. Like all creations of the other as monster, Jewish Supremacy is a pure manifestation of "loyalty" without opposition; a creation rooted in the mirror of Supremacy and Trauma. One of the most glaring and lethal applications of this false accusation of harm as a justification for cruelty in turn is the way Palestinian resistance to occupation has been pathologized instead of supported. As I wrote the first draft of this book over the summer of 2014, the world watched as a distinctly unjustifiable series of acts of destruction was unleashed by Israel on Gaza. And as it unfolded, all of the elements of false accusation were at play.

What made this assault different from previous events against Palestinians, or against other oppressed but pathologized people, was that it unfolded before our eyes, live on social media. Whereas in the past we were dependent on corporate television and print press to provide information and context, the killing of Gaza took place on Twitter and Facebook, at a level of graphic detail that made it possible to bypass official reports. Palestinians, who had been shunned and were therefore invisible to Americans, were now being seen and heard at the apex of human suffering. The events were brought to bear in a manner that was not available during other historical turning points of cruelty. As Palestinian-American filmmaker Nadia Awad said to me, "Imagine if the Holocaust had unfolded on Facebook, or slavery." I thought about the Warsaw Ghetto uprising and liquidation, a direct comparison to the killing in Gaza, displayed live for all to see.

Here I want to set out *the order of events* or "geneology" and recreate my own very personal experience of how I take in information from Twitter, and the expression of the digestion of that information via Facebook. This is to share my own individual recognition process through the first weeks of the massacre, from June 2 to July 24, 2014, in order to underline the terms by which distorted thinking, projection, shunning, and the insistence on the other in totalizing "monster" terms were visible, and how resistance to Abuse was reconstituted as its justification.

The Strategy of False Accusation

June 2, 2014

Two *New York Times* reporters assigned to Israel, Jodi Rudoren and Isabel Kershner, shared a byline on coverage of a groundbreaking event: "With Hope For Unity, Abbas Swears In a New Palestinian Government." After seven years of conflict, Prime Minister Ismail Haniya of Hamas, democratically elected to represent Gaza, and President Mahmoud Abbas of Fatah, democratically elected to represent the West Bank, declared that "a black page in history has been turned forever." The wording of the *Times* headline underlined not only the paper's bias towards Abbas and Fatah, but their insistence that his benevolence was at the core of this unification. After seven years of bitter division, Abbas confirmed, "Today we restore our national unity. We are all loyal to Palestine." The ceremony came six weeks after the Palestine Liberation Organization, dominated by Fatah, signed a pact with Hamas paving the way for one united government.

"The Palestinians," the *Times* reported, "are also bracing for punitive sanctions by Israel." The authors quote Benjamin Netanyahu, the Prime Minister of Israel, declaring in response that "Israel will not conduct diplomatic negotiations with a Palestinian government backed by Hamas." As a practitioner of shunning, Netanyahu would not negotiate because he would not have unilateral control. Secretary of State John Kerry, on the other hand, was clear that the United States would work with the new unity government. "Israel," said an advisor to Netanyahu, "is deeply disappointed by the US position." The *Times* goes on to report that the new government would be led by Prime Minister Rami Hamdallah, a linguist and former university president. The sixteen ministers in his cabinet included three women and four Gaza residents, who were barred by Israel from traveling to attend the swearing-in. Haniya, the outgoing Hamas prime minister, said, "We showed high flexibility in making this government successful. The government's task will not be easy, and we will cooperate with it and embrace it." Abbas acknowledged that Israeli sanctions were forthcoming. "We are aware that we will face difficulties," the *Times* reported him saying. "But the train of reconciliation has set off, and we will not go back to conflict and schism again."

June 12

Ten days later, three Jewish teenagers from Kfar Etzion, an illegal settlement in the West Bank between Bethlehem and Hebron, were kidnapped while hitchhiking home from their yeshiva. Later it would be revealed that one, Gilad Shaer, made a desperate cellphone call to Moked 100, Israel's 911. When the tape reached the security services the next morning—neglected for hours by Moked 100 staff—the teen was heard whispering, "They've kidnapped me" ("hatfu oti"), followed by shouts of "Heads down," then gunfire, two groans, more shots, then singing in Arabic. That evening, searchers found the kidnappers' abandoned, torched Hyundai with eight bullet holes and the boys' DNA. There was no question that they had been killed. But the Israeli government lied about their knowledge that the young men were dead. Instead they publicly blamed the kidnappings on "Hamas" and began to "search" for the boys as if they were still alive.

"This is the result of bringing a terrorist organization into the government," Netanyahu told John Kerry.

In fact, the crime had been committed by members of a local Hebron clan who did belong to Hamas, but were acting without the agreement or knowledge of Hamas leadership. Their original plan was to kidnap one Israeli and hold him for prisoner exchange; when they picked up one hitchhiker, he invited his two other friends to come along, and the kidnappers' Hebrew was too limited to separate them. The bungled plan backfired completely when the cell phone call was made and all three young men were murdered right then in cold blood. Khaled Meshal, the exiled political leader of Hamas, who in principle sees kidnapping for prisoner exchange as a legitimate action, said of Hamas leadership: "We were not aware of this action in advance." He said he "learned of it from Israeli investigations."

In Israel, grief and anger over the boys' disappearance grew rapidly as the lie that they were still alive stretched into a second and third week. Demonstrations took place across the country and in Jewish communities around the world. The worried parents appeared constantly on television pleading for their children's return. One mother spoke to the United Nations in Geneva to beg for her son's life. Jews everywhere were in anguish over the government's depiction of the monster, the ongoing, overwhelming totalizing threat of barbaric Arab terror plaguing Israel.

The so-called "search" centered initially on the Hebron area in the southern West Bank. Israeli soldiers forced their way into Palestinian homes, and widespread home invasions started to be reported throughout the West Bank. These were accompanied by mass arrests of West Bank residents said to be members of Hamas. The Israelis' actions quickly escalated into the largest military operation in the West Bank since the Second Intifada. Over the next eighteen days, under the pretext of "searching" for the Hamas members who were supposedly holding the teenaged boys, 400 Palestinians were arrested, 5,000 homes were raided, and six Palestinians were murdered by Israeli gunfire.

These actions reminded me of the anti-Jewish pogroms initiated against my poor ancestors in Russian *shtetls* or ghettos during the time of the Czar, or any pogrom-like event where large numbers of civilians are punished for the actions of a few. In this case, Israel's false claims that Hamas was holding the teenagers hostage when the government knew that they were dead inflamed already paranoid fascist elements in the Jewish population. Vigilantism and street rampages were reported widely by Palestinians.

June 29

An Israeli air attack on a rocket squad killed a Hamas operative. Hamas protested. The next day it responded with a rocket barrage, its first since 2012. The ceasefire was over.

July 1

Two days later, after three weeks of constant violation, arrest, and mob violence, the Israeli government announced that they had found the young men's bodies under some stones. Benjamin Netanyahu, in his announcement, cited the modernist Hebrew poet Hayim Nahman Bialik: "Vengeance ... for the blood of a small child, / Satan has not yet created." He added, "Hamas is responsible and Hamas will pay." The Prime Minister's office tweeted the lines as well. That same day the PLO's Hanan Ashrawi told Al Jazeera that the "Israeli escalation has already taken place, and now they have an excuse of further escalation."

Ali Abunimah
I have never heard BBC World Service cover a Palestinian funeral, let alone in the depth and emotion it covered the funeral of 3 Israelis.

Ali Abunimah
Media reflect the values of apartheid and colonialism: the lives and deaths of members of settler society more newsworthy and noteworthy.

Rania Khalek
Meanwhile the Israeli govt can issue bellicose calls for retribution against the whole Palestinian population with little challenge.

Also on that momentous first of July, a seventeen-year-old Palestinian named Muhammed Abu-Khdeir from the East Jerusalem neighborhood of Shu'fat was abducted by a racist Jewish gang. They poured gasoline down his throat and set him on fire.

July 2

My friend, a Palestinian architect, posted on Facebook:

> The extremist 'lynch mobs' attacking Palestinians on the streets of Jerusalem are not an anomaly. They do not stem from a state of exception but precisely from the everyday, where Palestinians are second and third class residents of the city, disposable, voiceless and 'Arab.' The same reality that allows for home demolitions and extra-judicial arrests in Palestinian areas of Jerusalem allows for extremist mobs to roam the streets and interventions occur only when the world is watching.

It was a runaway train. An entire nation having a borderline episode—impulsive acting out, justified by lies and the removal of any discussion of their own behavior. Complete shunning of Palestinian perspective, without any justification, cued the negative community to obey by either feeding the flames or standing by in silent acquiescence. And what did the surrounding world community do? Objections to this scapegoating and unmerited punishment and dehumanization were minimal. UN human rights spokeswoman Ravina Shamdasani said, "We urge all parties to refrain from punishing individuals for offences they have not personally committed or by imposing collective penalties." But little more than that whimper was heard.

A few hours later, Israel admitted to thirty-four air raids on the Gaza Strip. As governments around the world remained silent, the first significant response came from the Algerian World Cup soccer team, who donated their salaries to the people of Gaza.

July 3
My Facebook:

Algerian Soccer Team, The Conscience of the World.

At this point, the world still did not know that the Israeli government was lying about Hamas' role in the kidnapping/murders. But many things about their story did not seem right.

My Facebook:

Why would any political organization think this was a good strategic idea?
After all, Hamas had never before engaged in kidnappings of this nature. They had captured an Israeli soldier, Gilad Shalit, as a prisoner of war, but had no history of reaching out and initiating something like this. Shalit, after all, was not kidnapped. He was a captured soldier and was not killed, but instead was held until the Israelis agreed to a prisoner exchange. Also, when Hamas did something they traditionally claimed responsibility for their actions. And most importantly, they had just formed a unity government, so how would it serve them to commit such a useless killing?

July 4
Muhammed's fifteen-year-old cousin, Tariq, who was visiting his family from his home in Florida, was seized and beaten by Israeli police.

Electronic Intifada
Thousands turn out for Jerusalem funeral of murdered Palestinian teen Muhammad Abu Khudair pic.twitter.com/gx5hbUaUk6

Linda Sarsour
OUTRAGEOUS! Israel holds US citizen high school student without charge after nearly beating him to death

Ali Abunimah

teenager nearly beaten to death by Israeli police, video shows

Electronic Intifada

"There is no protection for Palestinians from the police or soldiers or army" says dad of US teen beaten in Jerusalem http://bit.ly/1msVwPY

July 5

The *New York Times* finally reports on the burning alive of Muhammed Abu Khdeir, but those of us on Facebook and Twitter and readers of Electronic Intifada (the daily web news source propelled by Chicago-based Palestinian refugee Ali Abunimah) already knew. We had all seen footage from security cameras showing two men forcing Muhammed into a gray Hyundai. Protests by Palestinians erupted that evening in Nazareth and nearby villages, resulting in injuries and thirty-three arrests. The next day, Hamas fired rockets into southern Israel. The Times coverage identified the three settlers: "Eyal Yifrach, 19; Naftali Fraenkel, 16, who also held United States citizenship; and Gilad Shaar, 16." But further in the article, the *Times* reported that "during a recent crackdown in the West Bank, six Palestinians were killed." No ages or names were given.

Habib Battah

For @nytimes dead Palestinians don't have names.

Jewish Daily Forward

Aunt calls beaten Florida cousin of Palestinian revenge victim 'fun-loving' all-American boy http://jd.fo/r4Kb1

Remi Kanazi

Is there a gag order on fair coverage of the shameful brutality that is being exacted against Palestinians? It seems that way

Palestine Video

Israeli crimes in Hebron included Israeli occupation soldiers forcing a child (who doesn't want to be identified) to drink their urine

sarah colborne
More than 1000 now protesting outside the Israeli embassy in London - and growing

Mondoweiss
PHOTO: Israeli soldier aims sniper rifle at Bethlehem protest thru opening in Separation Wall

NYU SJP
Why doesn't @rudoren mention that Tariq was denied medical treatment for 5 hours?

July 6

On a Sunday, Israel unleashed ten air strikes on the Gaza Strip. Nerdeen Mohsen, one of my students from The College of Staten Island, Students for Justice in Palestine, posted on Facebook from East Jerusalem:

Yesterday settlers stormed the issawiyeh and hid in every possible place you could hide in, no one knows why they did it. If they were just watching, planning something, attempting another kidnapping, we don't know. Settlers are scarier than the army here because they kidnap and torture openly. I mean the army does that too but not as flagrantly as settlers... I don't know how to explain it honestly. There is nothing holding the settlers back, they do what they want without facing any repercussions. Because of this and recent events my grandma is making me leave Palestine tomorrow): I feel like my heart is being ripped to shreds

Why am I forced to leave my own country out of fear from colonizers???It's not like I could've stayed more than 3 months though because the only reason I was able to enter was through my American citizenship. Forever being reminded that I can't visit or live in my own country without permission and authority of those who took it. Being a Palestinian is confusing and painful.

That same day, Gideon Levy, a writer for the Israeli newspaper *Haaretz*, published an article on the same phenomenon called

"Our Wretched Jewish State."

> The youths of the Jewish state are attacking Palestinians in the streets of Jerusalem, just like gentile youths used to attack Jews in the streets of Europe. The Israelis of the Jewish state are rampaging on social networks, displaying hatred and a lust for revenge, unprecedented in its diabolic scope ... These are the children of the nationalistic and racist generation—Netanyahu's offspring. For five years now they have been hearing nothing but incitement, scaremongering and supremacy over Arabs ... Not one humane word. No commiseration or equal treatment.

Inherent in Levy's critique are all the tactics of Conflict and Abuse. Not only grotesque overstatement of harm and projection as a justification for cruelty; not only a lack of self-criticism or a refusal to acknowledge one's role; not only the persistent encouragement of a negative community based on Supremacy bonds to blame, scapegoat, shun, and punish. But also the clear evidence that these tactics reflect and produce escalation and distorted thinking, which create long-term cumulative consequences of extreme injustice and destruction. Here we see the phenomena of asserting one's own pain as exclusive and paramount, and as the justification for cruelty towards others. Here, again, is pain from the past being blamed on the wrong party. Levy articulates the lack of empathy that we have been discussing:

> The media in the Jewish state wallows in the murder of three yeshiva students while almost entirely ignoring the fates of several Palestinian youths of the same age who have been killed by army fire over the last few months usually for no reason ... In the Jewish state there is pity and human feelings only for Jews, rights only for the Chosen people.

And then Levy addresses shunning:

> The new sabra (Jew born in Israel) ... has never met his Palestinian counterpart, but knows everything about him—the sabra knows he is a wild animal, intent only on killing him; that he is a monster, a terrorist.

There is that word again: "monster." Levy shows that when pushed to its ultimate expression, the insistence on shunning as a tool of

Supremacy creates fascism. And that the bully, the Supremacist that we discussed earlier, is no longer the spoiled son in a family controlling his mother, or the arrogant man in a small town whose partner ensures that no one tells him a truth that would challenge his sense of his own perfection. This bully, the one who can't ever apologize, has now become Benjamin Netanyahu. His is a clear path from the person who can't negotiate and so they blame, from the person who won't face their own participation and so they shun, from the person who calls the police rather than face and deal with conflict, to the person who calls out the army and kills civilians while blaming it all on "Hamas." And just as the person who overstates harm contrives resistance to their unilateral bullying as being, itself, a threat, Netanyahu commits an injustice based on false notions of loyalty. According to Levy:

> Being left wing or a seeker of justice in the Jewish state is deemed a crime, civil society is considered treacherous, true democracy an evil.

And the "bad" friends, the negative community, and the unself-critical family embed their values in an inescapable cocoon.

لينة
Zahi Abu Hamed was killed today after Israeli settlers ran him over with their car in #Tulkarem

Diana Buttu
When Palestinians are murdered by Israelis its called "nationalist" or "aberrations" not part of state sanctioned policy. #apartheid

sarah schulman
Demonstrations against Israeli violence are taking place all over the world. There will be one in NY on Wed at 5:30.

When We Need to Be "Abused," the Truth Doesn't Matter

July 7

After more than a week of intensive air strikes, Israeli Defense Force ground troops were launched. I started to focus, increasingly, on what I was hearing from Palestinians in person, on social media, and through their own press and those in solidarity. The more attention I paid, the more inadequate the US press became. I discovered that information that I reposted daily from originating sources was rarely included in the *Times* or on NPR. For example, none of the following appeared in the mainstream press.

Facebook: Report from Palestine in the last hour:

--Mass arrests continue. A wave of arrests now in Jdaidet al-Maker and Kafr Yasif in northern Palestine. More than ten arrested so far, and many who were not arrested have received summons to the police station.

--Four Palestinians have been arrested in #Akka before the demonstration even began! The Palestinian residents of Akka have been struggling against policies of Judiazation of the city for many years now. State-owned housing management companies are dishing out eviction orders as Israeli and foreign development companies buy up blocks of homes and undertake development projects across the city.

In fact, the more I hear Palestinian and solidarity voices, the more distorted and untrue mainstream US media is revealed to be.

Palestine Video
Report: Israeli warplanes carried out 85 airstrikes on Gaza Strip since dawn this morning (local Palestine time)

OccPal-Gaza
Huge explosion Gaza 857pm

Dan Williams
Preparing for possible Gaza escalation, Israeli military calls up 1,500 reserve troops and raises state of alert - @TalLevRam @GLZRadio

July 8

Remi Kanazi
Sad truth. Israel has executed 1 Palestinian every hour, today. #Gaza

Al Jazeera English
Israel vows 'lengthy' offensive in Gaza http://aje.me/1qGslJb

July 9

Democracy Now!
Today Marks the 10th Anniversary of ICJ Ruling on Illegality of Israeli Settlements, Separation Wall in West Bank http://owl.li/yXOXz

Ali Abunimah
CHILDREN MAY BE DYING IN GAZA, BUT HEY THERE'S AN AWESOME CLUB SCENE IN TEL AVIV SO IT'S OKAY.

July 10

Finally an article appeared in the Jewish newsapaper *The Forward*, formerly a Socialist daily, now publishing in New York in English under the leadership of Sam Norwich, a Yiddishist. Aside from some articles criticizing the Boycott, Divestment and Sanctions movement, I had not paid much attention to *The Forward* since the days my grandmother read it in Yiddish. This piece, "How Politics and Lies Triggered an Unintended War in Gaza," was written by someone named JJ Goldberg.

> The government had known almost from the beginning that the boys were dead. It maintained the fiction that it hoped to find them alive as a pretext to dismantle Hamas' West Bank operations.

Goldberg reported that Prime Minister Benjamin Netanyahu had immediately placed a gag order on the deaths. Journalists who heard rumors were told the Shin Bet wanted the gag order so their search would be unhindered. For the sake of the public, the official word was that Israel was "acting on the assumption that they're alive."

> It was, simply put, a lie ... It was clear from the beginning that the kidnappers weren't acting on orders from Hamas leadership in Gaza or Damascus. Hamas' Hebron branch—more a crime family than a clandestine organization—had a history of acting without the leaders' knowledge, sometimes against their interests. Yet Netanyahu repeatedly insisted Hamas was responsible for the crime and would pay for it ... His rhetoric raised expectations that after demolishing Hamas in the West Bank he would proceed to Gaza. Hamas in Gaza began preparing for it. The Israeli right—settler leaders, hardliners in his own party—began demanding it.

So there it was. Netanyahu lied about the order of events, and projected blame onto Hamas so that Israel could avoid facing the truth about itself. The bad family, an Israeli public primed for racism, hatred, and vengeance against the wrong people, propelled the hysteria and false blame. Goldberg went on to report that

> The last seven years have been the most tranquil in Israel's history. Terror attacks are a fraction of the level during the nightmare intifada years—just six deaths in all of 2013. But few notice. The staged agony of the kidnap search created, probably unintentionally, what amounts to a mass, worldwide attack of post-traumatic stress flashback.

Goldberg reported that when the bodies were found on July 1, the cabinet meeting "turned into a shouting match." Right-wing ministers demanded that the army reoccupy Gaza and destroy Hamas, now that there was popular momentum.

> In Gaza, leaders went underground. Rocket enforcement squads stopped functioning and jihadi rocket firing spiked. Terror squads began preparing to counterattack Israel through tunnels. One tunnel exploded on June 19 in an apparent work accident, killing five Hamas gunmen,

convincing some in Gaza that the Israeli assault had begun while reinforcing Israeli fears that Hamas was plotting terror all along.

July 11

sarah schulman
Yiddish paper, Jewish Daily Forward exonerates Hamas from settler killings, shows Israel bombed first. http://m.forward.com/

Ali Abunimah
Imagine bombing the refugee camps of the people whose land you stole. That is what Zionism means to its Palestinian victims.

Gaza Youth Break Out
Tonight was the night of the mosques. Israeli F16s targeted 8 mosques in #Gaza and destroyed them completely!

July 12

Electronic Intifada posted a remarkable video, submitted by Ronnie Barkan of Boycott From Within, showing elected Arab Members of the Israeli Knesset being shut down and thrown out of the Parliamentary chambers because they were trying to enter the names of the then one hundred Gazans murdered by Israeli bombs into the record. When Ibrahim Sarsour of the United Arab List party condemned the attacks, Moshe Feiglin, the deputy speaker of the Knesset, ordered guards to forcibly remove Sarsour from the podium and expel him from the room. "Those who refer to Israeli soldiers as murderers will not stay here another second," Feiglin said. Representative Ahmed Tibi of the Arab Movement for Change was also expelled. Finally, Masud Ghanayim, as he was being forcibly removed, shouted on tape: "You have massacred, you have murdered! And in Gaza up to this moment you murder. The army is an army of murderers and you may kick me off the stage." Electronic Intifada quoted a former Israeli general, Elazar Stern, who said that "saying IDF soldiers are murderers is incitement." This of course is the classic paradigm: that the telling of the truth is the crime, not the truth itself. And then he used the rhetoric of the compensatory mothers as a stand-in for nationalism and vectors of male control. "We only shoot when we know that one mother is destined to cry," he said. "I'm telling you that if a mother has to cry I'd rather it be the mother of the person trying to kill me and not my mother." Using the typical bullying tactic, he blamed the object of the cruelty for causing the bullying. In the nationalist/militaristic version of hurting someone because "they need 'help,'" Stern said, "When we shoot at a house in Gaza, it is also in order for Gazans to live better ... I'm telling you that the missiles we shoot into Gaza are not only to save lives in Tel Aviv and Ashkelon but also to save lives in Gaza." According to the United Nations, 77 percent of those first hundred Gazans whose lives he saved by killing them were civilians. Twenty-one were children.

July 12

sarah schulman
Most insane NY Times headline of the week: "In Gaza, Airstrikes and Economy Make for Tense Ramadan." How dishonest can a newspaper be?

susan abulhawa
There is no "cycle of violence" or "two sides". It's another Israeli massacre of Palestinians. http://fb.me/34yePtnWt

Ali Abunimah
Ynet: "IDF" to expel Palestinians from northern occupied Gaza Strip and invade area http://www.ynetnews.com/articles/0,7340,L-4542321,00.html

Palestine Video
Israel is about to commit a large scale ethnic cleansing of the Palestinians, under threat of leave or die

Tweet_Palestine
Breaking: doctors in #Gaza hospital confirm that Israel is using illegal weapon DIME Illegal lethal genotoxic in its attack on #Gaza

Max Blumenthal
reports from Al Shifa - Israel using DIME weapons on Gazacivilianshttps://twitter.com/mogaza/status/488080334802518016 ...What's DIME? http://www.independent.co.uk/news/world/middle-east/tungsten-bombs-leave-israels-victims-with-mystery-wounds-1418910.html

Al Jazeera English
#AJOpinion: The US should admit responsibility for the #Gaza crisis - by @NoraInPalestine http://aje.me/W72XS1

Scott Roth
Israel really covers all the bases: it destroys your home, kicks you off your land, keeps you a refugee then kills your family.

Tom Léger
Bertolt Brecht — 'As crimes pile up, they become invisible.'

July 13

My Facebook
So, what is on the front page of the NY Times today about Gaza? NOTHING.
Do you feel lied to yet?

My Facebook
Since I get info from Palestine I have seen many photographs of murdered people: children with their faces blown away, their torsos torn. I've decided not to repost them because if you don't get what's going on by now, images of their extreme suffering won't make a difference. I can't post those photos of Israelis in lawn chairs cheering the bombing of Gaza. I can't stand that either.

Omar Ghraieb
its a blessing to witness the sunrise in #Gaza, birds chirping, but blood cover the streets & smell of death is everywhere! #GazaUnderAttack

Jehan Alfarra
Israeli naval commandos clashed with Palestinian resistance in what appeared to be the first ground assault so far #Gaza #Israel #Palestine

Tayari Jones
I'm trying to figure out why what's going on in Gaza isn't connecting with the American public.

Ali Abunimah
The slaughter in Gaza is not front page news for @nytimes. Imagine if entire Israeli families, synagogues wiped out. #GazaUnderAttack

F.
Oussama Hamdan for Hamas: we have received threats from #Israel through Egyptian intelligence that a third of #Gaza will be flattened.

Urgent From Gaza
All over the world people are moving for #Gaza It's time to stop this aggression. #GazaUnderAttack

bangpound ebooks
Amnesty International calls for arms embargo on #Israel http://amnesty.ie/news/israelgaza-un-must-impose-arms-embargo-and-mandate-international-investigation-civilian-death-t ... (that's BDS in case you don't know) #GazaUnderAttack

Rania Khalek
Israel is deliberately killing civilians in Gaza. The targeting of families and children is systematic & intentional. http://electronicintifada.net/blogs/rania-khalek/israel-deliberately-targeting-civilians-gaza ...

July 14

My Facebook
Today's gesture. I signed a petition begging Israeli academics to take a stand against the war,

My Facebook
"You can't defend yourself when you're militarily occupying someone else's land. That's not defense." - Noam Chomsky

JewishVoice4PeaceNYC
700+ academics sign open letter urging Israeli counterparts to speak out. http://buff.ly/1m8OA4y @sarahschulman3 @ rfalk13

Nancy Kricorian
New Museum confirms Palestinian artist barred by Israel from attending show http://news.artnet.com/art-world/palestinian-artist-barred-from-attending-new-museum-show-61214 ...

Global Voices
Leading Muslim-American Activists Boycott the #White-HouseIftar, Refusing to Break Bread with Obama http://bit.ly/1qZDSDC

Nena
thank you for speaking out against Israeli aggression and for #bds @TaliShapiro

July 15

Rihanna became the first US pop star to respond to the murder of Gaza. She tweeted #FreePalestine, and then deleted it eight minutes later. But 7,000 people had already retweeted it.

Did Rihanna act naïvely, unaware of the political context? Did she simply, humanly, recognize the injustice? Did she understand that she was alone in expressing this view and that her celebrity coterie was especially silent? Was she informed that American history is filled with blacklists, official and unofficial shunning of both celebrities and civilians who take political stances on behalf of people without power? The irony of Rhianna, perhaps America's best known battered woman, transgressing a pervasive fear of loss of currency is notable. When questioned by the media, her response was, "I didn't even realize I tweeted #FreePalestine." She then corrected herself and tweeted, "Let's pray for peace and a swift end to the Israeli-Palestinian conflict. Is there any hope?" Her message was accompanied by a photograph of the backs of two men with their arms around each other, faces obscured; one is wearing a kafiya and the other a yamacha. It's an image of something that almost never takes place. I look at the picture wondering if they are both models.

Ali Abunimah
A handful of Israeli academics responds to call to condemn Gaza slaughter http://bit.ly/1n3LpBg via @intifada

Max Blumenthal
According to Jodi @Rudoren, a "quiet night" consists of Israel bombing 25 targets, killing 5:

Electronic Intifada
Foreign activists maintaining a presence at al-Wafa hospital in Gaza City as Israel threatens to strike it again http://bit.ly/W8Mlcn

Ali Abunimah
The slaughter in Gaza is not just Israel's crime. It is also an Obama crime. Obama could pull the plug but chooses to let the blood flow.

Electronic Intifada
Brian Eno blasts BBC for treating Palestinians lives as "less valuable" http://bit.ly/1kQv5hD

July 16

Demonstrations erupt in Ramallah in the West Bank as people protesting Israeli murders in Gaza were stopped by Palestinian Authority security forces. Then four young boys playing soccer on the Gaza beach are murdered by Israeli soldiers on camera. The New York Times' original headline, "4 Young Boys Killed Playing on Gaza Beach," is changed to "Boys Drawn to Gaza Beach and Into Center of Mideast Strife."

My Facebook
TODAY'S LETTER FROM A PALESTINIAN FRIEND:
"Schulman, the situation has become unbearable! I burst into bitter tears early, feeling completely hateful and helpless.. I don't know what else to do.. The murder of the 4 children at the beach just broke me. Im heart broken..

We are going on Anger demonstration on friday in Haifa. Will i get hurt? Will i get arrested? Will fear for my life and those marching against the shameful oppression along with me??

I dont know what to do! I fear for my son.. How will he grow up in this place??

Will send u updates from the demo And a link about the boys murdered on Gaza's beach, in their last attempt to escape Israel's missiles! I guess that even when they decided to swim for it, israel got them!"

My Facebook
I wish I could volunteer to stand trial in the world court as an emblematic war criminal whose taxes paid for the spilling of Palestinian blood. As a child, during the war in Vietnam, we saw murdered children on television and in Life magazine. But through my twitter feed and video links I am seeing tiny mangled bodies, and wailing destroyed adults all day, everyday.

JewishVoiceForPeace
Thousands protest for #Gaza in Cape Town, South Africa

JewishVoiceForPeace
Activists from @ChicagoDivests & @ChicagoJVP protesting *inside* @Boeing headquarters in Chicago #Gaza

MECA
Where's the outrage? 8 children killed today in Gaza - http://eepurl.com/Y-UZD

Electronic Intifada
Human Rights Watch: Israel targeting "civilian structures and killing civilians in violation of the laws of war" http://bit.ly/1r4IhoP

#GazaInOur❤s
Sadly, very true. There has been NO break for #GazaUnderAttack They are shelled day & night! #Ramadan

Saroumane
10 000 south Africans united to show their support to #Gaza #FreePalestine

kerry washington
Heart breaking "@Newsweek: A 1st-hand account of deadly strike on #Gaza port that killed 4 children: http://bit.ly/1mhoUmy via @GuardianUS"

July 17

Aswat: Palestinian Gay Women:
REAL QUEER LIBERATION BEGINS WITH ALL FORMS OF DECOLONIZATION

In light of the ongoing brutal Israeli military aggression on Palestinians in Gaza, and the cruelty of Israeli Police Forces in oppressing acts of solidarity and resistance, we LGBTQ activists and organizations call allies around the world to take stand in solidarity with Palestinians and pressure Israel to Stop its aggression on Gazan civilians, End its Occupation of Palestinian Land and End its Apartheid regime.

Israel's current assault on Gaza - "Protective Edge" - is the third in the past 5 years! In late 2008 the Israeli assault dubbed "Cast Lead" murdered more than 1,400 People. During the 2012 assault 'Pillar of defence' more than 150 people were murdered!

To date, since July 8th, Israel has launched more than 3594 attacks on Gaza which have resulted in displacement of more than 117,468 Palestinians, the injury of 4563, and has cost the lives of over 736 people.

The torture and the brutal murder of young Mohammed Abu Khdeir in Jerusalem a few weeks ago, the "Price tag" actions against Palestinian homes and holy places, the house demolitions and the ongoing assault and murder in the Gaza strip are all different forms of the Zionist occupation and should all come to an end!

In particular, we urge activists to:

Join demonstrations against the Occupation and the current aggression on Gaza;

Use your social media to increase awareness of the situation in Palestine;

Join your local Palestine solidarity movement.

Queer activists must mobilize their communities around the world to take action to hold Israel accountable for its continued collective punishment and war crimes against Palestinian civilians.

"*None of us is free until all of us are free.*" Martin Luther King, Jr.

Rawya Rageh
Min of health spox in #Gaza says dozens taken to hospitals in north reportedly choking from some sort of gas

Tweet_Palestine
Israeli army are invading Al Aqsa Mosque they are firing at people there and Israeli army firing at youth marching in #Jerusalem streets

Electronic Intifada
Foreign activists maintaining a presence at al-Wafa hospital in Gaza City as Israel threatens to strike it again http://bit.ly/1p94GhA

Mohammed Omer
Terrifying bombing now from #Israeli warships

Ali Abunimah
"I've had many senior journalists at the BBC saying they simply can't get the Palestinian viewpoint across" http://bit.ly/WfifDW @intifada

Rania Khalek
Israel testing a new weapon?
RT @Mogaza: #Israeli warships is using missiles that explode in two locations. I never experienced this #Gaza

Suzanne Gardinier
MT @3arabawy Israeli historian Ilan Pappé ">>>but now we need, as never before, a strong BDS campaign..." #Israel http://goo.gl/0CISnm #Gaza

Mark Ruffalo
@joelakayaki @markruffalo Sorry, I thought blowing up Hospitals was something that all human beings could agree was off limits.
Retweeted by sarah schulman

Mohammed Omer
The airstrikes are hitting all directions of #Gaza City
no one knows what is the target!

Rania Khalek
Israeli ambassador in Canada allegedly blamed parents of 4 murdered Gaza children for letting them play on the beach https://twitter.com/tariqramadan/status/489954132959461378 ...

Electronic Intifada
UN: 900,000 people, half of Gaza population, "without water supply" http://bit.ly/1l906QO

 Bethany Horne

Ecuador recalls their ambassador to Israel! RT @RicardoPatinoEC Gobierno del Ecuador ha decidido llamar a consultas a su Embajador en Israel

July 18

Phyllis Bennis, a longtime activist for Palestine, published a piece in *The Nation* in which she wrote: "The Jewish community is, thankfully, now profoundly divided on the question of Israel." That same day, France becomes the first country to specifically ban pro-Palestine demonstrations.

 My Facebook

It's stunning to hear colleagues still struggle for some convoluted way to defend Israel or deflect responsibility and criticism. It's weird to see large swaths of people ignore what's happening or refuse to speak out because of their narcissism and self-interest at any cost. This is a key event that illuminates all of us and our relationships to cruelty. Do we fear it, identify with it, or interrupt it?

I started noticing some patterns on my social media feeds. Some posts produced hundreds of "likes," substantive comments, and intense interactions. People who would normally never have access to each other were communicating on my page. Some of them were extremely ignorant about Palestine. They were uncritical of the US media, they regurgitated *Hasbara* (Israeli government propaganda) without thinking it through for themselves. But I also saw huge swaths of people who had no interest in any of these related subjects. And of all the different communities of which I am a part, it is the theater people who were the most absent. Actors, directors, producers, designers, and others were almost uniformly silent. Occasionally, an actor outspoken on other political issues would click "like," but only after a hundred people or more had already done so as well. One actress, who also has opinions, messaged me privately. But people involved in public presentation and public image were hiding. Two powerful men in the theater world messaged me privately asking for some information, which I provided, but they didn't express their opinions publicly. It's true that the theater is a highly narcissistic and punitive business with little accountability, and the fear of blacklisting exists as a matter of course. But I found this lack of response barbaric.

Then there were those who justified Israel's cruelty and expressed unexplored, fixed group identities or false loyalties, regardless of the actual values Israel espouses. They saw everything through their racial/family-based group lens, which trumped the reality of what was happening. Many of these people, some of whom I had known for a long time, expressed racial clichés, cultural Supremacy ideologies, and all of the components of overstating harm in order to justify acting out with cruelty. To them, everything Israel did was right. It's like the big man in a small town who can never apologize, and is surrounded by a partner, family members, and friends who reinforce his sense of perfection at the expense of the scapegoat, who embodies his very real flaws. But now it was an entire country. With an unrestrained military.

Despite everything I knew about "bad" groups, about a desire of the Traumatized to seek alliance with bullies, about group shunning, about the paradigms of perfections that keep us from taking responsibility for our part, or the origins of projection in both Supremacy and Trauma—despite all this understanding, I was still shocked. I was frustrated and upset to read on social media that people I knew personally were justifying, and therefore identifying with, this cruelty unfolding before them. Just as I was shocked, overwhelmed, and frustrated to watch people in their own romantic and group relationships bully, shun, and refuse to be accountable.

But even more so than the perpetrators themselves, bystanders are extremely dangerous. Obviously ringleaders, initiators, and enforcers of group cruelty originate the negative action, but those who don't talk back, don't interrupt, don't say, "What you are doing is wrong" is what I find so offensive, even shocking. Israel sends 900 rockets in Gaza's direction and kills over a hundred Palestinians. No Israelis are killed. This is falsely called "both sides."

Both Supremacy and Traumatized behaviors are by definition the denial of nuance, the refusal to recognize complicity in creating problems, and the rejection of mutual responsibility for solutions. Since those who act out on these behaviors cannot tolerate difference, they produce unilateral stories based in a profound fear of ever being wrong. Instead, it is the bystanders who actively avoid the responsibility of intervention by invoking the theory of "both sides." This claim allows cowards an excuse not to act, not to confront the self-righteousness of the bullies. The Jewish Bully, like any bully, cannot be wrong, therefore cannot negotiate, and so defends their lack of self with a claim to moral superiority. The bystander refuses to engage them and instead insists that "time" will produce change, so that they don't have to. This false claim is intended to obscure their avoidance of responsibility to intervene in a way that facilitates resolution instead of conflict.

"How would you feel if you were Palestinian?" I asked bystanders over and over again. But it's a question they couldn't answer because the shunning kept the information about what Palestinians were thinking and feeling out of their realm of consideration. How does it feel to be the person you are ganging up on? Refusing to negotiate with? Scapegoating for issues you don't want to face about yourself? In the meantime, on my Twitter feed, very graphic photographs and videos were coming from Gaza, one after the other: children with their faces blown off, their torsos severed. I looked. I watched.

Gaza Youth Break Out
32 people got killed today so far... #Gaza

Democracy Now!
TODAY: Israel threatens to "significantly widen" its #Gaza ground invasion. @sharifkouddous reports from Gaza City.

Electronic Intifada
As number of children slaughtered by Israel mounts, efforts to justify the killing becoming more desperate http://bit.ly/1teJLMT

CAIA
"To employ "both sides" rhetoric completely misrepresents the situation. It is not "both sides" who take... http://fb.me/1pMutLMog

July 19

Abby Martin
Americans should be outraged they're sponsoring the brutal occupation & massacre in #Gaza by giving Israel billions in military aid every yr

'hmad
Palestinian sabotage power line reaching to settlements west of #Ramallah @RoadToPalestine #XXXXXX_XXXXX pic.twitter.com/R98DbgmEyT

Elizabeth Tsurkov
Far-right wingers just burned the Palestinian flag and beat policemen in Haifa. Via @chickos99

benwedeman
So far today, 62 people in #Gaza have been killed, the highest daily death toll so far. And the day has 2 hours left. #Palestine #Israel

Hamish Macdonald
Israeli military now confirms that fighters from Gaza made it into Israel disguised as Israeli soldiers earlier today

Matthew Vickery
Pro-Palestine protests & marches are now illegal in France, but that didn't stop 1000s from marching in Paris today.

gily stein@
Haifa demo about to end,Tel Aviv ended. extreme-right wing groups walking surrounding streets looking for people to beat up #antifa972 #Gaza

gily stein@
Haifa demonstrator- police won't let anti-war demo disperse, and yet does not protect demonstrators from right wing attacks #Gaza #antifa972

Palestine Video
an analyst said: "Israeli army invaded 400 hundred meters into Gaza Strip, Palestinian resistance infiltrated 4 km behind them" & attacked

rizwan ansari
Right now: hundreds demonstrating in Tel Aviv against the massacre in Gaza #GazaUnderAttack #antifa972 pic.twitter.com/IKkCFJRpsT

Remi Kanazi
Last 48 hours: Hamas kills 5 Israeli soldiers. Israel murders 110 men, women & children, bombs civilian infrastructure & cuts electricity

Palestine Video
people calling for help

Ali Abunimah
"It's time to stop saying this slaughter of children has anything to do with self-defense"

July 20

My Facebook
Another day of constant messages and photos of Palestinians being murdered (sixty yesterday alone), dead bodies, fingers, heads in the street. I still can't post them because I fear the indifference of others. I know that my Palestinian friends held a march in Haifa where they were confronted by very scary Jewish racists and nationalists. Very little real opposition by Jews in Israel to their own government. The US Senate votes 100 to 0 to support this cruel unjust mass murder, but then we always do, don't we? Here is the image I choose to share with you: An Al Jazeera reporter breaks down in tears on the air, unable to describe what he has experienced.

I shared a video, from Al Jazeera in Arabic, of a stunned young reporter strapped into a helmet and bulletproof vest standing in front of a vista of bombed homes and apartment buildings billowing smoke. He starts to speak to the camera, then trembles, falters, and finally breaks down in tears. This, after all, is what we who were actually paying attention were seeing all day long: people wailing, people screaming, people's hearts literally torn out. The Palestinians, whom we shunned for decades, whom we have silenced so we could blame, were now in our lives daily and they were crying.

Netanyahu accused Palestinians of displaying their "telegenically dead."

As for my friends in Palestine, I didn't want to bother them. I also didn't know what to say to them. I let everyone know that I was sending them love, and each one answered warmly and with kindness. It's not that I worried that they would be hurt; they had already been harmed, even if they were still alive. One friend from Haifa sent me a photograph of the "Anger" demonstration that she wrote to me about on July 16. In the photo, a young woman in a kafiya is being assaulted by five Israeli riot police. Five of them. I posted it with this caption:

> Here you see Siwar, the Staffperson for Aswat: Queer Palestinian Women being assaulted by Israeli police at demonstration in Haifa.

Later, I posted a ten-minute video of the same demonstration. This was not in Gaza, but in Israel, the place that many commentators were extolling for its "democracy." The demonstrators represented a large cross-section of Palestinian society in Haifa and its environs. Honestly, it could have been taking place in New York. They were westernized, casual; some were religious, but not many. They carried Palestinian flags but no weapons, no protective clothing. Chatting with each other, many were smiling. Something was being expressed and it energized the crowd. Then, a few minutes later, a very large group of Israeli riot police appeared. They were armed and carried sticks, and wore helmets, visors, and bulletproof vests. This was not a demonstration that needed to be repressed or controlled. There was nothing dangerous or inappropriate or out of control. And yet this clearly didn't matter. The police ritual was designed to enforce obedience, an exercise in overreaction, overstatement, projection, dehumanization.

The Palestinians' reasonable reactions to the murder of their own people were responded to unreasonably by the very people who had caused the pain. Suddenly the police were grabbing, arresting, throwing people to the ground. The demonstrators were wearing t-shirts; the police, armor. And still some of the Palestinians talked back. It was incredible to watch. They may have been afraid, but they knew that what they were saying was true, whether they were saying, "Don't hurt him" or "This is our right." They spoke in Hebrew, which added another level of poignancy. But their refusal to obey unreasonable and unjustified demands enraged the Israeli police. It was a classic display of everything we have been discussing. How could this be happening? But of course I knew. I knew that it started with one person scapegoating another. And it grew when that person's bad group joined in. And it festered even further, when all the people around them said and did nothing. Then suddenly, it was genocide.

BBC Breaking News
At least 50 Palestinians reported killed in district of Shejaiya - #Gaza death toll rises to more than 400 http://bbc.in/1pr30Al

Janis Mackey Frayer
This is Shejaiyya in eastern #Gaza. Pounded all night until a short truce so Palestinian medics could remove bodies.

Mohammed Omer
Im at Shifa hospital. Dead bodies, ppl split into pieces. Fingers and heads are thrown in streets now as I see... #gaza

Ben White
Norwegian MP calls for boycott of Israel over its Gaza offensive http://shar.es/NR02E via @middleeastmnt

Diana Alzeer
So Tomorrow the entire Palestine including '48 goes on a general strike for #Gaza

Morgan M Page
The creation of the idea that Palestinians are the bad guys here is probably the most effective propaganda of the modern era.

Moustafa Bayoumi
Sick to my stomach. Head in my hands. #Gaza

Maysara Al Arabeed
A friend of mine frm #Gaza says" I just responded to a dead person's friend request! seems killed yst after d request" #shujaia_holocaust

AlterNet
Israel's harshest critics and most ardent defenders agree on one thing: The battle is really about America: http://ow.ly/zm4Cb

Ali Abunimah
US Jewish community needs to do more to prevent its youth becoming radicalized and going overseas to join "IDF" death squads in Palestine.

Sheren Khalel
HUGE protest in #Bethlehem tonight. 100s out. #IDF immediately responding with gas from jeeps. Biggest turn out yet. #Gaza #Israel

James Wolcott
How dare the dead telegenically splay their broken, butchered, unseeing bodies amid the rubble to court the pity of a pitiless world. #Gaza

Linda Sarsour
Today at 4am, right be4 morning prayers car w/ lights n sirens flying Israeli flags antagonized worshippers at mosque in Bay Ridge.

Talkoholic
"@adanielroth: Right-wingers beat Haifa deputy mayor during anti-war protest http://www.haaretz.com/news/national/1.606240 Right-wingers beat Haifa deputy mayor during anti-war protest http://www.haaretz.com/news/national/1.606240 " #antifa972

Roshan Rizvi
@georgegalloway Breaking: Clashes between youths and #Zionist #Israeli's in #Nablus #Palestine #PalestineUnderAttack pic.twitter.com/sygKtX3FDg

Omar Daraghmeh
#Nablus now: Violent clashes with the #PA forces after they suppressed a protest with #Gaza, live ammunition used!!! pic.twitter.com/i6g6lvXWXl

occupiedpalestine
Up till now 45 injured during clashes in #Hebron via @NasserBI

Jalal
Palestinian Authority Police firing teargas at demonstrators in Ramallah who came out in support of Gaza pic.twitter.com/aIrg65mQsh

Katie Osgood
Thousands gathered outside the Israeli Consultate in Chicago. #FreePalestine #GazaUnderAttack pic.twitter.com/WITKjSHDNj

Stefan Plebovich
When I tweeted 90 Palestinians killed by Israel, I did mean in ONE day. #SkynewsTotalBias #Gaza

Lisa Goldman
Hanan Ashrawi announces PLO will sign Rome Treaty & prosecute Israel for war crimes.

Saree Makdisi
Israel made all the same claims about human shields in 2006, 2008, 2012, and they were all systematically debunked by UN/NGO investigations.

Remi Kanazi
Zionist on campus, "My cousin lives in Israel..." 469 Palestinians no longer live in Gaza because they were massacred by Israel.

Joanne Michele
The UN Security Council should be convening momentarily for an emergency meeting on Gaza.

Vijay Prashad
It is obscene that the New York Times headline suggests that the death of soldiers & civilians in warfare is symmetrical.

Martin Nicholls
I've worked in a newsroom for more than a decade but the images coming out of Gaza are the worst I've seen. Utterly horrific.

Nick Mamatas
Queer Chicanos Against Occupation.

Javier Espinosa
Nelson Mandela's party calls for expulsion of Israeli ambassador in South Africa #Gaza #Israel http://m.polity.org.za/article/anc-statement-by-office-of-the-anc-chief-whip-on-the-situation-in-gaza-18072014-2014-07-18 ...

Alun McDonald
43% of #Gaza's total territory has now been warned to evacuate. But borders are closed. Where are people supposed to go?

July 21

The Forward published an article by Haggai Matar entitled "Tel Aviv Is Under Red Alert—In Many Ways" in which he wrote that the status quo double standard of the ways Palestinians and Jews living in Israel were treated differently by the state was shifting; Jews were now facing more restrictions on their ability to protest. The article described a peaceful demonstration by Jews on July 12 that was attacked by "several dozen extreme-right activists, some of them wearing T-shirts with neo-Nazi designs." Matar wrote:

> Now, I've been shot at, beaten, arrested and spent two years in prison for conscientious objection, but this brutal attack by dozens of bullies chanting, "Death to Arabs" and "Burn the leftists"—just two weeks after a young Palestinian boy was torched to death—was one of the most frightening experiences I've ever encountered.

He then outlined changes in rhetoric in Israel as an "ongoing process of delegitimization of Palestinian citizens and of the Jewish left," and pointed to legislation introduced in 2009 that started framing anti-war protesters and human rights NGOs as "traitors in our midst." Now that organized gangs had been patrolling the streets of Jerusalem and other cities since the kidnapping of the settlers was announced, "the government is nowhere to be found."

July 21

A Facebook post from my student Nerdeen Mohsen, who had just left Palestine:

> I blame you all for Gaza. I blame the students who didn't care to ask their universities to divest from companies that make this occupation and expansion of settlements possible. The citizens of states who didn't ask their government to stop sending military aid to Israel that ends up in the form of bullets in the chests of Palestinian children. Those who do not care enough to tell their government to sanction. Those who never told their favorite artists that playing Israel is like playing apartheid South Africa. Consumers who have

> options and are able to boycott Israel and purchase goods that aren't from stolen Palestinian culture and resources used to serve illegal settlements and terrorist military wings, but choose to purchase them regardless. You, yes you. The one who said "I'm one person, it's not going to make a difference." And "When Palestine is free it'll be the day of judgment." You have blood on your hands.
>
> You do not get to sit around and wait and pretend everything is okay until it takes 500 killed in Gaza with 80% being civilians and close to 3,000 injured to move your blood enough to scream "Free Palestine." Yes, protests are good to stand in solidarity. But don't forget you have the power to make a difference, and unless you use it you are also to blame.
>
> Gaza didn't just begin its suffering, the siege and blockade slowly kills people off everyday. Why does it have to be so quickly destructive for people to notice?
>
> If people are truly moved and will do everything in their power from now on to change this then more power to you. But if you know when this "dies down" you'll resume back to normal and forget Palestine and Gaza again, I want you to take a long hard look at yourself before you pretend you care about Palestinians at all. #BDS #Palestine #Gaza #GazaUnderAttack.

By contrast, my own Facebook page had more and more ignorant defenses and unbelievable questions posted by people I didn't even know. That same day, a woman with a Jewish name posted on my page:

> Here is a question. There are 57 Arab nations. Isn't 57 enough? Of course the killing is horrific. But what of this question?

This is the poison of Supremacy ideology: in this case, a clear dehumanization of the other through racism, so that the "monster," created by the poster's projections, can be reduced to "questions" devoid of empathy or recognition. I did my best to respond because shunning her guarantees no change, and informing her creates the possibility of change:

My Facebook

There are hundreds of Christian nations, does that mean that the people who live in them should be forced out of their homes, plunged into exile and controlled by another people? Anyway half of the Jews in Israel are Arab Jews. That idea that Jews and Arabs are separate peoples is propaganda. And that 57 number refers to Muslim majority countries, not Arab nations.

On a daily basis I was watching the reports from Gaza and then reading posts with every element of distorted thinking: the self is inscrutable, the other is turned into a specter. Different standards are imposed on the self and the other. There is no empathy, but rather an illogic, a distorted system of thought that is delusional about both the self and the other. The identification with the negative group is the machine that obstructs evolution of thought and feeling. Therefore the other's existence is treated as de facto Abuse. The other's refusal to obey unjust orders and accept undeserved punishment is treated as its cause. The other's resistance is intolerable, and therefore merits every possible cruelty.

I resolved that it was my responsibility to try to address these insanities directly and clearly, with meaningful information. Since these people espoused ideology that was shoring up unjust power, I had to counter it. And as long as they were not shunning me, i.e., as long as I was still allowed to speak, I was required by moral law to speak clearly and directly, to intervene.

That same day, the *New York Times* reported that the US government was now advising Americans to "Put off travel to Israel."

> "The security environment remains complex in Israel, the West Bank, and Gaza, and U.S. citizens need to be aware of the risks of travel to these areas because of the current conflict between Hamas and Israel," the State Department warning said.

I note the false opposition of "Hamas and Israel." It should either be "Hamas and Likud," the two opposing ruling parties, or "Israel and Palestine."

corey robin
"American audiences are seeing the story of the conflict, perhaps more than ever before, through Palestinian eyes." http://nymag.com/daily/intelligencer/2014/07/why-israel-is-losing-the-american-media-war.html ...

Bakari Kitwana
David Cameron: "Gaza cannot and must not be allowed to remain a prison camp."

Irene Nasser
I'm quite surprised, but there's actually a general strike in #Ramallah

Countercurrents.org
#WarCrime: Video Shows Sniper Killing of Wounded #Gaza Civilian By Ali Abunimah http://www.countercurrents.org/abunimah210714.htm ...

Zaid Jilani
Israel's foreign minister is trying to ban Al Jazeera from operating in Israel. Middle East's Only Democracy (TM) http://www.newsweek.com/israeli-foreign-minister-avigdor-lieberman-seeks-ban-al-jazeera-operating-260178 ...

Jalal
Witness report that the Palestinian killed near Ramallah was shot by an Israeli settler (Not soldiers), died instantly on scene via @Ayataab

Listening Post
Breaking News: #Israel looking to ban Al Jazeera says Foreign Minister http://aje.me/1o1OD7N

Linda Sarsour
Doctors Without Borders ask Israel to stop killing civilians and stop interfering with their work.

Inas Safadi
"There were no Hamas in 1948 neither in 1967 neither in 1982, So stop your ridiculous excuses Israel, you're simply murderers"

#GazaUnderAttack
WestBank: Clashes at Bethlehem right now. #Palestine #Gaza @iFalasteen pic.twitter.com/qbv9H7WisD

Gaza Youth Break Out
Many people evacuated their homes to somewhere else because they thought its safer then they got killed in the new place. #Gaza

Palestine Video
And thank you to all our comrades, brothers and sisters throughout the world for your active solidarity with our people

July 22

Rebecca Vilkomerson, the Executive Director of Jewish Voice for Peace, and seven others were arrested in New York for entering the office of Friends of the Israeli Defense Forces and reading out loud the names of Palestinians murdered in Gaza. The *Washington Post* reported that more than fifty former Israeli soldiers have refused to serve in the current ground operation in Gaza. The soldiers wrote:

> We found that troops who operate in the occupied territories aren't the only ones enforcing the mechanisms of control over Palestinian lives. In truth, the entire military is implicated. For that reason, we now refuse to participate in our reserve duties, and we support all those who resist being called to service.

Simultaneously, twenty-four American Jews participated in the first ever Jewish National fund JDate singles' trip to Israel, an insane juxtaposition.

Jon Stewart was the first American television figure to acknowledge Israeli aggression. On his show, he performed a routine sending up the lack of accurate media coverage of Gaza in the US. After the broadcast, he responded to critics: "Questioning in any way the effectiveness or humanity of Israel's policies is not the same thing as being pro-Hamas." This was going to be the new fallback position of those who have enough integrity to speak out. Former Israeli National Security Advisor Yaakov Amidror said, "A ceasefire will mean that anytime Hamas wants to fight, it can. Occupation of Gaza will bring longer-term quiet but the price will be very high." The *New York Times* reported that Birthright, the Israeli government-sponsored program that brought Jews from around the world to visit Israel for free ten-day tours, was still leading trips despite the war on Gaza and the US airlines' cancellation of flights to Tel Aviv. "We will find alternative flights if needed," an organizer said. Since the state of Israel had now murdered 600 people in Gaza because they claimed they were "defending" themselves, many people on social media were openly wondering how Israel could simultaneously insist that the place was safe enough for tourism.

My Facebook

How do I understand Israel's constant bombing of Gaza? I attribute all of this pain, suffering, cruelty and annihilation to bad groups. That horrifying false sense of "loyalty" where blaming, scapegoating, shunning, removing, occupying, and killing somehow means you're a good citizen. Where uniting to destroy other people means you are perfect, superior, and right. A system of no self-criticism, no honest negotiation, no efforts towards reconciliation, no recognition of your own mistakes. That's how we get genocide, folks. A bunch of provincial thugs living in a hall of mirrors have a chance to face themselves and choose instead to destroy everyone else's life.

I received numerous responses to this post from a broad range of people, including classmates from high school and college, lovers, long-time colleagues, neighbors, students, childhood friends, fellow queer writers, one of my closest friends, Muslims, Jews, Palestine activists, and even people who were entirely unknown to me:

Marie Caridad Pérez
I think the history of Israel comes wrapped up with lots of fear, persecution and the need for safety. Those factors can easily create a situation where the persecuted becomes the persecutor etc. Pain is a great teacher and sometimes we learn how to understand and how to be compassionate and sometimes we just absorb it and spit it back out inflicting it on others. And like you say, some people feel perfect, superior and right and they will dish out punishment without any pity. Sad and horrifying, as this is not the only time this shit has played out on this planet. It's playing out in other places right this second.

Sarah Schulman
Reasons for false "loyalty" can come from supremacy ideology as well as from trauma. Half of the Jews in Israel do not come from countries that experienced the Holocaust. The culture of re-traumatization has been systematized and institutionalized and become a political apparatus

Sarah Schulman
And all the false positioning of Palestinians as "the problem", for decades, without responsibility or self-criticism produces this moment.

Caroline Ely
Many Jews in Israel may not come from countries that underwent the Holocaust, but many do come from countries where they encountered mass hostility and mass expulsion not too long ago. A melancholy distinction....

Maria Caridad Pérez
Practically any political apparatus needs an enemy to exert power and one does not need to be personally traumatize to believe that one is in danger. To me, it is the lack of compassion, the systematic hardening of the heart en mass that also has helped to produce this moment and all the other moments like this one.

Eve Sikora
This situation has gone on and on with no real resolution. Which saddens me, because the Arabic and Jewish cultures do share many similarities. How do I know? Because I've dated people from both cultures.

Eve Sikora
If people could just learn to focus on what they have in common, rather than what separates them, in this and so many other situations---politics, marriages, friendships... then we would have more harmony in this world.

Suz Mal
Unprocessed trauma. The holocaust was unimaginable trauma that was never processed and when trauma is not processed it is repeated. In this case identification with the aggressor. How could it have been processed. There is no simple answer to this- when a whole culture had been traumatized. But we as human beings need to discuss and figure it out- because this is unacceptable!

My Facebook
Just to say, this is not a "mutual" problem where we just need to "get along." On the contrary, Jews have been subjugating Palestinians for 66 years. Yes, I agree that there is a projection of blame by Jews onto Palestinians, who did nothing to deserve it and that is a trauma paradigm, ie blaming the wrong person. But as someone who came to reality about all of this very late in the game, I have to recognize that there were Jews all along who knew this was wrong and said so. The rest of the group, me included, did not listen. And here we are, perpetrators of never-ending injustice and pain. Now the killing has to stop, the siege has to stop, the occupation has to end. And any vestiges of the kind of supremacy ideology that makes it impossible for people to admit that they were wrong, the group re-enforcement of that lethal pathology has to be dismantled as we spend the rest of our days in truth and real accountability for this sick nightmare of cruelty for which we (Jews and Americans) are responsible.

Emily Stern
I feel both less and more overwhelmed when I imagine that every person involved is part of both their family system (and all of those intricacies), which are then incorporated into the larger systems at play. If a country is the sum of its parts, and all of the parts are suffering historical and systemic unresolved pain, it will be a long and horrendous unraveling.

I think a lot of this work is pretty interesting- it was born out of the systemic impact of the holocaust on both the survivors and the Nazis.

Emily Nahmanson:
"Jews have been subjugating Palestinians for 66 years..." What other outcome could there possibly be given this irrefutable truth? Post-1947 Israel created Hamas.

Sarah Schulman
I don't know much about Hamas, but their terms for ceasefire are very reasonable: end the seige by opening the two crossings and a sea corridor, allow people to pray in Jerusalem. Etc. They are religious fundamentalists like the Orthodox Jewish parties. But they are also democratically elected. Palestine is a multi-dimensional society (ies) like any other.

Emily Nahmanson
You are so calm, sane and reasonable. I adore you and hang on your every word re: this mess.

Arlene Istar Lev
The terms of the cease fire are fair. The "crossings" however have been used to smuggle weapons, bombs, and humans rigged with bombs. How does one manage to just open those gates? It's a serious question.

Sarah Schulman
Arlene, the occupation is wrong and people resist it. There is no way to maintain an unjust system without reaction.

Audrey Roth
Sarah - how can you fully blame Israel without knowing much about Hamas? They are a group that cares little at all about their own people, in my humble opinion, and more about the destruction of Israel. I support many efforts to shift Israel's intransigence, but not to the detriment of Israel's survival as a nation. I think blaming Israel for defending its people from hundreds and hundreds of rockets launched in the past two weeks is wrong. I think blaming Israel for the continuing settlements is right. And I think the blockade is a very complicated issue, and needs to be negotiated after a ceasefire - not as a condition to one. If the U.S. government (and here I include Congress along with Obama) had the backbone to say to Netenyahu that no more help would be given until the settlements were closed and Israel sat down for serious talks with the Palestinians (not Hamas), we would have peace.

Susan Nordmark
Tell it, Sarah. Everything you have said in this thread, I want to hear you say on TV and in op-eds. I want you published and your wisdom disseminated. Audrey, similarly, anti-apartheid movements in SA generated considerable corruption, sociopathic behavior. Proximally unpleasant behavior by resisting populations is not uncommon and not limited to Hamas. It is not central to the issue. Sarah's thinking has been really brave in keeping its focus on what's foundational.

Sarah Schulman
Audrey, well, my main point is that we (Jews and Americans) are locked into ideology, actions and systems that are not viable. A concept of "defense" that relies on mass murder at the worst of times and oppression and denial of basic rights as status quo, is not acceptable. We have to change how we see ourselves so that decent and humane solutions can occur. If the only way to achieve a goal is through mass murder, it is the wrong goal.

Arlene Istar Lev
Sarah Schulman I think that we, and I'm including Roth here, agree on the fundamental issues. But you are not answering the questions but side stepping them. Hamas is clear it wants to run the Jews into the sea. There is nothing in their words, behavior, or history that suggests if you unlock the doors they will not use that opportunity for more violence. That issue has to be part of the discussions.

Sarah Schulman
I am answering this but thinking about it differently than you are and not sharing your assumptions. As long as we are acting unjustly, Palestinians will resist. Any plan that involves dominating or controlling Palestinians will produce pain. Israel's predominant self-conception is reliant on injustice and is therefore not viable. That is the origin and center of the conflict.

Jane DeLynn
Hamas elected in 2006. Eight years ago and counting. Gee, we might still have George Bush as president!

Jane DeLynn
To use the word "genocide" shows a shocking ignorance of history and debasement of language. If Israel wanted to wipe out the Palestinians it could use nuclear weapons or have those 50,000 soldiers sweep through gaza demolishing every single home and killing every single person. That's genocide. Whether or not you consider it justified this WAR.

Ryn Hodez
I do think "bad groups," are often a result of collective trauma—which can then be exploited (politically, economically, culturally, etc) to gain power - perceived to be the antidote to trauma. The existence of Israel, clothed in the story of Exodus and the trauma of the Holocaust, was also a strategic political move by the West to gain a strong military foothold in the region for their own purposes. Two peoples with nowhere else to go brought into bloody confrontation

by colonialism. The way through trauma is internal, self-reflective, and counter-intuitive in that it involves surrender/acceptance before a way forward can be found. We do not know enough about healing collective traumas.

Mohan Sikka
It makes me angry to read comments like "If Israel wanted to wipe out the Palestinians it could use nuclear weapons or have those 50,000 soldiers sweep through gaza demolishing every single home and killing every single person." I'm supposed to be grateful that you are not doing this? Why is this even up for discussion? What you are doing is ghastly enough. Also Hamas is a convenient scapegoat, a reaction of a system under unbelievable pressure. This is about more than Hamas. Release the pressure, end the siege and occupation, admit that the crime of dispossession was done to the Palestinians, get on the table and negotiate honestly, and then assess what happens. Even so, and even in this crazy situation -- I agree with Sarah that the demands for ceasefire put forward by the Palestinians are eminently reasonable. The fact that they are not even considered tells you everything about who has power and who sets the terms, and who doesn't count.

Audrey Roth:
Sarah - I don't disagree with much of what you say, although for me some of the language you use is upsetting and not geared toward resolution. I think terms like "genocide" and "mass murder" will never get the parties anywhere. Similarly, I think many of the terms that Israel uses, and certain constructs, are ill-advised and often offensive. For me, I'm thinking about affirmative steps that can be taken to move these two immovable objects (as it were).

Tania Hammidi:
I keep thinking about the disembodied surveillance technology at play... How the Zionist military "knew" (either exactly or generally) which houses to bomb. I mean of course they are bombing neighborhoods now just to blow

away everyone, but what i mean is that this perverted invasion of privacy and sovereignty employs (surveillance) the very technology US military etc do to keep an eye and follow the lives of those they know have power (either spiritual, political, social, economic or military). Ive been wondering how to dismantle that unethical relationship, in regards to this cruel and inhumane massacre, as well as the structure of colonial apartheid which supports it. Any thoughts about thugs with high definition digital toys, Sarah Schulman?

Sarah Schulman
Audrey. Seriously, please what is your definition of mass murder? They've killed five hundred people, wounded thousands, destroyed hospitals and destroyed 280 schools, plus 11,000 homes. That not only destroys many lives but also ways of life.

Maria Caridad Pérez
The most serious issue to me is that there is no foreseeable end to this horror. The way the situation is set right now it looks like whenever either party puts down the gun the other one will shoot. What is the solution? So far I have not read anything resembling one.

Janine Dunmyre
Waiting to see Muslims have global protests over how Sharia leaders burn, hang, mutilate, beat and torture their own people.

Sarah Schulman
There is an end to the one-sided massacre. It lies with the international community exerting pressure through Boycott, Divestment, Sanctions, public protest and pressure on our governments for an arms embargo.

Justine Saracen
Janine, the crimes of Muslims in other countries are irrelevant to this conflict.

Maria Caridad Pérez
There are no countries or powerful organizations suggesting to do anything like that so far. Or at least I am not reading any of it in the press. When Israel stops the attacks, ends the occupation etc, what will Hamas do? What country or powerful organization will make sure they do the right thing. Even if Israel started it, both sides are expected to show responsibility and self examination for coexistence. It definitely looks bleak at this moment.

Diana Reid McCague
Nuclear weapons or other WMD in Gaza won't be used, but not b/c the Israeli gov't doesn't want to commit genocide. The world's reaction to such a thing would be the end of Israel. They already lie about their intent -- say they are pinpointing attacks so as to minimize non-combatant casualties, though they use weapons that do anything but provide pinpointed results. If Israel wants to put Hamas out of business, they need to win over regular Palestinians by providing freedom, respect, autonomy, statehood.

Janine Dunmyre
Israeli troops entering again Gaza last week uncovered 18 tunnels used by Hamas to send armed terrorists into Israel. It is estimated that Hamas used 800,000 tons of concrete to build these tunnels.

What else could that concrete be used for? Hmmmm. The world's tallest building, Dubai's Birj Khalifa, used 110,000 tons of concrete. Hamas could have given Gaza seven high rise apartment buildings. Or schools. Or maybe equipped their kindergartens with bomb shelters. Like Israelis did in Sdiderot.

Ryn Hodez
The response above about Sharia is a typical deflection, an example of baiting, anti-Muslim bias, and is exactly the blaming, scapegoating, shunning that Sarah is talking about. Are you not accountable for your own actions? You can run amok until all other atrocities are resolved? What the hell

is the point of that? It's bad behavior and when perpetrated by groups of people *with power* has catastrophic consequences.

Mohan Sikka
I'm putting a line in my mental sand about deflecting arguments that start with "Waiting to see how Muslims, etc." None of those conflicts are underwritten, supported and "allowed" by us. None of those conflicts are referred to as anything except abominable. Iraq, Syria, Sudan, wherever. Terrible. Does the US Congress pass resolutions 100-0 saying thumbs up to that kind of killing and destruction anywhere else. We give Israel a pass on whatever it does. Whatever it does. I ask all the people who want to keep saying Hamas Hamas. What level of destruction by the IDF will make this mayhem not acceptable

Justine Saracen
SOO, Janine. Then it's all right to wipe them out. Right? All a matter of defense. You build a wall, you create a ghetto, you block escape by sea and nothing helps. You just can't stop the little rats, can you.

Sarah Schulman
I am consistently stymied by the desire to justify these killings. Like I said in my original post, there is something terribly wrong with group identifications that produce excuses for this distorted thinking and deadly brutality.

Samuel Delany
What do you do, morally, when someone says, "Hey, here's a house you can have. No one really lives there. Just move in". So you do--to much celebration by your own family and the lots of friends, who keep saying about you, "You people who never had a home of your own and now have one. Isn't it great." Only you discover that there's a family already living in it, who says, "Hey, this is our house. We've been living here for generations. The people who gave it to you had no right to give it. it wasn't theirs. And though people

that you have a language and cultural relation to, but very little genetic relation to--otherwise you'd look like us--were living here two millennia ago, we're living here now, today." So you hang on for 60 years and a whole newer generation has now been born and brought up in that house, as have the people who have been there all along. Several armed wars have occurred between you. What's the way to handle it? I know how some very idealistic young Jewish men and women handled in the early sixties, when the situation was only fifteen or sixteen years old. They went over, expecting to find they had a home, and, when they got there, they were appalled at what they found--and they came back to America, and sat in my kitchen and broke down crying because they were so outraged at what they'd seen. I can still hear them, talking around my lover's kitchen table in our apartment on St. Mark's place, Bob and Carroll saying it was like a parody of what was going on in the American south among the segregationists who a few years before had been throwing rocks at the Black students entering the schools in Arkansas. They described Moroccan Jews being pushed off the sidewalk into the gutter by European Jews, the way their family's said they been treated in Germany before the war. It was clearly racial. The last time I brought this up in a conversation, maybe three months ago, with someone a dozen years younger than I--a woman perhaps sixty who had started a conversation with me on the train back to New York from Dover Plains--she told me no one could have felt that way in the sixties about Israel. Then why do I remember the tears? Why do I remember the details? Why do I remember the outrage of these young folk who couldn't take it? Why do I recall the kids who had gone there, planning to stay forever, coming home after three months so disillusioned? Now, three months after that train conversation and fifty years after that evening when Bob and Carroll came back and were sitting there with their suitcases and duffels around the table legs, rockets and bombs are being traded back and forth--again. Bcause it's happened before.

Diana Reid McCague
Janine, many governments use a grossly disproportionate amount of resources on "defense" at the expense of services and infrastructure to benefit their general populations. US is a perfect example. Do the people of all of these countries deserve death and destruction? Expose yourself to more sources of commentary and information -- you are parroting the words of Israeli representatives.

IS Horst
For what it's worth I have read Janine's exact comment about the concrete elsewhere from someone else. It's not in front of me now but it sure sounds word for word right down to the "Hmmm".

Justine Saracen
IS Horst, you think it is simply some paid Israeli apologist who is cutting and pasting the same argument in a dozen places? That would account for why so many Zionist arguments sound repetitive.

Mohan Sikka
From Mondoweiss: Yousef Alhelou reports from Gaza where news of another massacre is unfolding. Based on early reports, Khoza village, situated in the eastern part of Khan Younis in the southern Gaza Strip, is facing a similar fate to Shijaeyah which was almost flattened by Israeli tank shelling and air strikes over the weekend. Scores of people have been killed and injured as the village is now besieged by Israeli snipers, and people are being fired upon as they flee the bombardment. Above, Palestinians flee their homes following heavy Israeli shelling east of Khan Younis earlier today.

IS Horst
Well I've read of such things. I was really struck by the repetition of the "Hmmm." But I don't know.

Diana Reid McCague
Janine's comment is a talking point being used by Israeli mouthpieces. I could have written the same thing from having heard it so often.

Maria Caridad Pérez
Look at this thread. We argue, argue, argue. Some vent, some attack, some kiss ass, some ignore and hardly anyone learns, soothes, looks to unite ideas and find solutions. A mirror. I'm lost.

Janine Dunmyre
I'm not sure the bias of this particular news source but I appreciate a Muslim writer recognizing the complexity of the lack of Muslim outrage worldwide when Muslim terrorists damage countless humans.

Janine Dunmyre
I disagree Maria. I appreciate this space as a space where people disagree without being attacked. People disagree with me. Short of being called an Israeli talking point mouth piece, no one is attacking me or bullying me. I come to learn too. Sarah and I disagree with the point of Zionism. She calls it an occupation. I call it a Jewish homeland. I know we both agree that nationalism sucks. I just happen to see it as reality on the ground. But I do love and appreciate her idealism. I definitely do not come here to look in the mirror.

Maria Caridad Pérez
Janine. Perhaps you have misunderstood what I wrote. I do appreciate this space, otherwise I would not be here. The reasons why you write on a Facebook thread might be different than mine, or someone else's.

Ian Iqbal Rashid
Sarah: "this sick nightmare of cruelty for which we (Jews and Americans) are responsible." This article speaks to that notion: http://www.huffingtonpost.com/.../aipac-americas-israel... AIPAC Is the Only Explanation for America's Morally Bankrupt Israel Policy

Minus Smile
So when elections come up, people tend to focus on problems with Hamas and how Hamas was elected. For people in favor of Israel's actions, that is supposed to justify the collective punishment being inflicted on Gaza.

I know it sounds harsh but... is it also not true that the current Israeli government was elected, and that the Israeli electorate is thus entirely responsible for their atrocities - that indeed they mandated exactly these atrocities be committed? (At least the portion of the electorate that supported parties making up the current coalition?) I'm just wondering if the same criteria that justify collective punishment apply to both parties or just one.

Ian Iqbal Rashid
Jane DeLynn and Audrey Roth: Nazi Germany didn't choose the word 'genocide' either. The slant of history did. Israel may have the weapons and the power but they do not and will not get to name this tragedy.

Sarah Schulman
Ian Iqbal Rashid Thanks for the article on AIPAC. Honestly, the prevalence of Christian Zionists (like George Bush) in the majority religion here creates a context for AIPAC's extremist views.

Dudley Saunders
There has been a long term, openly-discussed push for the creation of what is called "Greater Israel" through the confiscation of Palestinian land, sometimes with the call to overthrow Jordan leadership and ship the Palestinians off to resettle there, in a kind of Middle East version of our Trail of Tears. The settlements and Kafka-esque oppression is clearly aimed at slow-walking this direction. But In the last few days, at least one member of Knesset has called for Palestinian genocide.

Tayyaba Tabby Sajid
Can I please share this status update? Because it is unbelievably brilliant....

Marion I. Lipshutz
Sarah Schulman, I think that Hamas is also a bad group, albeit a non-state actor, but a bad group in the senses that you mean it too. Do you agree?

Sarah Schulman
"Hamas" is an excuse to justify all kinds of cruelties. It's a Monster or Spectre that has been invented as a dehumanized repository of everyone's blame. I am not religious and I don't support religious parties.

Diana Reid McCague
Do all US Senators support Israel's current war on Palestine b/c they are afraid of the political attack that will ensue? I do not believe that Franken, Sanders and Warren *really* believe Israel is justified in perpetrating the current horror.

Marion I. Lipshutz
Sarah, I am taken aback by your response. Are you saying that this does not exist? Is this merely a "Spectre" that Human Rights Watch invented? http://www.hrw.org/.../under-cover-war-hamas-political... Under Cover of War: Hamas Political Violence in Gaza

Sarah Schulman
No. I am saying that there are a lot of religious forces that use violence, and the singling out of Hamas as an excuse for the mass killings of Palestinians is a tactic.

Diana Reid McCague
http://forward.com/.../-israeli-reservists-refuse-to.../ 50 Israeli Reservists Refuse To Serve in Gaza War

Eric Solstein
Mr. Delany, I know why a Jew would cry for the injustice committed by his own people, but that does not frame the larger situation, not even half of it. Who do you think cried for the 600,000 Jews expelled from their homes throughout the Middle East?

Michael Rosenthal
But Mr. Solstein, do we continue trading injustice for injustice forever and ever? That won't end until one side is exterminated. Israel has the overwhelming power to determine if this ends in peace, death, or ever.

The internalizing of the creation of "Hamas" as the kind of monster that Kaspar Saxena described was now everywhere, a specter forbidden to respond, only to be destroyed. After all, Hamas was a *government* that was democratically elected. Jimmy Carter oversaw its election and declared it to be free and fair. There are religious parties all over the world: Hindu, Christian, Muslim, Jewish. Hamas is within this tradition, not some rare species from Hades. It represents a people who have been profoundly oppressed, in a condition long recognized by the United Nations as illegal, and in violation of international law. These people have been under siege, which means entirely controlled by an outside force. And the Gazans have been reliant on smuggling through tunnels to get food, supplies, and even visitors and cars. The government bringing *terror* into their lives is the Israeli government, whose violations of law and ethics calls itself *democracy* and their negative object: *terrorists*. For Israel, Hamas is an entity that must be dehumanized by being entirely shunned, an object that is not real, but that only exists to be projected onto and acted upon. A non-human at the service of the Traumatized/Supremacist bully. And I realized I have to deepen my thinking so that I could understand and address this fact. The US government has murdered far more people than Hamas, yet we don't advocate bombing every home and town that holds a registered Democrat.

Ali Abunimah
US airlines' suspension of all flights to Ben Gurion Airport likely to do huge economic and "brand" damage to Israel.

The Associated Press
BREAKING: Delta cancels all flights to Israel indefinitely, cites report of rocket near Tel Aviv airport.

Rania Masri
"Palestinians are expected, nay required, to refrain from any kind of resistance to Israeli occupation." http://english.al-akhbar.com/content/western-standards-palestinian-resistance ...

Anna Baltzer
While we mourn so many killed, we must strengthen our work for Palestinian rights: http://bit.ly/1kkqsuG #BDS

Electronic Intifada
Gaza civil society leaders reject claim Hamas uses them as "human shields"

Dan
hi, I'm a conservative, I want to overthrow the US government because my lightbulbs are dimmer now but Palestinians have no right to resist

JewishVoiceForPeace
Jews around the world protest Israel's #Gaza slaughter, call for Boycott, Divestment & Sanctions #BDS

Diana Buttu
So I thought that it is so unsafe for Israel that they need to bomb Gaza to bits. But yet it is safe enough for tourists? #GazaUnderAttack

JewishVoiceForPeace
Carolyn Klaasen: "Calling the IDF a defense force is absurd; it's an illegally occupying army"

E | Resistance
BREAKING NEWS: #Israeli occupation forces stormed the city of #Nablus #Gaza #Palestine

Ronna Syed
Air Canada joins U.S. airlines in halting flights to Tel Aviv

Hend
I've seen more concern from the Israeli government over lost flights than over lost lives.

syndicalist
Clashes between Palestinian youth & Israeli troops tonight in #Hebron, West Bank. Pal authorities made some arrests.

mcwbr
A humanitarian ceasefire is "not on the agenda right now," says a senior Israeli official. Well, nothing remotely human is. #Gaza

Joe Catron
Bolivian Ambassador at the UN speaking to the security council wearing Palestinian scarf. via @perdana4peace #Gaza pic.twitter.com/p4noAOM889

July 23

Ben Ehrenreich
Well this could get interesting: Mahmoud Abbas' family secretly leaves for Jordan. http://www.jpost.com/Middle-East/Abbass-family-abandons-West-Bank-for-Jordan-368496 ...

Ben White
African Literature Association endorses academic boycott of Israel http://electronicintifada.net/blogs/jimmy-johnson/african-literature-association-endorses-academic-boycott-israel ... via @intifada #BDS

July 24

My Facebook
The new Palestinian demands for ceasefire: The opening of borders and freedom of movement for Gazan residents; the release of prisoners, permitting Gazan fishermen to sail 12 miles from shore; Hamas and the Palestinian Authority also demand an international committee be set up to guarantee implementation of the agreement. Are there any of us who would agree to less for ourselves?

Shaima' Ziara
Israeli soldiers open fire at anything moving in Khusa'a! People can't move "the pieces" of the dead people in the streets! #GazaUnderAttack

Electronic Intifada
PHOTO: Palestinian police stop Ramallah protesters from reaching Israeli settlement http://bit.ly/1nidILE

Steven Salaita
#ISupportGaza even though my president is too cowardly to do the same.

Ben White
Israeli agency bans radio clip naming children killed in Gaza http://www.haaretz.com/news/diplomacy-defense/israel-gaza-conflict-2014/1.606908 ...

AJELive
BREAKING: At least 30 people reported killed and 100 injured in the shelling of a UN school in Gaza. http://aje.me/1kXSzSd

Al Jazeera English
Israeli shells hit UN shelter in Gaza http://aje.me/1nXrkau

Al-Akhbar English
Breaking: Reports of 1 dead, tens wounded at #Qalandia checkpoint clash in occupied West Bank #Gaza #48KMarch

By late August, the war on Gaza had claimed over 2,000 lives and more would follow. Most of them were civilians, and many were children. Another 10,000 Palestinians were wounded. By contrast, sixty-five Israeli soldiers were killed and three civilians and several hundred Israeli soldiers were wounded. One-quarter of Gazans were made homeless; most of the country was in literal ruins. Israel destroyed their power plant, thereby knocking out electricity, contaminating water, and halting sewage processing. The destruction included a university, many mosques, most hospitals, 146 schools, and several UN-run shelters filled with civilians, even though the UN gave Israel the coordinates seventeen times in one case and thirty-three in another. Disease became rampant; bodies were everywhere. The US Senate voted 100 to zero to support Israel, and President Obama signed $225 million in further aid. Samantha Power and Susan Rice obstructed UN efforts to condemn Israel. Only one Congressman, Keith Ellison of Minnesota, spoke out in support of the people of Gaza.

In the midst of the fighting, poet Peter Cole, writing in the *Paris Review*, returned to the line of poetry by Hayim Nahman Bialik that Netanyahu had quoted when pretending to discover that the three settler boys were dead: "Vengeance ... for the blood of a small child, / Satan has not yet created."

Cole pointed out that the poem was not Israeli:

> It was written long before the state was founded and very far from it. "On the Slaughter" was the thirty-year-old Odessan Hayim Nahman Bialik's immediate response to the April 1903 pogroms in the Bessarabian town of Kishinev, where some forty-nine Jews were slashed, hacked, and cudgeled to death, or drowned in outhouse feces, and hundreds were wounded over the course of several days. Women and girls were raped repeatedly. The Jewish part of town was decimated. Netanyahu quoted just two lines, carefully avoiding the one preceding them: "Cursed be he who cries out: Revenge!"

Like the woman who called the police on her partner as a consequence of her predatory father who had never been made accountable, the Israelis continued to re-enact their own historic trauma on the people who were not its cause. European Jews suffered the multi-generational trauma of a genocide perpetrated by European non-Jews that we already understand travels psychologically, culturally, and biologically through time. Then, via a spectacle of protection-through-dominance, they used the tactics of myth-building and accrued might, rooted in themes of European racial Supremacy. They built an assault apparatus committed to the principle that the Holocaust proved the necessity of a Jewish state. This was based on the belief that their earlier trauma justified their contemporary Supremacy ideology: the mirroring of Trauma and Supremacy. The state encased Arab Jews inside this trauma, who joined the collective projection onto Palestinians through elaborate tactics of the overstatement of harm, shunning, and the bad group "loyalty" that cannot be nuanced or self-critical. Not only were Palestinians not the perpetrators of this trauma or its extension, but they are, in fact, its victims.

Cole went on to explain that the title of the poem Netanyahu selected, "On Slaughter," alludes, "with the darkest irony," to the prayer recited by the *shochet*, the kosher meat slaughterer, before killing the animal. It also refers to Jewish martyrs in the Middle Ages who committed suicide before their Christian oppressors could murder them directly. It is a cry of hopelessness, the impossibility for rescue, futile fury in the face of dehumanizing cruelty. It's a poem that deeply resonates with the Palestinian experience. But only if Palestinians are embraced, instead of blamed, does that become clear.

The Israelis need to maintain the false notion of the Palestinian monster because it is only in opposition to that monster that the Israelis can construct themselves. When that "other" asserts its needs and realities, as Palestinians have tried to do, even by reading the names of the dead in the Knessset, they become the new accused. Yes, the Palestinians do pose a threat, but to what? A threat to a distorted self-concept of the Jews who support the Occupation. A threat to the mental illness, the collectively supported distorted thinking produced by both actual Trauma and the fetishization of Trauma. It is the identification of traumatized people with bullies, who cannot be opposed or acknowledge mistakes. The Jews have an opportunity to deprogram themselves, as some of us have chosen to do when faced with the Palestinian challenge. We change our self-perception, our myths about ourselves. We challenge the terms of our group belonging to families, religion, state, and nation that are bonded together by bullying, shunning, perfectionist views of ourselves, and the dehumanization of others. But many Jews resist the change, viewing change itself as a *threat of violence*, pretending away the fact that this violence is one that we Jews are ourselves perpetrating.

Conclusion | **The Duty of Repair**

> Being treated as a non-person may be the most crushing kind of oppression that there is.
>
> —JOHN BOSWELL (1986 lecture at the University of Wisconsin)

OUR TRANSFORMATION into a conscious, accountable, and healing culture requires an openness about differentiating real danger from projected danger. If we discuss this with each other with casual grace, it will cease to be viewed as stigmatizing and become a common-sense practice.

"Do what feels right" is unfortunately considered the individual's best guide to ethical action. But this can be a capitulation to the controls of impulsivity, rooted in trauma and egged on by bad friends and negative family relationships. There is a gross distortion in this ideology as an excuse to do what you "want." Pretending that what is comfortable and easiest is inherently what is right is a tragic self-deception. Or as painter Rochelle Feinstein has described, it is a condition in which a person can't process the situation they have created and in which they play a role.

What's So Impossible about Apologizing for Your Part?

I, like many people, have had marking experiences of group bullying, sometimes so overwhelming, pointless, and mean that they have been life-threatening. One was in a wealthy provincial city some hours away. The community had the trappings of urbanity, but a very, very small-town system of social enforcement. Sometimes I felt like I was in *In the Heat of the Night* or some other melodrama of a small dustbowl town where the most upstanding citizens—the sheriff, the mayor, and the minister—all secretly belong to the Klan. No matter how many efforts I made to communicate, the other parties were rigid in their group Supremacy identification. And many people I know who had moved away from this clique warned me that group punishment was notoriously their cultural mode. As a result of a normative and regular disagreement about our understandings of a situation, some people who did not know how to discuss differences acted out by doing some grotesquely mean things. When I tried to discuss it with them, they refused to talk to me. This made it impossible for us to find an alternative.

Finally, Yom Kippur came, and I wrote to each person saying that I apologized for my part. My friend Stephen, the boyfriend of one of the clique members, was skeptical. "They should be apologizing to you," he said. But I knew they had no self-reflexivity, so I took the initiating step.

Now, none of these people had been brought up Jewish and so perhaps they didn't get the Day of Atonement thing, but behaving as a group instead of as individuals, they assigned one representative to respond. Her basic argument was that since I had apologized, that meant that I was confessing that I had been wrong. And since only one person can be wrong, that meant that they were right. So instead of my gesture serving to open the door, it was used as a confirmation of their unilateral Supremacy.

I answered her (by email, because part of their group bullying tactic was the refusal to speak) that generally Yom Kippur is a *collective experience*. And that my history with it showed that people usually responded to apologies with "Thank you," or said nothing, or also apologized for their part. Usually, Yom Kippur is not used to deepen the accusation. She wrote back: "Never contact us again." The concept of mutuality was unbearable.

Later that week, Hillary Clinton was on *Fresh Air* on National Public Radio, and host Terry Gross asked her about her changed position on the issue of gay marriage. Now, Gross herself has a very spotty history when it comes to covering queer ideas and politics before they become status quo, but nonetheless, she was right to ask Clinton to be accountable. Clinton evasively would not acknowledge having taken a position earlier against gay marriage. Reporting on this, journalist Melissa Dahl cited recent studies revealing that "digging in and refusing to admit an error feels pretty great." Yes, she quoted an Australian study published in 2013 which found that when people refused to acknowledge that they had made mistakes, they reaped *more* psychological benefits than those who copped to their errors. The study showed that people who refused to admit wrongdoing felt greater self-esteem and more in control than those who did apologize, even if they were liars.

In the spring of 2014, Professor Dorit Naaman, an Israeli living in Canada who teaches at Queens University, published a personal essay titled "I am a Palestinian Jew Or At Least I Will Be" that she posted on Facebook. She wrote:

> Certainly in my lifetime this place will be called Palestine and I will be a citizen of Jewish-Israeli heritage. By saying I am a Palestinian Jew I am being neither flippant nor provocative ... instead I am analyzing the current reality.

She went on to explain her belief that Judaism and Israeli identity would survive, but Zionism would not. This was, to me, a kind of apology. She acknowledged that an earlier strategy, in which she was implicated, did not work out, and had produced pain. She acknowledged that that system not only should not continue, but could not continue. At the same time that she recognized reality, many fellow Israelis were participating in delusional thinking, imposing every kind of possible cruelty to keep from ever having been wrong, to keep continuing a wrong. Dorit Naaman didn't do this—she was ending the wrong. She was changing how she saw herself. She would no longer be an Israeli Jew, she would be a Palestinian Jew. She recognized the other, heard them, and as a consequence, was transformed.

This is my favorite kind of apology. It is not a Christian-style confession; there is nothing abject here. There is no martyrdom. There is only the recognition of a reality. That's it. It's factually correct.

Dorit was acting morally, ethically. She was raised a certain way, was born in a certain place, she was imbued with a family-based negative ideology rooted in group Supremacy. But she figured out that she didn't have to always be that way. She didn't have to defend it. She didn't have to pretend that it was okay. She didn't have to re-inscribe any of its injustices. She could simply embrace change, of her own identity and self-concept. She could become a Palestinian Jew. And so, literally or metaphorically, can we all.

Feeling Better vs. Getting Better

On some level it all comes down to Feeling Better versus Getting Better. Repressing information about ourselves or our friends, creating scapegoats as a way to avoid our problems, using shunning to unite a clique and create group identity—all of these make people feel better because it makes them feel superior. But the only way to truly get better is to face and deal with each other, sit down and communicate. And I think the difference between these two choices is determined by what groups (cliques, families, nations) we belong to. If we are in groups that cannot be self-critical and therefore punish difference, we will join in on the shunning, excluding, and cold-shouldering. But if we are in groups that promote acceptance, intervene to create communication, and recognize that people have contradictions, we will be able to face and deal with the true nature of Conflict: that it is participatory, and cannot be solved by being cruel, spreading rumors, enacting laws, or incarcerating, invading, and occupying.

I keep returning to those refugee psychiatrists who escaped from Nazi Germany and Austria, bringing to America the concept that people do things for reasons, and that these reasons may be rooted in early experiences which are worth identifying so that we don't blame the present for the past. They recognized that there is an unconscious, i.e., that we have motives and associations which propel our actions, of which we may not be aware. Some of these refugees, whose families and friends were murdered by fascists, actually wished to treat their tormenters, to have them as patients. They didn't want them to go to jail or be killed. Instead, the refugee practitioners wanted to talk to their persecutors about their feelings. I find this to be remarkable. That, like Edith Weigert, some of these refugees saw fascism as a neurosis, a compulsion to act out on anxieties about Jews and Communists. And her beautiful vision, *The Courage to Love*, expressed that, by talking to them in a therapeutic relationship, she could help them separate the anxiety from the action. They could understand the roots of the anxiety so that the fascist didn't have to bond together with others, similarly neurotic, to shun, isolate, exclude, scapegoat, blame, incarcerate, and mass murder those whom they blamed for their anxieties.

I also feel this way. Sometimes we find ourselves in history, and Weigert's perspective is one that I identify with. I feel that if I could talk to people who are projecting their anxieties onto me, some pressure could be reduced. It is so easy to whisper about, isolate, and shun someone whose pain you can cause without having to see the person. But it is another thing to hear about what your group-bonding ritual is actually doing to another human being's life. This is why I am not surprised to learn that many Israelis or Jews who support the Israeli government have never actually heard from Palestinians directly about what their lives are like. Instead, they are filled with misinformation and projections in an insular circulation. And in my own case, the more contact I have with Palestinians, the more I learn to see the world from a place influenced by their information. In fact, in my experience, it is the person who is suffering who wants things to get better, while the person who is repressing their own conflicts usually wants to be the one to feel better. So, it is the person with HIV, the Palestinian, the object of group shunning, who wants to talk, to be heard, and thereby to transform.

Of course, the person who shuns from a place of Supremacy—the big man in a provincial town—is the least likely to risk opening up his mind. He has everything to lose: his inflated stature, the comforts of his life, the ways that his partner and the people around him obey him in order to have a social role. But the person who shuns from a place of Trauma is the one who benefits the most from change, because the exhausting cycle of projection has a chance to rest.

In the years of writing this book, I gave many talks and had many conversations developing these ideas. One of the most productive was at an elite liberal arts school in the United States. There was an audience of about a hundred students, and I noticed a group of five young women sitting together near the front. During the Q and A, one raised her hand.

"I am a survivor," she said. "We are all survivors here," indicating her friends. "And our abuser is walking around this campus. Do you think that's right?"

Now, normally when someone tells me that they are a *victim* and someone else is *abusive*, I first determine if they are in physical danger. If not, I then ask them a lot of questions so that I understand what has happened before I join in on condemning another human being. I don't simply jump on the bandwagon because certain words were used. I ask what the other person would say happened. I ask for the order of events. But since this was not a private conversation, we got into a very rich and fruitful back and forth about some of the larger questions of accusation and punishment on college campuses. We started talking about the case at Columbia University in which a woman charged a man with sexual abuse and wanted him to be expelled. Rather than debate the details of that case, we went to an even larger conversation about the question of expulsion itself. I proposed that expelling a man who has committed a sexual assault from an elite private school simply unleashes him on the world of women who don't go to elite private schools. It may remove him from the class-based gated community, but it launches an angry, disenfranchised, and stigmatized perpetrator into the world of women who don't have deans and college councils to defend them.

We discussed what the alternative would be, and how it may be more responsible for these wealthy institutions to develop ways of dealing with or treating male offenders, rather than passing them on to the masses. And this, in turn, raised the question of whether or not we want people to be treated or to be punished. We then got into the question of what exactly a "male offender" is. None of this rich and textured mutual learning experience could have happened through email. We had to face each other.

At one point I quoted a casual, off-the-record conversation I had had with a friend who was hired to set reasonable response systems in place for another private, elite institution around male assault. She was finding, as a result of talking to a wide range of students, that there were a small number of men who were pathological assaulters, and that it was the violation of consent, itself, that was the motivator. But at the same time, she discovered a large percentage of young men who were confused by women. They didn't understand women's messaging. They were confused by women's conflicts about sexuality. They couldn't figure out how people got from one place to another in the trajectory of a sexual relationship. How sexuality and romance depicted in film, television, or online influences how people think they are supposed to behave, and also influences how other people read and interpret those behaviors. And for some, authentic communication is something that they grow into, or it is learned or acquired through therapy or life experience. My friend is also lesbian, and she and I had a moment of recognition over that one. We also knew that women have deep conflicts about behavior, expectation, and image, and we ourselves are often confused and don't understand ourselves and other women. And we are adult enough to know that recognizing contradiction is not "blaming the victim" but instead is necessary to finding real solutions.

I then repeated for the audience some of the research from this book about how the early feminist anti-violence movement emphasized "patriarchy, racism, and poverty" as the causes of violence against women. I expressed how this focus on cause, or understanding, has been replaced by a focus on punishment which enhances the power of the police, but leaves the causes of violence unaddressed. At this point, one of the other women in this group of survivors became upset. She was angry and shaking.

"You're saying that when I was ten years old and my father was beating me, someone should have sat me down and said ..."—and here she sarcastically mimicked a super-sweet condescending adult voice—"he only did that because of patriarchy, racism, and poverty."

Fortunately this conversation was live and in person, because if she had made that accusation by email and I had responded, she never would have heard me. But because we were together in that room, because we had facial expressions and our tone of voice could be recognized, and most importantly because other people were there with us, we could actually get somewhere. Now, I knew that I had obviously never said such a thing. And I knew that the other hundred or so people in the room also knew that. So I carefully, respectfully, and kindly—all tonal elements that would have been invisible in email or text—delineated that that was not what I said. That I did not believe that a person should tell a ten-year-old child who was beaten by her father that what happened to her was caused by "patriarchy, racism, and poverty." Then I asked the room: how many people thought that that was what I said? No one raised their hand. So I respectfully, kindly, and carefully underlined that the girl should have been loved and cared for. That what her father did was wrong. Simultaneously, central to my talk that evening—in fact, its very core subject—was the precise emotional event that had taken place that led this young woman to hear something that had not been said. That, in fact, this is exactly what my work is about. The mis-hearing, i.e., the accusation.

So I asked her, softly—which cannot be conveyed in email or text—"Do you think that you were feeling anxious while I was talking?" Because we were all there in person and she could see that no one else in the room heard what she heard, I knew that she was listening. "Is it possible that the anxiety, and remembering what happened to you, and imagining that I might be taking that away from you, overwhelmed what was actually being said in the present?" And the young woman actually considered what I was saying. And then, as the gift of this in-person interaction, I had a new insight that I never would have had if she had blocked me on email or refused to talk on the phone. "Wouldn't it be amazing," I said, "if we could turn to our friends and say, I felt anxious and so I exaggerated, and instead of them using that as a reason to ignore us, disparage us, or punish us, whenever we say *I feel anxious and so I exaggerated*, our friends would put their arms around us, hug us and kiss us and thank us and praise us for telling the truth?"

At the end of the talk, I went up to her, we shook hands. I told her I looked forward to seeing her again. That night, when I got home, I went on twitter, and this same young woman had sent out a message. "Sarah Schulman came to talk at my school tonight. And she was fantastic."

If she had shunned me, if she had refused to sit down in person and talk things over, if she had cold-shouldered me because someone whispered a rumour about me to her that she refused to check out, neither of us would have come to this positive relationship, these insights, or this moment.

Working on this book has been a profound experience. I had to go very, very deep. I had to look honestly inside myself and honestly inside the people around me, especially the ones who refuse to engage. And I think some basics emerged: shunning is wrong. It is unethical. Group shunning is the centerpiece of most social injustice. To bond, or to establish belonging by agreeing to be cruel to the same person, is dehumanizing and socially divisive. It causes terrible pain, and is unjust. If someone asks you to hurt another person, to refuse to speak to them, to cold-shoulder them, to refuse to sit down and hear what they have to say about the consequences of your actions on their lives, then you are being invited into a Supremacy system. The best thing to do when being asked to hurt another person is to ask the scapegoated object herself what she thinks is going on. Just pick up the phone. If you have a conflict with another person, tell them how you feel before implementing punishment. Ask and listen. Talk face to face. Learn from the art of fiction writing: all people are real. Your actions have consequences on other people.

Intervention is the only moral response to another person being group-bullied, or another group of people being shunned, excluded, incarcerated, or occupied. Especially when someone asks us for help, we must intervene. Usually intervention means confronting the head bully or the central clique, and usually this means risking marginalization ourselves. Most of us—probably all of us—have times in our lives when we risk losing favor by standing up for someone who is the object of everyone else's blame, whether it is people with HIV, the homeless person on the subway, or our friend's ex-girlfriend. Those of us who present ourselves as "progressive," who support others, or help out, or take stands, are the ones most responsible for bucking the trend of cruelty. When we don't refuse cruelty, ultimately we stand for nothing; we are hypocrites, and our public selves are phony. Progressive people do not shun, and in fact they intervene when group shunning is being organized. Finally, ultimately, when groups bond over shunning or hurting or blaming another person, it is the state's power that is enhanced. Because the state doesn't want to understand causes, because the state doesn't want things to get better, it doesn't want people to understand each other. State apparatuses are there to maintain the power of those in control and punish those who contest that power; that is what bad families do, and that is what bad friends do. And nothing disrupts dehumanization more quickly than inviting someone over, looking into their eyes, hearing their voice, and listening.

Acknowledgments

SO MANY PEOPLE influenced this book; nothing I have written before has ever been so populated. Some transformed my understanding by their strength and depth, their willingness to change and question, their compassion, self-criticism, and commitment to engage. Others opened my eyes by being shallow, cowardly, provincial, frightened, and defended. All were fascinating, and each informed and thereby enriched this project by their example.

Deep gratitude to the Corporation of Yaddo, and the MacDowell Colony where much of this book was written. And to Ted Kerr, Kelli Dunham, Tom Léger, Nadia Awad, Matias Viegener, Bryn Kelly, Dean Spade, Darren Patrick, Adam Fitzgerald, Suzanne Carte, Matan Cohen, Maureen Fitzgerald, Daniello Cacace, Ian Iqbal Rashid, Jim Hubbard, Gardenia Flores, Jasmine Rault, Catherine Lord, Heidi Schmid, Laura Benkov, Theo, Marcilyn Cianfranciso, Zoe Whithall, Claudia Rankine, Farzana Doctor, Michelle Pearson Clarke, Jackie Reingold, Ghadir Shafie, Danny Glenwright, Savannah Garmon, Sa'ed Atshan, Patty White, Claire Potter, Christina Hanhardt, Ger Zielenski, Andrea Houston, Tayari Jones, Jane Walsh, Kim Emery, Jordan Arseneault, Tracie Morris, Kim Koyama, Mattilda Bernstein Sycamore, Leslie Gevirtz, Tom Waugh, Jack Waters, Peter Cramer, Kaspar Saxena, Aidan Cowling, Rachel Epstein, Alex McClelland, Scott Berry, Amy Fung, Rowan McNamara, Sur Rodney Sur, Andy Parker, and James Shack for compassionate insights, open conversation, support, and enlightened understanding, whether momentary or ongoing. Thanks to Allison Danzig and Amy Ellingson for generously hosting me in San Francisco. And thank you to researchers Kelly Roberts, Ann Simonds, Patrick DeGauw, Daniela Silvestre Jorge Ayoub, and Josh Valentine Pavan.

Hats off to the distant aura of Judith Butler who gave me the word "specter" to describe the shunned individual as an object of projection.

Special thanks to Zab Design.

My thinking on brain disease, consequences of trauma, denial of mental illness, and the general question of being "defended" have long been influenced by Liz Garbus and Rory Kennedy's 2007 HBO documentary *Addiction*.

Sometimes a person says one word or phrase that is so starkly true that doors of understanding open forever. It's the kind of knowledge that can be denied but not unlearned. Thanks to Rebecca Garrett for the words "barbaric" and "repulsive" to describe a particularly gruesome act of group bullying, and for explaining the fear of being targeted if one doesn't comply. Thanks to Avi Lewis for acknowledging that "Motherhood is all about guilt" and, in deep recognition of the responsibility to intervene with unjust bullying, pledging twice that "We're going to fix this." Thanks to Misha Abarbanel for the wisdom to recommend "Stop blaming others and stop blaming yourself, just fix it," and to Stephen Andrews for using the word "realignment" for conscious shifting away from bad groups, and for saying the word "shunning," for bravely speaking openly to community about bullying and for identifying the phenomena of those who "never apologize." Thanks to TL Cowan for being the first to point out to me the phenomena of a bullying group falsely "constructing" someone "as an abuser" in order to avoid responsibility for their own actions, and for illuminating the role of the observer as a participant. Wendy Coburn strategically offered the word "dysfunctional" and the phrase "It's about feminism" in a key conversation. And Tony Souza told me that some people would rather follow instructions to punish than "take the time" to help a friend face the complexities of their past. Thanks to Roy Mitchell for the insight that if we believe that someone "needs help," "we should help them" instead of punitively yelling, "You need help," and then shunning them. And to everyone else who spoke honestly, and directly, and listened in turn, even for an instant. Your truthful words have enlightened me permanently from the moment that you offered them, which has never been forgotten.

Thanks to Nan Alamilla Boyd for the word "elevator" to describe a narrative device that carries a complex idea throughout the life of a book.

Vivian Gornick's book *The Romance of American Communism* first articulated for me that people who believe themselves to be progressive can violate their own stated values through an identification with a negative group relationship that supercedes and thereby violates any actual commitment to justice.

I am grateful to the patient, encouraging folks at Sixth Street Pilates, who have been present for evolution, no matter the circumstances, and to Jeffrey Van Dyke for his healing craft and skills.

I am especially grateful to those who generously and productively read and commented on the full manuscript, sometimes responding to multiple drafts: My publisher Arsenal Pulp Press has been a caring and productive partner for many years. Daniel Allen Cox, Will Burton, and Lana Povitz were true friends and engaged intellectuals. I am particularly grateful to Matt Brim, with whom I am in constant dialogue about everything that matters, and to Dudley Saunders who has read, critiqued, and fully engaged my books-in-progress and life-in-progress lo these many decades.

Works Cited

Ahmed, Sara. "A Campaign of Harassment." *feministkilljoys*. 26 May 2015. Web. 20 January 2016. http://feministkilljoys.com/2015/05/26/a-campaign-of-harassment/

___________. *The Promise of Happiness*. Durham, NC: Duke University Press, 2010.

American Psychiatric Association. *Diagnostic and Statistical Manual of Mental Disorders*. 5th ed. Arlington, VA: American Psychiatric Publishing, 2013.

Arendt, Hannah. *Lectures on Kant's Political Philosophy*. Ed. Ronald Beiner. Chicago: University of Chicago Press, 1982.

Baldwin, James. "As Much Truth as One Can Bear." *New York Times Book Review*, 14 January 1962.

Barner, John R. and Michelle Mohr Carney. "Interventions for Intimate Partner Violence: A Historical Review." *Journal of Family Violence* 26.3 (2011): 235-244.

Bartlett, Tom. "The Science of Hatred." *The Chronicle Review*. Chronicle of Higher Education, 24 November 2013. Web. 20 January 2016. http://chronicle.com/interactives/bosnia

Behrendt, Hadar and Rachel Ben Ari. "The Positive Side of Negative Emotion: The Role of Guilt and Shame in Coping with Interpersonal Conflict." *Journal of Conflict Resolution* 56 (2012): 1116-1138.

Bennis, Phyllis. "Why Opposing the Israel Lobby Is No Longer Political Suicide." *The Nation*. 15 July 2014. Web. 21 January 2016. http://www.thenation.com/article/room-criticize-israel-grows-are-policy-changes-table/

Blake, William. "The Marriage of Heaven and Hell." *The Portable Blake*. Ed. Alfred Kazin. New York: Penguin, 1985. 249-266.

Boyd, Nan Alamilla. "Sex and Tourism: The Economic Implications of the Gay Marriage Movement." *Radical History Review* 100 (2008): 222-235.

Brach, Tara. "Attend and Befriend - Healing the Fear Body (3/30/12)." YouTube lecture. 28 May 2012. Web. 21 Jan 2016. https://www.youtube.com/watch?v=k5w4Mh28wn4

___________. "Awakening through Conflict." YouTube lecture. 23 April 2014. Web. 21 January 2016. https://www.youtube.com/watch?v=50W4MSxQ79g

Brown, Jacqueline Nassy. *Dropping Anchor, Setting Sail: Geographies of Race in Black Liverpool*. Princeton, NJ: Princeton University Press, 2009.

Butler, Judith. "Public Assembly and Plural Action." Alexander Lecture at University College, University of Toronto, Toronto, ON. 11 February 2014.

____________. *Precarious Life: The Powers of Mourning and Violence*. London and New York: Verso, 2004.

Cole, Peter. "On the Slaughter." "The Daily," *The Paris Review*. 30 July 2014. Web. 21 January 2016. http://www.theparisreview.org/blog/2014/07/31/on-the-slaughter/

Cross, Gary. "Jaded Children, Callow Adults." *The Chronicle Review*. Chronicle of Higher Education, 10 March 2014. Web. 21 January 2016. http://chronicle.com/article/Jaded-Children-Callow-Adults/145117/

Dahl, Melissa. "Why Hillary Clinton Was (Psychologically) Right Not to Admit She Was Wrong." "Science of Us," *New York Magazine*. 13 June 2014. Web. 21 January 2016. http://nymag.com/scienceofus/2014/06/hillary-was-right-not-to-admit-she-was-wrong.html

Daly, Mary. *Gyn/ecology: The Metaethics of Radical Feminism*. Boston: Beacon Press, 1978.

Darwish, Mahmūd. "Edward Said: A Contrapuntal Reading." Trans. Mona Anis. *Cultural Critique* 67 (2007): 175-182.

Davis, Laura. *Allies in Healing: When the Person You Love Was Sexually Abused As a Child*. New York: Harper Collins, 1991.

Eloit, Ilana. "Sarah Schulman on 'Conflict Is Not Abuse': Rethinking Community Responsibility Outside of the State Apparatus." *Engenderings*. London School of Economics Gender Institute, 7 July 2015. Web. 20 January 2016. http://blogs.lse.ac.uk/gender/2015/07/07/sarah-schulman-on-conflict-is-not-abuse-rethinking-community-responsibility-outside-of-the-state-apparatus/

Email #132247. *Wikileaks*. WikiLeaks. 22 July 2014. Web. 20 January 2016. https://wikileaks.org/sony/emails/emailid/132247

Even Or, Yael. "We are Israeli reservists. We refuse to serve: A petition." *Washington Post*. 23 July 2014. Web. 21 January 2016. https://www.washingtonpost.com/posteverything/wp/2014/07/23/we-are-israeli-reservists-we-refuse-to-serve/

Gladstone, Rick. "U.S. Advises Americans to Put Off Travel to Israel." *New York Times*. 21 July 2014. Web. 21 January 2016. http://www.nytimes.com/2014/07/22/world/middleeast/us-advises-americans-to-put-off-travel-to-israel.html

Goldberg, J.J. "How Politics and Lies Triggered An Unintended War In Gaza." *The Forward*. 10 July 2014. Web. 21 January 2016. http://forward.com/opinion/israel/201764/how-politics-and-lies-triggered-an-unintended-war/

Grant, Isabel and Jonathan Glenn Betteridge. "A tale of two cases: urging caution in the prosecution of HIV non-disclosure." *HIV/AIDS Policy & Law Review* 15.3 (2011): 15-23.

Hanhardt, Christina B. *Safe Space: Gay Neighborhood History and the Politics of Violence*. Durham, NC: Duke University Press, 2013.

Hass, Amira. "Israel's Moral Defeat Will Haunt Us for Years." *Haaretz.com*. Haaretz, 28 July 2014. Web. 20 January 2016. http://www.haaretz.com/israel-news/.premium-1.607550

Heidegger, Martin. *Being and Time*. Trans. John Macquarrie & Edward Robinson. London: SCM Press, 1962.

"How To Have Sex In A Police State." *How To Have Sex In A Police State: One Approach*. Tumblr. 26 March 2015. Web. 20 January 2016. http://howtohavesexinapolicestate.tumblr.com/post/114884057757/this-is-not-intended-as-legal-advice-please

Kershner, Isabel. "6 Israelis Held Over the Killing of Palestinian." *New York Times*. 6 July 2014. Web. 21 January 2016. http://www.nytimes.com/2014/07/07/world/middleeast/israel-palestinians-muhammad-abu-khdeir.html

Levy, Gideon. "Our Wretched Jewish State." *Ha'aretz*. 6 July 2014. Web. 21 January 2016. http://www.haaretz.com/opinion/.premium-1.603232

Lis, Eric et al. "Neuroimaging and Genetics of Borderline Personality Disorder: A Review." *Journal of Psychiatry & Neuroscience* 32.3 (2007): 162–173.

Mason, Paul and Randi Kreger. *Stop Walking on Eggshells: Taking Your Life Back When Someone You Care About Has Borderline Personality Disorder*. Oakland, CA: New Harbinger, 1998.

Matar, Haggai. "Tel Aviv Is Under Red Alert—In Many Ways." *The Forward*. 21 July 2014. Web. 21 January 2016. http://forward.com/opinion/202383/tel-aviv-is-under-red-alert-in-many-ways

Matthews, Nancy A. *Confronting Rape: The Feminist Anti-Rape Movement and the State*. New York & London: Routledge International Library of Sociology, 1994.

Mikhalovskiy, Eric and Glenn Betteridge. "Who? What? Where? When? And with What Consequences? An Analysis of Criminal Cases of HIV Non-disclosure in Canada." *Canadian Journal of Law and Society* 27.1 (2012): 31–53.

Millett, Gregorio A. et al. "Comparisons of disparities and risks of HIV infection in black and other men who have sex with men in Canada, UK, and USA: a meta-analysis." *The Lancet* 380.9839 (28 July 2012): 341–348. Web. 20 January 2016.

Naaman, Dorit. "I am a Palestinian Jew, or at least I will be." *+972 Blog. +972 Magazine*, 17 June 2014. Web. 21 January 2016. http://972mag.com/i-am-a-palestinian-jew-or-at-least-i-will-be/92175/

National Coalition of Anti-Violence Programs. *Lesbian, Gay, Bisexual, Transgender, Queer, and HIV-Affected Intimate Partner Violence in 2013*. New York City Gay and Lesbian Anti-Violence Project, 2014. Web. 20 January 2016. http://www.avp.org/storage/documents/ncavp2013ipvreport_webfinal.pdf

New York City Department of Health and Mental Hygiene. *Intimate Partner Violence Against Women in New York City*. 2008. Web. 20 January 2016. http://www.nyc.gov/html/doh/downloads/pdf/public/ipv-08.pdf

"PACBI Guidelines for the International Cultural Boycott of Israel (Revised July 2014)." *Palestinian Campaign for the Academic & Cultural Boycott of Israel*. 31 July 2014. Web. 21 January 2016. http://www.pacbi.org/etemplate.php?id=1045

Pappe, Ilan. "Genocide in Gaza." *The Electronic Intifada*. Electronic Intifada.net, 2 September 2006. Web. 20 January 2016. https://electronicintifada.net/content/genocide-gaza/6397

"Police Family Violence Fact Sheet." *National Center for Women & Policing*. Feminist Majority Foundation, n.d. Web. 20 January 2016. http://womenandpolicing.com/violenceFS.asp

Puar, Jasbir. *Terrorist Assemblages: Homonationalism in Queer Times*. Durham, NC: Duke University Press, 2007.

Richie, Beth. *Arrested Justice: Black Women, Violence and America's Prison Nation*. New York: New York University Press, 2012.

Rosin, Hanna. "The Over-Protected Kid." *The Atlantic*. Atlantic Magazine, March 2014. Web. 21 January 2016. http://www.theatlantic.com/magazine/archive/2014/04/hey-parents-leave-those-kids-alone/358631/

Rudoren, Jodi and Isabel Kershner. "With Hope for Unity, Abbas Swears In a New Palestinian Government." *New York Times*. 2 June 2014. Web. 21 January 2016. http://www.nytimes.com/2014/06/03/world/middleeast/abbas-swears-in-a-new-palestinian-government.html

Said, Edward. *The World, the Text, and the Critic*. Cambridge, MA: Harvard University Press, 1984. Print.

Schulman, Sarah. *The Gentrification of the Mind: Witness to a Lost Imagination*. Berkeley, CA: UC Press, 2012.

____________. *Israel/Palestine and The Queer International*. Durham, NC: Duke UP, 2012.

____________. *My American History: Lesbian and Gay Life During The Reagan/Bush Years*. New York & London: Routledge, 1994.

____________. *Ties That Bind: Familial Homophobia and Its Consequences*. New York: The New Press, 2009.

"Sex workers and HIV/AIDS: stigma, discrimination and vulnerability." *Sex, Work, Rights: Reforming Canadian Criminal Laws on Prostitution*. Canadian HIV/AIDS Legal Network. 2006. Web. 20 January 2016. http://librarypdf.catie.ca/PDF/P30/22749.pdf

Stoever, Jane K. "Enjoining Abuse: The Case for Indefinite Domestic Violence Protection Orders." *Vanderbilt Law Review* 67.4 (2014): 1015-1098. Print.

Tangney, June Price, Patricia E. Wagner, et al. "Relation of shame and guilt to constructive versus destructive responses to anger across the lifespan." *Journal of Personality and Social Psychology* 70.4 (1996): 797-809.

Thomson, Helen. "Study of Holocaust survivors finds trauma passed on to children's genes." *The Guardian*. 21 August 2015. Web. 20 January 2016. http://www.theguardian.com/science/2015/aug/21/study-of-holocaust-survivors-finds-trauma-passed-on-to-childrens-genes

Tjaden, Patricia and Nancy Thoennes. *Extent, Nature, and Consequences of Intimate Partner Violence: Findings From the National Violence Against Women Survey*. Washington, DC: U.S. Dept. of Justice, Office of Justice Programs, National Institute of Justice, 2000.

Weigert, Edith. *The Courage to Love: Selected Papers of Edith Weigert*. New Haven, CT : Yale University Press, 1970.

Citations by Page

15 Baldwin, James. "As Much Truth as One Can Bear." *New York Times Book Review*, 14 January 1962.

24 Hass, Amira. "Israel's Moral Defeat Will Haunt Us for Years." *Haaretz.com*. Haaretz, 28 July 2014. Web. 20 January 2016. http://www.haaretz.com/israel-news/.premium-1.607550

25-26 Bartlett, Tom. "The Science of Hatred." *The Chronicle Review*. Chronicle of Higher Education, 24 November 2013. Web. 20 January 2016. http://chronicle.com/interactives/bosnia

31 Pappe, Ilan. "Genocide in Gaza." *The Electronic Intifada*. Electronic Intifada.net, 2 September 2006. Web. 20 January 2016. https://electronicintifada.net/content/genocide-gaza/6397

55 Said, Edward. *The World, the Text, and the Critic*. Cambridge, MA: Harvard University Press, 1984.

56 Stoever, Jane K. "Enjoining Abuse: The Case for Indefinite Domestic Violence Protection Orders." *Vanderbilt Law Review* 67.4 (2014): 1015-1098.

63 Schulman, Sarah. *The Gentrification of the Mind: Witness to a Lost Imagination*. Berkeley, CA: University of California Press, 2012.

68 Schulman, Sarah. *Ties That Bind: Familial Homophobia and Its Consequences*. New York: The New Press, 2009.

75 National Coalition of Anti-Violence Programs. *Lesbian, Gay, Bisexual, Transgender, Queer, and HIV-Affected Intimate Partner Violence in 2013*. New York City Gay and Lesbian Anti-Violence Project, 2014. Web. 20 January 2016. http://www.avp.org/storage/documents/ncavp2013ipvreport_webfinal.pdf

76 Arendt, Hannah. *Lectures on Kant's Political Philosophy*. Ed. Ronald Beiner. Chicago: University of Chicago Press, 1982.

82 New York City's official statistics for 2003-2005 show that 44 percent of reported and confirmed cases of violence experienced by women were Intimate Partner Abuse. *Intimate Partner Violence Against Women in New York City*. New York City Department of Health and Mental Hygiene, 2008. Web. 20 January 2016. http://www.nyc.gov/html/doh/downloads/pdf/public/ipv-08.pdf

83 Matthews, Nancy A. *Confronting Rape: The Feminist Anti-Rape Movement and the State*. New York & London: Routledge International Library of Sociology, 1994.

84 Barner, John R. and Michelle Mohr Carney. "Interventions for Intimate Partner Violence: A Historical Review." *Journal of Family Violence* 26.3 (2011): 235-244.

87 Schulman, Sarah. *My American History: Lesbian and Gay Life During the Reagan/Bush Years*. New York & London: Routledge, 1994.

88 Richie, Beth E. *Arrested Justice: Black Women, Violence and America's Prison Nation*. New York: New York University Press, 2012.

89 Brown, Jacqueline Nassy. *Dropping Anchor, Setting Sail: Geographies of Race in Black Liverpool*. Princeton, NJ: Princeton University Press, 2009.

91 Eloit, Ilana. "Sarah Schulman on 'Conflict Is Not Abuse': Rethinking Community Responsibility Outside of the State Apparatus." *Engenderings*. London School of Economics Gender Institute, 7 July 2015. Web. 20 January 2016. http://blogs.lse.ac.uk/gender/2015/07/07/sarah-schulman-on-conflict-is-not-abuse-rethinking-community-responsibility-outside-of-the-state-apparatus/

110 "Police Family Violence Fact Sheet." National Center for Women & Policing. Feminist Majority Foundation, n.d. Web. 20 January 2016. http://womenandpolicing.com/violenceFS.asp

113 Ahmed, Sara. "A Campaign of Harassment." *feministkilljoys*. 26 May 2015. Web. 20 January 2016. http://feministkilljoys.com/2015/05/26/a-campaign-of-harassment/

119-120 Mikhalovskiy, Eric and Glenn Betteridge. "Who? What? Where? When? And with What Consequences? An Analysis of Criminal Cases of HIV Non-disclosure in Canada." *Canadian Journal of Law and Society* 27.1 (2012): 31-53.

126 "Sex workers and HIV/AIDS: stigma, discrimination and vulnerability." Sex, Work, Rights: Reforming Canadian Criminal Laws on Prostitution. Canadian HIV/AIDS Legal Network. 2006. Web. 20 January 2016. http://librarypdf.catie.ca/PDF/P30/22749.pdf

128-130 "How to Have Sex In A Police State." *How To Have Sex In A Police State: One Approach*. Tumblr. 26 March 2015. Web. 20 January 2016. http://howtohavesexinapolicestate.tumblr.com/post/114884057757/this-is-not-intended-as-legal-advice-please

131 Puar, Jasbir. *Terrorist Assemblages: Homonationalism in Queer Times*. Durham, NC: Duke University Press, 2007.

133 Grant, Isabel and Jonathan Glenn Betteridge. "A tale of two cases: urging caution in the prosecution of HIV non-disclosure." *HIV/AIDS Policy & Law Review* 15.3 (2011): 15-23.

135 Butler, Judith. "Public Assembly and Plural Action." Alexander Lecture at University College, University of Toronto, Toronto, ON. 11 February 2014.

139 Heidegger, Martin. *Being and Time*. Trans. John Macquarrie & Edward Robinson. London: SCM Press, 1962.

141 Email #132247. *Wikileaks*. WikiLeaks. 22 July 2014. Web. 20 January 2016. https://wikileaks.org/sony/emails/emailid/132247

147 Tangney, June Price, Patricia E. Wagner, et al. "Relation of shame and guilt to constructive versus destructive responses to anger across the lifespan." *Journal of Personality and Social Psychology* 70.4 (1996): 797-809.

147-148 Behrendt, Hadar and Rachel Ben Ari. "The Positive Side of Negative Emotion: The Role of Guilt and Shame in Coping with Interpersonal Conflict." *Journal of Conflict Resolution* 56 (2012): 1116-1138.

154 Hanhardt, Christina B. *Safe Space: Gay Neighborhood History and the Politics of Violence*. Durham, NC: Duke University Press, 2013.

154 Ahmed, Sara. *The Promise of Happiness*. Durham, NC: Duke University Press, 2010.

155 Davis, Laura. *Allies in Healing: When the Person You Love Was Sexually Abused as a Child*. New York: Harper Collins, 1991.

157 Daly, Mary. *Gyn/ecology: The Metaethics of Radical Feminism*. Boston: Beacon Press, 1978.

165 Butler, Judith. *Precarious Life: The Powers of Mourning and Violence*. London and New York: Verso, 2004.

168-172 Weigert, Edith. *The Courage to Love: Selected Papers of Edith Weigert*. New Haven, CT: Yale University Press, 1970.

173 American Psychiatric Association. *Diagnostic and Statistical Manual of Mental Disorders*. 5th ed. Arlington, VA: American Psychiatric Publishing, 2013.

174 Lis, Eric et al. "Neuroimaging and Genetics of Borderline Personality Disorder: A Review." *Journal of Psychiatry & Neuroscience* 32.3 (2007): 162–173.

175 Thomson, Helen. "Study of Holocaust survivors finds trauma passed on to children's genes." *The Guardian*. 21 August 2015. Web. 20 January 2016. http://www.theguardian.com/science/2015/aug/21/study-of-holocaust-survivors-finds-trauma-passed-on-to-childrens-genes

177-178 Mason, Paul and Randi Kreger. *Stop Walking on Eggshells: Taking Your Life Back When Someone You Care About Has Borderline Personality Disorder*. Oakland, CA: New Harbinger, 1998.

181-183 Brach, Tara. "Awakening through Conflict." YouTube lecture. 23 April 2014. Web. 21 January 2016. https://www.youtube.com/watch?v=50W4MSxQ79g

184-185 Brach, Tara. "From Fight, Flight, Freeze to Attend-Befriend." YouTube lecture. 3 May 2014. Web. 21 January 2016.https://www.youtube.com/watch?v=a25T4KlaQDs

189 Blake, William. "The Marriage of Heaven and Hell." *The Portable Blake*. Ed. Alfred Kazin. New York: Penguin, 1985. 249-266.

190 Tjaden, Patricia and Nancy Thoennes. *Extent, Nature, and Consequences of Intimate Partner Violence: Findings From the National Violence Against Women Survey*. Washington, DC: U.S. Dept. of Justice, Office of Justice Programs, National Institute of Justice, 2000.

195 Boyd, Nan Alamilla. "Sex and Tourism: The Economic Implications of the Gay Marriage Movement." *Radical History Review* 100 (2008): 222-235.

201 Cross, Gary. "Jaded Children, Callow Adults." *The Chronicle Review*. Chronicle of Higher Education, 10 March 2014. Web. 21 January 2016. http://chronicle.com/article/Jaded-Children-Callow-Adults/145117/

202 Rosin, Hanna. "The Overprotected Kid." *The Atlantic*. Atlantic Magazine, March 2014. Web. 21 Jan. 2016. http://www.theatlantic.com/magazine/archive/2014/04/hey-parents-leave-those-kids-alone/358631/

210-211 Rudoren, Jodi and Isabel Kershner. "With Hope for Unity, Abbas Swears In a New Palestinian Government." *New York Times*. 2 June 2014. Web. 21 January 2016. http://www.nytimes.com/2014/06/03/world/middleeast/abbas-swears-in-a-new-palestinian-government.html

216 Kershner, Isabel. "6 Israelis Held Over the Killing of Palestinian." *New York Times*. 5 July 2014. Web. 21 January 2016. http://www.nytimes.com/2014/07/07/world/middleeast/israel-palestinians-muhammad-abu-khdeir.html

217-219 Levy, Gideon. "Our Wretched Jewish State." *Ha'aretz*. 6 July 2014. Web. 21 January 2016. http://www.haaretz.com/opinion/.premium-1.603232

221-223 Goldberg, J.J. "How Politics and Lies Triggered An Unintended War In Gaza." *The Forward*. 10 July 2014. Web. 21 January 2016. <http://forward.com/opinion/israel/201764/how-politics-and-lies-triggered-an-unintended-war/>

233 Bennis, Phyllis. "Why Opposing the Israel Lobby Is No Longer Political Suicide." *The Nation*. 15 July 2014. Web. 21 January 2016. http://www.thenation.com/article/room-criticize-israel-grows-are-policy-changes-table/

243 Matar, Haggai. "Tel Aviv Is Under Red Alert—In Many Ways." *The Forward*. 21 July 2014. Web. 21 January 2016. http://forward.com/opinion/202383/tel-aviv-is-under-red-alert-in-many-ways

245 Gladstone, Rick. "U.S. Advises Americans to Put Off Travel to Israel." *New York Times*. 21 July 2014. Web. 21 January 2016. http://www.nytimes.com/2014/07/22/world/middleeast/us-advises-americans-to-put-off-travel-to-israel.html

247 Even Or, Yael. "We are Israeli reservists. We refuse to serve: A petition." *Washington Post*. 23 July 2014. Web. 21 January 2016. https://www.washingtonpost.com/posteverything/wp/2014/07/23/we-are-israeli-reservists-we-refuse-to-serve/

267 Cole, Peter. "On the Slaughter." "The Daily," *The Paris Review*. 30 July 2014. Web. 21 January 2016. http://www.theparisreview.org/blog/2014/07/31/on-the-slaughter/

273 Dahl, Melissa. "Why Hillary Clinton Was (Psychologically) Right Not to Admit She Was Wrong." "Science of Us," *New York Magazine*. 13 June 2014. Web. 21 January 2016. http://nymag.com/scienceofus/2014/06/hillary-was-right-not-to-admit-she-was-wrong.html

273 Naaman, Dorit. "I am a Palestinian Jew, or At Least I Will Be." *+972 Blog*. *+972 Magazine*, 17 June 2014. Web. 21 January 2016. http://972mag.com/i-am-a-palestinian-jew-or-at-least-i-will-be/92175/

Also by Sarah Schulman

Nonfiction

Israel/Palestine and the Queer International

The Gentrification of the Mind: Witness to a Lost Imagination

Ties That Bind: Familial Homophobia and Its Consequences

Stagestruck: Theater, AIDS and the Marketing of Gay America

My American History: Lesbian and Gay Life During the Reagan/Bush Years

Novels

The Cosmopolitans

The Mere Future

The Child

Shimmer

Empathy

Rat Bohemia

People In Trouble

After Delores

Girls, Visions and Everything

The Sophie Horowitz Story

Plays

Carson McCullers

Manic Flight Reaction

Enemies, a Love Story (adaptation from IB Singer)

Mercy

Films

Jason and Shirley, dir. Stephen Winter
United in Anger: A History of ACT UP, dir. Jim Hubbard
Mommy is Coming, dir. Cheryl Dunye
The Owls, dir. Cheryl Dunye

Awards and Honors

Guggenheim Fellowship (Playwriting), Fulbright Fellowship (Judaic Studies), 3 New York Foundation for the Arts Fellowships (Fiction and Playwriting), 2 American Library Association Stonewall Awards (Fiction and Nonfiction), MacDowell and Yaddo residencies, Kessler Award for Lifetime Contribution to LGBT Studies. Selected by *Publishers Weekly* as One of the Sixty Most Underrated Writers in America. Fellow at the New York Institute for the Humanities at New York University, Distinguished Professor of the Humanities at the City University of New York College of Staten Island, Advisory Board of Jewish Voice for Peace, Faculty Advisor to Students for Justice in Palestine.

PHOTO: DREW STEPHENS

SARAH SCHULMAN was born on July 28, 1958 in New York City. Perhaps as a consequence of being handed *The Diary of Anne Frank*, at age six she began a diary and wrote "When I grow up I will write books." Her maternal grandmother had two sisters and two brothers who were exterminated in the Holocaust, and she was exposed to many discussions about mass-murder, the abandonment of the scapegoated, and the responsibilities of witnesses and third parties. The first socio-political idea that she heard was that "other people stood by and did nothing" while the Jews of Europe were destroyed. This became a central tenet of her point of view, and a foundation to her method of understanding social structures and human dynamics. However, *The Diary of Anne Frank* also produced new knowledge in that it made plain that girls could become writers of work that spoke for marginalized experience and carried meaning and gravitas. This was re-enforced a few years later by the novel *Harriet the Spy*, by Louise Fitzhugh, again about a girl writer, but this time a queer girl separate from expectations of traditional femininity, who had a queer boy sidekick, with whom she discussed the truth, as she documented her own time in a little notebook that she carried in her back pocket. In this way, these two writers, Anne and Harriet, helped make Sarah's life possible.

Being a New Yorker in the 1960s, living in the pre-gentrification Open City, meant being exposed to a wide range of arts and artists. She saw Yiddish Theater and she saw American theater. She knew the children of dancers, painters, actors. She had the freedom of an urban child of the era and walked the streets of the city, observing, feeling, and living. In this way she had the luck of place and time. A lifetime of walking through her city has re-enforced the early lesson that other people are real, they suffer, they live in simultaneity, they are flawed, anxious, petty, and fragile. This recognition has been at the core of her aesthetics as a novelist, playwright, and screenwriter. And she applies this recognition in her role as a friend, teacher, colleague, and mentor to many emerging and advanced writers, in a variety of social relationships.

Conflict Is Not Abuse is Sarah's eighteenth book.